MY PARENTS WERE
PEDOPHILES

*A Survivor's Journey Through
Abuse, Broken Systems, and
the Sacred Fight to Heal*

BY LISA PLUMB

Edited by Lil Barcaski

Published by: GWN Publishing
www.GWNPublishing.com

Cover Design: Kristina Conatser

ISBN: 978-1-965971-34-5

For my family,
I love you more than can be measured.

TABLE OF CONTENTS

PROLOGUE

The soft hum of the sound machine fills my office, blending with the rustle of trees outside my window. Sunlight spills through the glass, scattering into a warm, golden glow across the room. Late afternoons used to feel dangerous, so many of my worst memories happened in that light. But now, this time feels sacred, a reminder of how far I've come. I soak the light and shadows in, grateful for my own peaceful space after years of working in the trenches of mental health agencies. Now, in private practice, I answer to no one but myself, free to create the kind of healing space I once desperately needed.

Every detail in this space was chosen with care. Shelves hold books, some that carried me through my own healing, others waiting for the right moment. The sheer volume of the ones I have yet to read makes me chuckle sometimes but they are a reminder that growth and learning never end. The couch and chairs cradle the stories of survivors who have sat here, trusting me with their pain. Their courage is a living reminder that healing is real. Redemption is real. This is the room I once needed and couldn't find.

There was a time I couldn't even imagine a life like this, stable, peaceful, purposeful. As a child, I only knew fear, confusion, and the dull ache of being unprotected. I carried that ache for years, numbing it with substances before I ever reached adulthood.

Healing didn't come quickly. It began when I finally got away from the abuse, when I learned to speak gently to Little Lisa, the small, hurting version of me who still lived inside. The pace was slow because it had to be; my nervous system could only take so much at once. Answers were scarce, even from therapists, so, I became determined to find my own. Step by step, I wrestled my way forward, collapsing under the weight of old pain and rising again.

As an adult, when the damage done to me came flooding into my life, I begged for healing. I fought for it. I uncovered insights, found clarity, and clung to hope, even in the darkest moments. And now, sitting here in my office, I get to witness others stepping onto this same path of healing, the bravest journey a person can take. I remind them, as I remind myself, that *we were never responsible for the harm done to us.* But we *do* get to choose healing. That power belongs to us now.

Eventually, I became a marriage and family therapist, not only to help others heal, but to give words to what had been stolen from me, to speak the truths Little Lisa never heard.

As I wrote this book, I realized I wasn't just telling my story to expose evil or educate others. I was still healing. Each chapter became another conversation with Little Lisa, another layer of shame stripped away. I worked with my own therapist through the writing, learning how to hold myself with compassion in places I had once only held pain.

Some of what follows is heavy. Some may trigger memories or feelings in you. But please know this before you turn the page: I survive. I heal. I have joy. What was meant to destroy me has become the foundation of my purpose.

At the end of each chapter, you'll find a "Little Lisa Takeaway," a conversation from the therapist I am now to the child I was then. These are tools and truths for the hurting child in all of us. My hope is that my conversations with Little Lisa will inspire you to begin your own with your "little you."

The darkness doesn't win. Light always rises. Healing isn't easy, but it is worth it. And so are you.

CHAPTER 1

The camper shell door groaned open, releasing a stale cloud of cigarette smoke. Don's thick arm gestured inside.

"Okay, get in."

Heat pressed down, but I didn't care, and even though there were no soft places on which to rest my bony thirteen-year-old body, I liked the idea of being alone in the back. No cramped seat next to Don, no brushing against Jody's long legs, my mind could wander without much interruption. But solitude wasn't part of the plan today. We were picking up other girls.

I smirked when I saw Don and Jody together. Today, they'd even dressed in matching colors, like some odd couple from a cartoon. Don was built like an aging bodybuilder with a beer belly. Jody, at twenty something, was half his age and nearly half a foot taller. She had light blond hair, a thin frame, and one unmoving blue eye that made me self-conscious. When she wasn't looking, I sometimes covered one of my eyes, testing what it might feel like to see the world the way she did. I felt bad that she was missing an eye, but it didn't seem to faze her one bit.

By the time all the girls climbed in, six of us crammed together, the truck was lurching through turns, tossing us into each other. They were giggling; I stayed quiet. We were on our way to a photographer's studio to see about becoming models. The other girls seemed excited, but I did not want to go. We wore dolphin shorts and T-shirts, typical casual 1980s attire, not the glamorous outfits you'd see on fashion models.

When Don first told me I could be a model, I laughed.

"No way! I'm not pretty enough, and I'm fat."

He rolled his eyes, pulling me close. "You're my pretty baby."

"I don't like having my picture taken," I stammered, already bracing myself for whichever of Don's endless lectures might follow. The most likely would be why it was perfectly fine to take pictures in their apartment, but that could easily shift into how my feelings were wrong and how he and Jody were right. More often than not, those talks turned into lessons about why the things happening in their apartment were supposed to be good for me. He noticed the sadness in my face and tried to coax me out of it. "Lisa, it's going to happen, so you might as well enjoy it." He grinned, reaching over to tickle me, trying to force a smile onto my face too.

As the truck rumbled toward the studio, I leaned against the wheel hub, daydreaming I was a Polynesian dancer on a warm, sandy beach enjoying the cool water lapping at my feet, when I was interrupted by something unusual. A calm yet powerful male voice spoke above me: "Lisa, memorize how to get there." Startled, I lifted my eyes, but only the roof of the camper shell stared back. No one was there. The other girls seemed untouched, unaware, as though the moment had been meant for me alone. I tried to return to my daydream, but the voice came again, steady, direct, yet filled with love. Its tone carried both urgency and tenderness, like a guardian sent to guide me. "Lisa," it said, "memorize the way to the photographer's."

I obeyed, not questioning why. I normally never noticed where I was being taken, but this time I felt compelled to obey the voice. I pressed my face toward the window, forcing myself to memorize every detail. With sharp focus, I repeated the names of the streets like a chant, "Fourteenth Street, Fourteenth Street, Fourteenth Street." Then we turned, and I did it again. "Seventh Street, Seventh Street, Seventh Street." Tan brick building, corner lot. The moment I'd locked it in, the urgency faded.

"Go to the second floor," Don said as he opened the tailgate to let us out. He pointed to the studio, and we raced to the top of the stairs. I got there first, stopped, and waited for Don and Jody, the first girl to follow in behind them. My eyes immediately locked in on the Rubik's cube in the middle of a large desk. The man behind the desk seemed too young to have all that gray hair. His white button dress shirt and slacks seemed out of place for a glamorous profession. Nonetheless, he appeared ready for business. The dull office and monotone colors were not what I pictured at all! I blurted out, "Can I play with the Rubik's cube?" Our eyes met. Immediately, dread flooded over me. He did not respond to my question, just stared at me coldly. His dark eyes locked onto mine. I looked away first, flinching from his vile, accusing stare. *What had I done wrong?*

I quickly scanned the room and dropped into the nearest chair. I didn't dare ask another question. He remained silent, not a single word directed at me. *Don't look at him.* I held my breath, trying to make myself smaller, sinking into the seat. My heart thudded so loudly I wondered if anyone else could hear it.

He finally went in the other room with Don and Jody and then, one by one, we were each called into the room by name. "Come on get your pictures taken!" Jody encouraged us, happily. I was last. When I heard my name, I strained to stand. I cautiously walked to the lone stool in the room. In my peripheral vision I could see him staring at me. I turned my focus to my legs dangling from the tall stool. *Don't look at him.*

At last, he spoke. "Look over here at the camera, honey. Smile. Relax..." The words carried a practiced gentleness, but his deep voice trembled with strain. I avoided his eyes, though they hovered just beside the camera lens. His forced grin, tightened into a glare, made my hands grip the stool until my knuckles ached. I followed his instructions as best I could, relief washing over me when he finally said he was finished. He, Don, and Jody moved to a far corner, whispering among themselves. I sat frozen, waiting for permission to move, shifting my legs back and forth, my skin sticking uncomfortably to the wooden seat. My eyes stayed fixed on the floor as I strained to catch fragments of their conversation. When it ended, the photographer passed by, brushing so close his arm grazed me. A wave of chills rippled through my body.

"Lisa, come on, "Don instructed, and I jumped off the stool and rushed out quickly joining the rest of the girls in the office.

"Bye-bye, girls," the photographer said, his voice low and guttural. I bolted for the stairs, desperate to escape, nearly stumbling in my rush to get away.

The next day, as usual, it was just me in the apartment with Don and Jody. As I was sipping my drink, I overheard Don on the phone: "Yes, Lisa will do nude pictures."

11

I gasped, "No, I won't!" Surprised by my brazenness Don turned to me and mouthed quietly yet forcefully, "Shut up!" and pointed to the couch, his eyes raging.

I sank reluctantly onto the couch, as if shoved there, eavesdropping the rest of the conversation. I swallowed a heavy gulp of my drink, then choked as the searing burn of the strong alcohol tore down my throat, dragging tears to my eyes; tears aching for release.

Don's tone changed to reassuring when he told the photographer, "No, there won't be any problems, she will do it." After he hung up, he sat right next to me on the couch and turned my head towards his, "Don't you ever interrupt me on the phone again!" Ignoring my tears, he placed me firmly on his lap while gesturing to Jody to fill up our drinks.

As we pulled into my driveway the next day, Don turned to me and said, "Lisa, it'll be fine, don't worry." He tugged me close and gave me a hug just as Jody stepped out, reaching over to help me from her side. "See you next week," she said, hugging me quickly and giving me a slap on the backside as I walked away.

Behind me, Don's voice followed: "Can't wait to see you next week, wish you could stay longer. I'll be looking forward to your call."

I had to call by Tuesday. It was up to me to call and arrange the pick-up time. Mother used to handle it, but now the responsibility had shifted to me. Don would decide whether he could come on Friday after school or wait until Saturday, depending on their schedules.

He continued, "But if your mom kicks you out again, call me anytime so you aren't wandering on the streets alone. We love you and we are here for you!"

When Tuesday came, I called and Jody answered. She heard my voice then snapped. "Don't ever contact us again," she said, before slamming the phone down. My heart burned. Was this some kind of joke? I dialed back immediately, no answer. My head throbbed with confusion. I tried again and again, but still nothing. My throat tightened, a hard lump rising as I fought to understand. In a daze, I swallowed it down and slipped into my hiding place in the bushes. I couldn't make sense of any of it. Afraid of getting in trouble for not arranging the pick-up, I kept it to myself. *Maybe they'll call me later,* I told myself.

A couple of days later, gym class was interrupted when I was handed a slip telling me to report to the office. In my gym clothes, I walked the empty hallways, wondering if this was about my attendance. The thought made me groan. I hated missing gym, and I didn't want another lecture in the office. For a moment, I considered slipping off campus to hide, but instead, I pushed forward, hesitant, and stepped inside.

The first face I saw was Ms. Brewer's. *Ugh.* She had always been quick to scold me for my spotty attendance, usually meeting me with a glare. But this time, she wore a nervous smile. *That's strange.*

"Hi Lisa, come over here," she said, gesturing toward two men in suits, radios clipped to their belts, guns at their sides. I instinctively took a few steps back, but she shook her head and waved me forward. My stomach dropped. I kept my eyes averted from the intimidating men, wishing I had slipped away when I had the chance. Then she introduced them: "This is Detective Mendez and Detective Romero."

Little Lisa,

That photographer's office wasn't safe, you sensed it. None of that was. But you weren't allowed to trust yourself. You should never have been handed over to people who smiled while planning harm. You were just trying to survive, finding the tiniest freedoms, like lying down alone, or pretending to be a dancer on a faraway beach. Your imagination was sacred, a secret lifeline.

That voice urging you to memorize the way? It was a gift. It was protection. It was love, watching over you.

You weren't confused because you were weak. You were confused because it was confusing. They hurt you and then told you it was love. But it wasn't. Love never violates, never threatens, never discards a child.

13

You didn't deserve to be tricked, humiliated, or silenced. The way you were cut off left you gasping for answers. You thought they loved you because, for you, those who love you, hurt you.

You are not a bad girl. You are not to blame. You were preyed on and harmed, and still, you kept going.

You are precious. And I am always here for you.

CHAPTER 2

Around eight years earlier…

"Hurry!" Mother screamed from the far side of the house. I sprinted to deliver the exact towel she demanded. "Why are you shivering? It's ninety degrees outside!" she barked into my ear, her voice so sharp it made me flinch sideways. Sweat clung to my skin, but I didn't feel cold. I lifted my shoulders in a small, uncertain shrug. When her fury shifted to my brother for not mopping fast enough, I slipped away unnoticed and stood beneath the air conditioner's steady stream of cold air. I blew my breath into the brisk wind, laughing at the vibrating sound as it tangled my hair across my face and into my mouth. A giggle bubbled out as I imagined how silly I must have looked.

"You kids better hurry! My guests will be here by seven, and this house better be in flawless condition by then!" Mother's sharp command rang out; each word clipped with irritation. Her grumpiness clashed with the polished image she had crafted for herself. Bright eyeshadow framed her amber eyes, and her crimson lipstick stood out boldly against the platinum blond of her carefully sculpted updo. The way her hair stayed frozen in place all week fascinated me; it seemed untouchable, almost unreal. Each week, at the salon, the hairdresser curled her locks high above her forehead, shaping them into a stiff ocean wave, then sealed the style with layer upon layer of lacquered hairspray until it hardened like armor.

A sudden smack cracked through the room, followed by a curse. I darted away, heart pounding, slipping behind the couch in the other room, hoping to disappear. From my hiding place, the sunlight caught on the chrome handlebars of my new bike just outside the sliding glass door, a birthday gift I treasured. My heart leapt with the idea of escape. I slid the door open slowly, but instead of the stealthy getaway I'd imagined, it slammed open, the glass rattling violently in its frame.

Mother's fury whipped toward me in an instant. "What are you doing? How dare you treat my house this way, you little b…!" The slap cracked across my face, her words dripping with venomous profanities. Without pause, she spun toward my sister, shrieking that the glass had to be spotless so no one would think we were uncivilized.

She dragged me to our bedroom, yanked our toothbrushes from the bathroom, and flung them onto the floor. "Scrub every inch of the kitchen floor with these, you pigs!" she barked. Then, as she scanned the room, her eyes landed on the dresser. One drawer was open a little bit infuriating her. She tore that drawer open and dumped the contents onto the floor. Then she frantically pulled out the rest of the dresser drawers and picked them up one by one heaving contents onto the carpet, fabric raining down like confetti, tossing the drawers on top of each layer. "These need to be folded perfectly, not crammed in like animals live here! If I have to wake you in the middle of the night again to get this house the way it should be, I happily will!" she roared.

Then she stormed off toward my brother's room to unleash the same chaos.

The moment her back was turned, I bolted. My legs carried me straight to one of my secret hiding places, the thick bushes at the side of the house, where I could fold myself into the leaves, and buy a little time until I was summoned again.

While huddled in the bushes, trying to soothe myself, my thoughts drifted to my grandmother's noodles. A smile crept across my face as I pictured being in the kitchen with her. Just a month earlier, in March of 1973, Mother had gone away for a few weeks, and my grandmother had come from Indiana to stay with us in California. It was the first real time I had ever spent with her, and everything about her visit felt new and special.

She was delighted by the endless orange groves surrounding our neighborhood. "We may not have this citrus smell in Indiana," she said with wonder, "but smell this." She held a bowl up to my face filled with the batter for her secret noodle recipe. "Just wait until you know what real noodles are supposed to taste like." She handed me a small bowl, then showed me, step by step, how to make them.

In all my five years of life, I had never tasted anything as glorious as my grandmother's noodles. As she rolled the dough out across the table, her voice softened. "I wish you didn't live so far from me, but it is nice here in Riverside. You aren't too far from Disneyland! Maybe we can go there together someday." She smiled at me as she spoke, her words filling me with a warmth I carried long after.

I had been born in Riverside and had never once been to Indiana, but the way Grandma described it made it sound magical. They even had snow in the winter, something I had only seen in pictures. She went on, "Maybe your birth would have been easier on you and your mom if I had been here." Taking my small hand gently in hers, she guided me as we cut noodles together.

"I'm just glad you and your mom are okay now," she said softly. "You know you were born by an emergency cesarean section. You came into the world just a month after Martin Luther King Jr. was assassinated, and your mother barely survived your birth." I stared up at her, amazed, trying to take in all the details. Then she smiled as she added the part that fascinated me most: "Your foot was actually born a day before the rest of you!"

"I know people don't often speak of these things," Grandma said gently, "but maybe it will help you understand your mother. She was just a teenager in the 1940's when she found herself pregnant and unmarried. She had an operation to make the baby go away." Her voice dropped, heavy with shame. "It left her with complications, and after so many miscarriages, it's truly a miracle she was able to have you at forty. Your mom should be fine when she comes home. I'm sorry you had to see her that way."

The last time I had seen my mother was in her bedroom, the shades pulled down, lights off and a sadness flooded over her that stung me. I was scared for her. I remembered her saying she didn't want to be here anymore.

"Your parents' divorce has been really hard on her. She didn't want to go on, you know, but she is changing that attitude now. I'm here right by your side while she is getting better," Grandma continued.

My parent's divorce was a new battlefield for them. Sometimes, they told us things when the other wasn't around, cruel words whispered about the parent who wasn't there. Other times, we witnessed it all, standing in the crossfire as they hurled accusations at each other, their anger spilling into every corner of the house.

One day, when the arguing was done, Father gathered his things and headed for the door. I followed him outside, my feet quick, heart pounding, I rushed up to him, worried about his hurt, "Daddy," I asked softly, "can I have a hug?" He stopped, looked down at me, and shook his head.

"No."

I frowned, confused. "But… why not?" I asked softly.

"I don't want your brothers and sisters to feel jealous because they're adopted, and you're not."

The words landed like a stone in my chest. I bit back tears, my mind pleading, *But just hug them too.* Not waiting for a response, he walked on, leaving me standing in the yard.

"Lisa! Where are you?" Mother's angry voice shook me out of the memory. I immediately started praying, "God, excuse me, please bless my mom and please bless my sister and my brother and…" My brother found me, yanked me up, and shoved me inside towards my raging mother, but I kept praying.

"What are you doing, Lisa? Stop that! I'm sick of hearing you pray all the time!" Mother's voice cut through the room as she lined us up in the living room like soldiers awaiting inspection. She barked her orders with precision. "When the guests for my singles party arrive, you will not cross this line." She jabbed her finger toward the narrow space between the wall and the bookcase. "And you will not speak for any reason."

Her barking tone dropped suddenly when a knock sounded at the door. She turned to us with wide, warning eyes, glaring as she pressed a finger to her lips, her silent command to stay quiet. Then, in a heartbeat, her whole demeanor shifted. She pivoted toward the door, opening it while keeping her movements graceful, her face radiant. And as it opened, she greeted the guest with a polished smile and a sweeping gesture of her arm. She sang out, "Welcome to my home!" "There's Hollywood mom, now," my brother whispered to us. Her voice now matched her perfect makeup, hair, and special form-fitting clothes.

We stood on our assigned line and kept quiet as guest after guest arrived. We attracted a lot of attention, and when the guests said hello to us, Mother nudged us. "Say hello to my friends," she said in her smooth Hollywood voice. One of the guests asked if he could share some of the hors d' oeuvres with us, looking into my eyes with a smile. Mother told him, "Of course," and motioned that we could sit on the couch. With her teeth clenched at us, she said, "But only till eight."

Little Lisa,

I watched you that day, running for towels, shrinking under words too heavy for little shoulders, hiding in the bushes, praying to a God you barely understood but somehow trusted. You did nothing wrong. You didn't deserve to be slapped for trying to escape. You didn't deserve to be silenced for praying. You were just trying to survive an unpredictable, painful world.

I know how hard you tried to keep up, to run fast enough, to clean enough, to be small enough so no one would get mad. But their anger wasn't because of you. Their chaos wasn't yours to fix. You were meant to play, to ride your bike, to feel safe in your own home, not be caught between their storms and staged smiles.

I see you, Little Lisa, chasing father into the yard, softly asking for a hug. He told you no, that it might make your brothers and sisters jealous because they were adopted and you weren't. His words pressed hard against your small heart. You knew it didn't make sense! Inside, your thought was simple and true, then hug them too. You deserved arms around you, not reasons that left you empty.

Still, you found small pockets of peace, the hum of the air conditioner, the smell of Grandma's noodles, whispered prayers. Those little joys were your spirit refusing to be crushed.

You're safe with me now. And one day, your home will hold only real love, the kind that doesn't change when the doorbell rings.

CHAPTER 3

John Lippert quickly became one of Mother's favorite new friends from her parties. Unlike many of the others, he went out of his way to be kind to us kids, drawing us into the festivities as if we belonged. Before long, he was a steady fixture in our home. With the divorce finalized at the start of my fifth year, Mother often leaned on him for the "men's work" she said she couldn't manage alone. He fixed our struggling air conditioner, patched up fences, and cleared drains with practiced ease.

Lean and muscular, the veins that bulged across his arms almost pulsed with too much intensity. His brown hair, dusted with gray, gave the appearance of age, yet the energy behind his movements carried a restless edge. Mother seemed pleased, too pleased, with her new helper.

The Summers in Riverside sweltered, but I found solace in the shade and in crunching ice cubes. Cold treats provided relief. When the melody of the ice cream truck rang through the streets, we scrounged for money. When found, we raced to get in line before the truck moved on the next street.

John, ever observant, noticed our eagerness for the cold delights. He started to offer to take us kids to Thrifty's to get ice cream when he was done with his chores on Saturdays. The ice cream trips soon became a ritual. Sometimes, he would just take me to get ice cream, and initially, I felt special about that. Treats required hugs in gratitude. Afterwards, was play time involving wrestling. It always started easy and often ended up with me in tears from being thrown too hard or squeezed too tightly.

John was kept so busy by mother that he had to start coming over during the week. His best time was in the late afternoons. When he came over, at that time, I was usually home alone, Mom was working, so she left me with a key around my neck to let myself in after school.

Sometimes, John showed up just as I was walking home, other times, he arrived minutes after I stepped through the door. If it was unlocked, he let himself in. If it was locked, I let him in, just as I'd been instructed.

One afternoon, he came carrying a gift, a brand-new coloring book and a box of crayons. He knew I loved to color and my excitement bubbled up instantly. Normally, I sat at the table to color, but John pointed to a corner of the living room.

"Here. Lay on your stomach. Color here."

I obeyed, stretching out on the carpet and flipping through the pages until I found the perfect picture. My focus narrowed to making sure I didn't rip the paper as I tore it free. At first, I barely noticed his hand scratching my back. Then it slid lower, down my legs, under my dress.

I froze. When I tried to roll away, his grip clamped hard on my thigh, forcing me back. "Relax, Lisa," he whispered, arranging my legs, touching where my underwear should have kept me safe. My chest pounded, but I buried the shaking inside me, pressing my crayon hard across the page, eyes locked on the picture.

"It's fine. Don't move."

After a while the front door banged open. My sister walked in and stopped dead, her body stiffening as her eyes locked on us. John jerked upright, yanking my dress down in a rush, his face flashing with sudden alarm. For a split second, the room froze, heavy with what she had just seen. Then her eyes flared wide, narrowing into something sharp, cutting through me like a blade.

"Lisa! What is going on?!" she snapped, her voice cracking the silence like glass shattering.

My mouth wouldn't work. My breath became shallow, my head dizzy. I didn't understand, only that something felt wrong. Her glare cut through me. "What is going on?" she demanded again, her voice sharper this time. I had no words. I just lay there, quiet.

John slipped out fast, leaving me where he had placed me. She stormed off, angry, while I stayed frozen on the carpet, too stunned to move. When I finally rose, I tossed the coloring book and crayons aside. My stomach churned as I crept outside to the bushes, my only safe place, curling into the leaves to hide.

It was the very next day, after my sister had caught him and John had bolted out of the house, when my sister called me into the kitchen. They were already there, John seated at the table, across from my mother, my sister at the end of the table.

I stepped through the doorway, my body stiff. I stayed standing, arms at my sides, feeling cornered. John's eyes locked on me, steady, almost daring me to speak. I kept mine glued to the floor, to the shapes in the linoleum, anywhere but him. My mother leaned in, her expression sharp with interest, not tenderness. She looked hungry for a story, not aching for my pain.

"Tell her, Lisa," my sister urged, her voice fierce. "Tell Mom what he did to you."

My chest burned. My mouth wouldn't work. I didn't have words. I didn't understand, only that something inside me felt wrong.

"John touched you, didn't he?" she pressed, louder now. "You need to say it!"

The kitchen tilted. I shifted my weight from one foot to the other, dizzy, silent.

John leaned back in his chair, calm, almost smug. My mother tilted her head, studying me as if I were some puzzle she wanted solved. Not once did she soften, not once did she reach for me.

And I stood there, mute, silence screaming in place of the words I could not form.

Little Lisa,

You were just a little girl, longing to belong, to feel safe, to have arms that sheltered you. John fixed things, smiled, even included you in the fun, but his attention carried shadows. That was the confusion: some-

times the very people who harm also hand out sweetness. It was never your fault that you couldn't tell the difference.

And when your body responded with feelings you didn't understand, that was not desire, not choice, not consent. That was simply biology, your body doing what bodies do. It never meant you wanted it. It never made it right. Innocence was yours; responsibility was his. Always.

The very next day, the kitchen became a stage you never asked to stand upon. John lounged in his chair, calm and smug. Your mother leaned in; eyes lit not with care but with a hunger to be entertained. Your sister's voice cracked the silence: "Tell her, Lisa. Tell Mom what he did."

You stood frozen, words locked in your throat, staring at the floor while their eyes pressed against you. You didn't even understand what had happened. You had no words to give. And still, instead of gathering you close, your mother only watched.

Freezing, fawning, clinging to small joys, coloring, ice cream, sunlight in Riverside, these were not silly escapes. They were survival strategies, shields of light in a dark world. Even in silence, even in confusion, you fought to live. That resilience has always been yours.

CHAPTER 4

The next day, I was first to father's car, waiting for my siblings to come. The stillness pressed in, broken only by the faint tick of cooling metal. I sat in the back seat, in the middle because I never got the window seats. Through the rearview mirror, my father's eyes caught mine. "I heard you were molested," he said evenly, like stating a fact.

My throat closed. I stared at the seat in front of me, heat rising up my neck. He let out a breath, slow and controlled. "Don't make a big deal out of it." His tone carried the weight of instruction, not comfort. He broke eye contact, looking back to the windshield as if the matter was settled.

I stayed silent in the back seat until my siblings climbed in, and then we drove off like it was any ordinary day.

The *Brady Bunch* was on, my absolute favorite! I liked *Gilligan's Island* too, but the *Brady Bunch* was a dream world to me. I sat right in front of the TV, sitting up straight with perfect posture, smiling at them as they smiled back at me. I wondered what they thought of me. When my sister caught me waving at the screen, she burst out laughing. "They can't see you, stupid!" Heat rushed to my face as embarrassment sank in. I quickly pulled my blanket tight around me, cocooning myself for safety. *They can't see me?* She marched straight over to the TV and switched it off. "Go away, I don't want to see you right now." I froze, unsure what to do, but before I could even move, she turned and headed for the door instead.

"Can I come with you?" I pleaded, my voice small. The sky outside was already dimming, and the thought of being left alone in the dark made my chest tighten. My brother joined in, teasing me then spitting on me, wiping his own snot in my mouth.

"No! You can stay home, alone." She snickered, her words sharp and final. Tears welled up, and panic pressed in on me. I couldn't stop myself from begging. She rolled her eyes. "Stop crying! You are such a baby." Still, I pleaded, desperate to go with her, but her answer only grew harsher. "No! Get away from me!"

The heavy dread of being left alone settled over me like a weight. My brother decided to pile on. Instead of helping, he teased me, mocking my helplessness. He whined exaggeratedly, shifting an imaginary gear stick, first, second, third, pretending to drive. "Mom...Mom...Mom..." he chanted, his voice dripping with cruel amusement.

A knock at the front door gave me a brief reprieve. My sister hurried to answer it. "Come on in!" she called. A boy stepped inside, and when his eyes landed on me, he asked, "Is this your sister?" My sister shrugged. "Yeah, but she's not my real sister. I'm adopted and she's not, so we're not really sisters."

"Same here," my brother chimed in, then shoved me with his foot as if to punctuate the rejection.

"Don't do that!" I shouted at him.

He only smirked, "And what are you going to do about it?" He moved closer and clamped his legs around my waist squeezing the breath out of me. His snicker told me he already knew the answer, there was no help for me, and he knew it.

"Yes, we are real," I choked out after I finally caught my breath", looking at my siblings with sadness, though my words carried no weight. Moments later, my sister and brother walked out with the boy.

"Don't follow us!" was the last thing they threw back at me as the door closed behind them.

The silence of the house pressed in on me, and fear rose like a tide. I sat in silence, my bladder filling up. The pain grew and I held my pee as long as I could, terrified of leaving the safety of my blanket, but eventually the pressure was too much. Heart pounding, I sprinted to the bathroom, certain monsters lurked in every shadow, then bolted back just as quickly, diving under my blanket. I wrapped it tight around me, convinced it was a shield strong enough to keep out all evil. I didn't dare move again. Hunger gnawed at my stomach, but I ignored it, sure that if I shifted even a little, the monsters would notice me. At last, exhaustion pressed down harder than fear. I gathered the courage to slip deeper into my blanket cocoon, tugging the cover over my eyes. I convinced myself that if a bad man ever broke in, he would see that I couldn't see him, and then he wouldn't need to kill me, because I wouldn't be able to tell what he had done.

Little Lisa,

You were so young, longing to be seen, cherished, and included. The Brady Bunch wasn't just a show; it was the picture of a family you wished you could step into. Smiling at the TV, sitting tall with perfect posture, even waving, you were trying to connect in the only safe way you knew how. In your child mind, the line between real and pretend was hazy. When your sister laughed or your brother mocked you, it stung all the more, reinforcing the lonely message you already carried, that you didn't belong.

The fear of being left alone in the house was real. Children aren't meant to shoulder that kind of terror, yet you had no choice. You crafted survival strategies, your blanket as a shield, your stillness as protection, your imagination as a barrier between you and the monsters. Even covering your eyes was your brave little brain trying to outwit danger. These weren't silly fears; they were survival instincts of a child forced to face overwhelming vulnerability without the safety of caring adults.

And then, in that still car, when your father looked at you through the rearview mirror and said, "I heard you were molested. Don't make a big deal out of it," you learned another crushing lesson: that even when the truth came to light, the response could be denial instead of protection.

Yet you survived. You found ways to hold yourself together when no one else did. That strength, that courage, is still inside you today.

CHAPTER 5

"We're going again? We don't like going to Glen Eden!" my sister complained, speaking for all of us. Then she caught herself. We all knew better than to argue with Mother's new boyfriend. Larry Feldman's irritation was instant and visible. His pale skin flushed the same red as his hair, and his scowl made my brother stumble backward. "Your kids are so disrespectful!" he snapped at Mom. She immediately turned on us, barking orders to gather what we needed for the nudist camp.

The last time we went to Glen Eden, I thought I was going to drown. A hairy man at the pool had scooped me up and flung me extra hard over his shoulder, his hand grabbing my private area as he tossed me. Pain shot through me. "Ouch!" I yelled just before my face hit the water, stinging my nose all the way up flooding it with chlorine water. Coughing and gasping, I pushed off the bottom, desperate for air. When I surfaced, I could barely speak. "That hurt!" I stumbled to a bench, wrapping my arms tightly around myself, covering as much of me as I could. At Glen Eden, there was no choice, everyone had to be naked, even the kids.

"Come on, everyone, let's go!" Larry's voice snapped me back to the present. He flung the front door open and waited, watching each of us pass by him one by one.

The ride to Glen Eden was tense, Mother filling the car with sharp lectures about how we had to behave. Every word a warning. The entrance was long and winding, the driveway twisted ahead of us, like a snake, empty and still, with no one in sight, until the very last turn. Then as if out of nowhere there were naked people. The man at the entrance booth said, "Hello you guys! Ready for a great day?" I tried to avoid looking at them, but their aging bodies were like a car wreck, disturbing, yet impossible to ignore. No matter how hard I fought it, curiosity took over. We parked and found a spot on the big grassy area. "Ok kids, get your clothes off." Larry barked, my brother glaring at me to look the other way, I hadn't noticed I was watching him. He and my sister begged to go to the pool and I ran off with them. At the big pool, the so-called "doctor" was already doing his usual underwater laps when we kids arrived. The kids warned us that he had his goggles on and even touched a kid's foot. We didn't want that, and we all bolted for the sauna.

Sitting in the sauna with other naked kids didn't last long. One boy started to kiss a girl and the rest of the kids got grossed out. My brother said, "Let's go watch the tennis players!" It was a game to the kids, laughing at the bouncing body parts as each ball was struck, the adults flopping around, trying to look athletic. After tennis watching became old, we all went to the café. Smelling the food made my mouth water. "Hey kids, where are your towels, no sitting down without a towel to sit on!" the waitress scolded us. Back to the pool, we decided it was worth the risk of the doctor watching us to have a place where we could play. But after getting dunked over and over by my brother, leaving me gasping for air, I was able to escape. I ran off to a waiting towel next to mother and Larry. I couldn't understand why the men all looked so different down there, but I dared not ask. I looked away as fast as I could, squeezing my eyes shut. If I couldn't see them, then maybe they couldn't see me.

My reprieve lasted only a minute or two before Larry told me it was time to put lotion on him. "I don't want to burn," he smiled as he handed me the cream. Obediently, I did as he asked, struggling with the coarse hair covering his body, a barrier that made the task even more difficult.

Little Lisa,

You should never have been taken anywhere that made you feel unsafe. It wasn't okay for adults to make you be naked in front of them, or for anyone to touch you like that, or make you touch them, not in play, not ever. You had every right to say no, to be angry, to cover yourself, I'm sorry you couldn't. Feeling ashamed, confused, or afraid in these moments is a normal response to something abnormal.

The adults around you kept pushing you into something that made you feel sick inside. That's not love. That's neglect. No wonder your stomach clenched when Larry was near. Your body was warning you: This isn't safe.

Even your memories knew when to yell "Ouch."

Your body remembers what your mind tried to forget. Listening to those body cues is part of your healing now.

I want you to know you are not alone now. Grown-up me is here with you now, and I will protect you. You don't have to be brave in silence anymore. I see your pain, and I believe you.

CHAPTER 6

The next day, strange, frightening noises drifted from my mother's room.

"Mom, are you okay?" I called, my voice uncertain.

"Yes," she answered, her words breathless.

Then Larry's voice followed, "Come in here."

When I stepped inside, he motioned to a chair. "Sit down. Watch."

I couldn't make sense of what they were doing, only that it was strange, awkward, scary, and unlike anything I had ever seen before.

"Mom, are you OK? Does it hurt?"

She mumbled, "I'm fine."

When it was finally over, Larry turned his eyes on me.

"I show you these things for your benefit," he said. "I don't want you to grow up frigid. Now get out of here but stay inside."

I moved slower than he wanted, so he yelled it louder, including instructions for making sure the kitchen table was clear. He yelled out, "Kids, go to the kitchen now!"

All three of us kids moved to the kitchen, wondering what lesson was next. Sometimes Larry's "lessons" were just for me or for my sister, but this time it was for all of us. He handed my brother the camera and told him to take pictures. Then Larry and my mother climbed up onto the kitchen table and began doing the same things I had just witnessed in her bedroom. As I stood there watching, confusion washed over me. My siblings' giggles tangled with my own. The awkwardness was painful, until the scene before me became hazy and distant. I didn't know if I should stand or run, but leaving was not an option.

The next day's "lesson" began with Larry ordering me to run him a hot bath. While I was in the bathroom running the water, my brother booked it out of his bedroom cussing at Larry. Furious, and naked, Larry stormed out of the bathroom, returning the anger with worse words and threatening him to never speak to him that way, adding "I'll teach you!" then he grabbed my eight-year-old brother by the ankles, flipped him upside down, and plunged his head into the toilet again and again.

I stood frozen, my breath caught tight in my chest, tears burning out. I couldn't move. *How can I help him?* I couldn't figure out how and then, finally, Larry dropped him like trash onto the floor. My brother scrambled up and ran, but before disappearing, he shot me a furious glare, his rage focused on me. Then Larry turned, fixing his eyes on me.

"Lisa, come on now."

With my whole body trembling, I did what he said. Every step was so heavy, as if my feet were sinking into the floor. Larry lowered himself into the bath and then guided me closer, instructing me on how to wash him, everywhere. My hands moved stiffly, my stomach twisted, doing exactly what he told me to do.

"Ok, good job girl, let's go get some dinner now, go get my clothes" I walked in the bedroom where my mother was waiting to hand me what Larry requested.

Weeks later, when Larry broke up with my mother, she was furious and devastated. She wanted to marry him. She waved the letter he'd left in us kids' faces. She forced us to read it out loud, "Your kids are too much to handle. I can't do it anymore."

"You rotten brats! I finally had a man I loved, and you chased him off. You kids ruin everything. Always have, always will. Nothing good ever lasts because of you."

A wave of relief washed over me, was he really gone? But it tangled instantly with guilt, heavy and sour in my chest. I felt crushed beneath the weight of her disappointment. She stormed off to her room and slammed the door, refusing the comfort I offered. The three of us slipped outside, taking advantage of her absence.

We joined the neighborhood kids for a game of hide-and-seek, but before long, the older girls drifted away. My brother's grin widened as he said to the other kids, "Let me show you something I just learned." Before I could react, he lunged, slamming me to the ground, then barked orders to the boys around him, "Grab her arms, grab her legs."

They pinned me down, unable to move, I screamed for help. As he pulled off my pants one boy covered my mouth. My brother laughed, pretending to take pictures.

When a neighbor came outside, the boys scattered. But that wasn't the end. Pantsing me became a regular game for them. It always started with them chasing me. I tried to outrun them but I never could. After catching me, pantsing me, groping me, trying to use objects on me, they would abruptly stop, leaving me alone in a heap. Left alone, I'd slowly pull my clothes back on, wipe my tears and go back to play.

Once, after it happened, I ran to my mother in the front yard, desperate and begging for her help. She rolled her eyes and sighed. "Oh, here we go again, Sarah Bernhardt."

"Who's Sarah Bernhardt?" I sniffled.

"She was a famous actress, overly dramatic," my mother replied, dismissing me as she turned back to laugh with the neighbors.

"Don't let them see it bothers you, then they won't keep doing it," she called after me.

I went to the bushes, staring at the leaves on the ground. After I was calm, I went inside. Mother was there blocking my way. "Uh-uh, get out. And don't come back this time." She disappeared into her room, then returned with a box. "This is your baby book, your baby shoes, anything that proves

33

you were once my daughter. You are not my daughter anymore. Now get out!"

It didn't matter that I was five. It didn't matter that it was dark. I took the box to the bushes and hid it away.

Little Lisa,

None of this should ever have happened to you. Not the touching. Not the watching. Not the shaming or the chasing. Not the abandonment. You lived in a world where the very people meant to protect you were the ones who hurt you, or stood by and let it happen.

Larry stole your safety. Your brother replayed what he had seen. And your mother, the one person who should have wrapped you in her arms to say, "I'll protect you," blamed you instead. That is a terrible betrayal.

When she mocked you as "Sarah Bernhardt," she taught you that asking for help would only bring rejection. But you weren't dramatic. You were desperate for someone to see your pain.

I would've taken that box from your arms and said, "You are always my Little Lisa. No one gets to throw you away."

You were never too much. You were never the problem. You were a child doing her very best to survive.

CHAPTER 7

"Mom, ouch!" My head snapped back from the hard yank of the hairbrush.

"You're six years old now, you shouldn't be so whiny. I'm sick of you crying every time I brush your hair! That's it, I'm cutting it all off."

"No! Please don't. I promise, I won't cry anymore," I begged, but she wouldn't be swayed. She dragged me to the hairdresser, and though shame burned hot in me, I tried to swallow my tears. Still, my traitor of a chin quivered, giving me away.

"Give her a pixie cut," Mother ordered.

The hairdresser nodded in agreement, ignoring my despair. "Just sit still, sweetie. Do what your mom says," she coaxed, her scissors already snipping as she chatted lightly, as if nothing important was happening. But with every lock that slid to the floor, I felt a piece of myself slipping away. I had always dreamed of long, flowing hair. Now it was gone.

"It'll be so easy to care for now," the hairdresser said, trying to cheer me up. I kept my eyes above the mirror, refusing to look at the stranger staring back at me.

The next day, at Dad's house, my brother and I walked to the store. "Hello, young men," the man behind the counter said, looking straight at me. At first, I felt humiliated. But then, like a rush of fresh air, I realized I looked like a boy! If I looked like a boy, maybe I could be invisible. I lowered my voice, smiled, and walked out savoring my new identity.

Little Lisa,

Your tears over your hair weren't about vanity, they were about loss. With every lock that fell to the floor, a piece of your hope went with it. You were silenced when you were in pain, instead of comfort, you were told to stop crying, told to accept someone else's control over your body. That cruelty trained you to believe your needs didn't matter, and it left you vulnerable to being hurt again and again. Children who are taught not to resist, not to speak, become easier targets for those who exploit them.

And yet, even in that moment of humiliation, you found a way to survive. When the man at the store mistook you for a boy, your shame shifted into relief. You discovered a disguise, a way to be invisible, to protect yourself from the gaze of men who never should have looked at you. What was forced on you as punishment became, in your small hands, a kind of armor.

You shouldn't have had to protect yourself, but you tried, again and again. You are so courageous! Today I want you to know: you never lost your femininity, your softness, or your worth. They were always there, waiting for the day when you would finally be free to choose for yourself who sees them.

CHAPTER 8

"No, you can't come, it's for older kids!" my sister snapped, again shoving me aside as I begged to go with her. Panic rose fast and hot inside me. Murderous images flooding my mind, intruders breaking in, shadows turning into monsters. "Please," I pleaded, my voice cracking, "I'll be good."

She didn't soften. "If you try to come again, we'll throw another rock at you!" she threatened. My hand instinctively rubbed the knot still tender on my head, a reminder of what had already happened. Just a day earlier, I had tried to follow, desperate not to be left behind. Instead, her boyfriend hurled a rock at me, splitting the air before it struck. Pain exploded, my vision blurred, and I crumpled to the curb, briefly blacking out while they walked away without looking back.

I knew better now. I shut up quickly. There was no chance of being allowed this time. So, I went to my ritual. I turned on the TV, grabbed my blanket, and positioned myself in front of the screen before she could leave. I wrapped the blanket tight around me, cocooning myself. As she closed the door behind her, she tossed one last laugh over her shoulder: "Lisa, look out for monsters!"

Her laughter lingered in the air as the silence swallowed me whole. Fear rooted me in place. Forcing away scary thoughts by counting and moving my eyes in the shape of the window, over and over.

That night, after everyone had gone to bed, I woke up with my bladder screaming, the pain twisting in my belly. The house was silent except for the pounding of my own heart. I called out into the darkness, "Mom! Mom! I have to pee!" My voice cracked with desperation. No answer.

My sister groaned from her bed, half-asleep. "I'll take you," she mumbled. But I shook my head. I wanted Mom. I needed her. I cried louder, over and over, until finally, after what felt like forever, she appeared in the doorway of her bedroom.

Mom stood there, arms crossed, her face hard in the shadows. "What now? Do you ever stop whining?" she snapped. Then, with a sharp flick of her hand, she gestured for me to move. The bathroom was right there, attached to our bedroom. The pain intensified with every step I took toward it. "Come on Lisa, I don't have all night."

Mom yanked my underwear off and sat me on the toilet, the light glaring, but I couldn't go. She loomed in the doorway, glaring at me like I was a burden. "Hurry up, I thought you had to go!" she hissed. My body froze. I couldn't go with her eyes burning through me. Shaking, I willed my bladder to let go. *Just go bladder.* Finally, I forced just enough out to ease the pain, then scrambled off the seat.

I ran back to my bed and dove under the blanket, clinging to my only protection. My heart still raced as I tried to disappear into the dark, yelling out to mother, "I love you."

Little Lisa,

Siblings are meant to protect and include; not leave you crumpled on the curb with pain bursting through your head. That rock was more than an injury, it was a declaration that you didn't matter to them, that your safety could be sacrificed without a thought. It planted panic inside you, a terror of being left alone, because you already knew what being discarded felt like. Being shut out went deeper than the knot on your head. That kind of cruelty taught you to expect rejection, to brace for abandonment, and to live with fear pressing in at every turn.

Even your body carried the weight of this fear. Children's bodies hold their fear. Fear of ridicule, fear of punishment, fear of everything kept your body clamped down, even when the pain screamed for release. Sitting frozen on the toilet under your mother's glare, straining for a trickle, was the body of a child adapting to an impossible environment.

And still, your heart reached outward. Even in the silence of night, you whispered, "I love you," hoping it might finally open a door that always seemed to slam shut. That longing showed the depth of your tenderness, the strength of your spirit, and the way hope continued to live inside you.

CHAPTER 9

One morning near the beginning of second grade, I woke up with the same usual sick feeling I usually had, lodged in my chest. "I have a headache. My stomach hurts," I cried, hoping, begging, to stay home. But Mother insisted I go, barely letting me wake up before shoving me toward the door. I was still wearing yesterday's clothes, my short hair sticking out in every direction.

When I walked into class, the most popular girl looked me over and smirked. "Your hair looks crazy," she mocked loud enough for a few kids to hear. Heat shot through me, shame first, then something sharper. I didn't say a word back. I stored her meanness away like a small, glowing coal. Recess was coming, and payback would come down hard on her.

I raised my hand in class to go to the bathroom to wet my hair. On the way there I stumbled upon a scene that instantly lit a fire in me. An older boy was mocking a kid with special needs. Fury surged through me. "Why don't you pick on someone who can fight back?" I shouted, my voice steady with defiance. I raised my fists, slipping into the stance my brother had taught me.

The bully froze, startled by my boldness. I felt a rush of pride. "Come on, pick on someone who can fight back," I challenged again. He stepped closer, towering over me, laughed, then turned away, shaking his head as he walked off. Triumph flooded me. I stood up for someone who couldn't. And if he had swung at me? So, what, I could take a punch.

I stared at my scruffy hair in the bathroom mirror, my mind drifting back to the way my brother had trained me. That training was how I first met my best friend, Andy. "Go! Jump on him, hit him!" my brother had ordered. Compliant and quick, I leapt onto Andy's back. In an instant, he buckled beneath me, crashing to the ground. Following my brother's command, I straddled him, holding him down. "Sit on him, use your body, and punch his face!" my brother urged.

Andy's tears snapped me out of my trance. "Please stop hitting me, I'm not allowed to hit girls!" he pleaded. My fists froze. I climbed off of him and stood aside as he rose to his feet, wiping at his wet eyes.

"I'm Andy," he said, his voice gentle but heavy with sadness. *He doesn't want to hit me back?*

"Hi… Andy." I stared at him, taking him in. He was taller, stronger, a big Hispanic kid. He asked me my name and what grade I was in. Bigger than me but a grade younger, he asked if we could be friends. My brother lost interest and Andy walked me home. From that day on, we had each other's backs.

I caught my reflection smiling in the bathroom mirror at the memory of Andy, then turned to the sink to wash my hands. Another memory surfaced of how my brother had forced an older neighborhood girl and me to settle a spat in the "ring", an area in our garage with ropes barricading us in. When it was clear I was losing, sweat and tears streaming, he dragged me into the kitchen, rummaging through cupboards. "Uh… try this pickle juice! It'll help," he said, laughing as I gulped it down without question.

Then it was back to the ring. The crowd of kids chanting and cheering. I followed his instruction and yanked open my opponent's button-up shirt, which brought the fight to a sudden halt, at least until she returned in a T-shirt. She soon had me pinned. Dana dominated the match, but I stayed in the fight until he finally called it.

My brother turned to the pack of kids crowding the garage and boasted, "Lisa will fight any of you, if you're not too chicken." Then he pulled me into the role of his sparring partner. He held back just enough, but his blows still stung. "This is how you fight," he laughed, easily overpowering me as the kids looked on.

The bell jolted me out of those memories, and I headed out to recess. Time to get back at that girl. I slammed a foursquare ball straight into her chest, acting like it was an accident. She gasped and bolted away in tears. Lucky for her it hadn't been worse. *That'll teach her to disrespect me.* I stayed on the court, cool and steady, taking over the game, even beating the boys.

It was one of those glorious days when school let out early, and my little boyfriend, Donny, suggested we ride bikes. He was just half an inch shorter than me, though whenever we stood back-to-back, he'd stretch up on his toes to claim the edge. The only blonde in his family, he once told me he liked me because I was a brunette.

We were the youngest of the neighborhood crew, though Donny was a little older and took it upon himself to show me the ropes. "Let's go get some candy," he grinned. Then, lowering his voice, he added, "I'm jonesing for a cigarette, and my sister and brother won't give me any. Do you have some?"

"I've got a few," I offered. We smoked the last of them in our fort in his backyard, plotting how to score more.

"Dang it! My bike's got a flat, so you'll have to ride me on your handlebars," Donny declared. He climbed on, and I pedaled us out, through the field, then along the busy street. I swerved around cars with practiced ease, cut across Tyler Street, and rolled into the parking lot with full confidence. Donny then commanded, "Let's hit Treasury's first, then Zody's." My confidence shattered as the reality of taking what wasn't ours again hit me. I lumbered along after Donny, following his directions. Candy, string cheese, and most importantly, cigarettes, were our mission. Donny pointed out, "Even though we're only eight, we're the best at stealing in our group aren't we? My brother wants us to grab him some smokes too." He laughed as he ripped a fresh hole in my windbreaker. "There, now you can carry a lot more."

I trailed behind as Donny darted briskly through aisles, guiding me like an expert, me a dutiful girlfriend. When the heist was complete, we bolted from the store, him hopping back onto the handlebars as I pedaled furiously toward safety.

Back in his fort, we celebrated, sharing candy and stolen drags, pausing for quick peck-kisses between bites and smoke. Sometimes, he timed our peck kisses, seeing how long we could hold that position.

When the fort lost its thrill, we tagged along with the older kids to Poppy Hill, a wealthy neighborhood with sprawling, manicured yards. We plucked pomegranates, kumquats, and other citrus straight from the trees as if they were ours for the taking, ducking behind shrubs whenever a car passed to hide our loot.

The older kids let us join them in sliding down the irrigation canals that fed the orange groves, our own secret water slides. Donny's brother barked instructions: "Start there, and when you hit the bottom, paddle hard left or you'll get sucked into the drain!" The water churned and disappeared into another canal system. We never knew where it went, and we didn't want to find out. One of the bigger kids stood ready to yank the next rider out. Too small to help, Donny and I happily let ourselves be pulled up again and again, soaked and breathless with laughter.

When that game wore out, someone suggested the storm drain that stretched toward Victoria Avenue, the tree-lined boulevard half a mile away. We followed single file through the tunnels, slipping on slime, dodging bugs, and clinging to the faint glow of someone's lighter. Darkness pressed in until we finally reached the built-in metal ladder. One by one we climbed up and spilled out onto the highway.

Later, we raided our favorite grove, filling the fronts of our shirts with sweet fruit. We ate until we were stuffed, then used the leftovers for target practice.

Though our tract housing sat just a mile from the freeway, the horse corral, open fields, and orange groves gave it a rural feel. They were our playground, a buffer between us and the busier city beyond. As the streetlights flickered on, our little gang drifted through the neighborhood, doorbell ditching, throwing rocks at cars, and planning how to get the next round of alcohol. Passing one house, I caught sight of the girl I'd slammed with the foursquare ball. Her bedroom window was visible. I hadn't known she lived there. I stopped in my tracks, mesmerized, while the other kids moved on, plotting who to doorbell ditch next. Through the window, I saw her in cozy pajamas, her mother gently brushing her freshly washed hair. The warm, safe scene made something boil up in me and I wanted to hurl a rock straight through the glass. Instead, I tugged my jacket tighter around me, lit a cigarette, and sprinted to catch up with the older kids.

Little Lisa,

Sweet girl, you carried so much fire inside you. You stood up to bullies, defended kids who couldn't defend themselves, and found pride in your own strength. That spark of courage of yours, it showed your heart and your fierce sense of justice, even when no one was there to guide or protect you.

I see the loneliness behind your toughness. You learned fighting, stealing, smoking, and dares because that was how you were taught to survive, how you were pulled into belonging. You didn't get cozy pajamas and a mother brushing your hair at night, you got training in fists and the pressure to prove yourself. No wonder that warm, safe scene through the window made you ache with anger. You deserved that tenderness too.

Lisa, the fact that you longed for it shows how deeply human you are. That longing was never weakness; it was your heart sharing what safety should feel like. Even while you lit your cigarette and ran to catch up, a part of you still knew you were meant for more. And I want you to know now: your fire and your longing can live together. You are both fierce and tender. You were never meant to be hardened into stone, you were meant to be seen, cherished, and kept safe.

CHAPTER 10

My third-grade class was going on a field trip and I needed to be at school early. As I got ready, I had to endure another of Mother's random tirades against Christianity, one of her favorite ways to unleash her rage. I remember wondering, even then, why she couldn't just let people believe what they wanted without it shaking her so deeply.

That morning, she had actually agreed to drive me to school, a rare gift. Just as we were about to leave, the doorbell rang.

"Got it!" I called, hurrying to answer.

On the other side stood a Black man, unusual enough in our neighborhood but especially at our door so early. His smile was warm, wide, and contagious, and something about his presence carried a gentleness. His arms were full of Fuller Brush cleaning supplies.

"Hi, darling, is your mother home?" the man asked with an easy smile. I was surprised by his kindness and called out, "Mom, someone wants you at the door!"

She joined me and spoke briefly with him before stepping aside to let him in. I lingered long enough to catch part of his Fuller Brush presentation before it was time to leave for school. Mother seemed energized by his presence, her tone brighter than usual. She offered him a seat, poured him a cup of coffee, and told him he could wait until she returned from driving me to school.

Hours later, when I returned home from school, the sound of laughter and lively conversation floated from the kitchen. To my surprise, the Fuller Brush man was still there.

Mother introduced us. "This is Raymond McKnight. He'll be staying for dinner."

I nodded shyly and slipped back to my room, puzzled about why this man was still in our house. But from that day on, Raymond became a frequent visitor.

At nine years old, I had no reason to trust him. Still, Raymond seemed fine enough, most of his time was spent with Mother, not us kids and I kept my distance. Whenever he came over, his attention was almost always on her. They'd disappear into her room, go out to eat, or sit for hours in deep conversation at the kitchen table.

My hesitation around him didn't go unnoticed. He often teased me about it. "Don't worry, Lisaaaa, I won't bite you," he joked once, roaring with laughter and punctuating it with a wink. I felt a strange pull toward him, almost enthralled, but I quickly looked away whenever his eyes met mine. After a few weeks, he moved in with us and the house was quieter for it.

Raymond slowly grew on all of us. even the neighborhood kids. He was friendly in a way that drew people close, and when he spoke, it felt like a blanket wrapping around you on a cool evening. With me, his tone was always gentle. "Where's that beautiful smile of yours? Why are you hiding it from me?" he'd tease, his voice smooth and warm.

I heard that voice not only in conversation but also in his chanting. As a practicing Buddhist, his rhythm and tone carried a strange comfort. "Come kneel by me," Ray invited one afternoon when he caught me watching from across the room. "Let me show you how to chant. Repeat after me: Nam myoho renge kyo." His voice bellowed soothingly, each syllable deep and resonant.

He performed every step of the ritual with quiet reverence, showing me how to burn the incense, dedicate offerings to the Butsudan, and join him in prayer. "Whatever you want, you can pray for it," he told me, pulling out paper and pencil. He wrote something down, folded it, and tucked it into the prayer drawer. "Now your turn. Don't show me, just write what you want. Then you can chant for it, and you'll get it."

Immediately, John Lippert's threatening face flashed in my mind, then left as if it never happened. All I could think of to chant for was, *Please don't let my mom die.* I folded the paper just as Ray instructed, placed it carefully in the drawer, and chanted with all the urgency I could muster. *Please.*

Raymond's main job was working as a cook in the merchant marines. When he wasn't out at sea, he spent his time doing sales in neighborhoods across Southern California. We believed he was a professional cook because some of the best meals we ever tasted were created from Raymond McKnight's long dark hands.

One day, Mother and Ray told us they were going away for the weekend. When they pulled back into the driveway a couple of days later, I rushed outside to greet them. Raymond stepped out in a suit, Mother in a dress. Smiling at Ray she made her announcement: "We got married! This is your new stepdad."

A rush of anger hit me first. Then confusion, then the sting of hurt. We hadn't been included in the wedding; hadn't even known it was happening. My disappointment was impossible to hide. Out of the corner of my eye, I caught the sadness in Ray's face when I didn't mirror their joy. I hated seeing that look on him.

"It will be okay, baby," he said softly, reaching out to hug me. I dodged his hug and darted off to my special place in the bushes. But eventually, it did become okay, better than okay.

From the start, Raymond fit right in. He noticed things other people didn't, like how we kids were treated and how we treated each other. He cared enough to step in, teaching us with gentle words and kindness and necessary firmness at times.

Since I was the youngest, he called me "baby" at first. But soon he leaned down with a smile and said, "Call me Chocolate, and I'll call you Vanilla." The words were just for me. When he said it, his eyes stayed on mine, waiting for my answer, like I mattered. At first, the names felt strange. I liked chocolate candy way more than vanilla, and I wasn't sure I wanted to be called Vanilla, ugh. But his skin really was the color of chocolate, mine was closer to vanilla, and after a while it felt special, like we belonged together. I wanted to be connected to him in any way I could and soon loved our special titles, Chocolate and Vanilla.

Soon, I was the one reaching out for hugs. When he called me Vanilla, Little Lisa, or Sugar, I felt his joy in every word. And every time, I felt wrapped up in warmth and love.

I still cried out at night, calling for my mother. But instead of her, it was Ray who came. He would scoop me up gently, his arms strong but careful, whispering, "It's okay, Sugar, it's okay," as he carried me to her bed. He would lay me beside her and then quietly take his place on the couch.

Mother never turned toward me, never reached back when I was placed there. But Ray's steady presence, his voice, his arms, his choice to comfort me, made the hurt in my chest feel smaller.

Ray did his best to protect me. He saw the fights between us kids and stepped in. One time, when he caught my brother hitting me, Ray's voice boomed: "Boys are not supposed to hit girls! Don't let me catch you doing that to your sister ever again!" After that, the pantsing stopped and the hitting slowed down, at least when Ray was there.

And when he was there, I was with him. Always. "You're stuck to me like glue," he'd laugh, and it was true. I wanted to go wherever he went. Riding in his van felt like riding in a magic ship, the air filled with jazz pouring from the speakers. He'd take me to his favorite restaurant, and we'd split pastrami sandwiches that tasted better than anything I'd ever eaten. At home, we cooked together, and it felt like we were making secret treasures in the kitchen.

Every day with Ray was an adventure. Sometimes he brought me to neighborhoods I had never seen, where his friends lived. I was the only white kid there, but I felt special and welcomed, like I was being let into a hidden world.

I felt especially welcomed by Mr. Lear, a devout, robe-wearing Muslim man who opened his ceramics studio to the neighborhood kids. Like Ray, he welcomed me with kindness and made me feel like I belonged.

Another of Ray's friends had a daughter, a beautiful and gentle girl who was older than me. Whenever Ray and I visited, she took me in as her little tagalong. One of her favorite things to do was sit on a brick wall in the alley behind her house, chatting with the boys who slowed their cars to get her attention. While they admired her, the things they said about me weren't always nice. But she always defended me, scolding them sharply: "Be nice to my girl."

Raymond told me he wanted me to call him Dad. And whenever he introduced me to anyone, he never said "stepdad." He simply said, "I'm Lisa's father." Each time, my whole heart lit up. I wondered if I looked like him at all? I pretended I did. Raymond McKnight, the coolest, kindest man in the neighborhood, was my dad.

Not everyone liked having a Black man in our home, but Ray showed us how to handle it. He taught us to look the other way, to meet ignorance with patience and kindness. We kids adored him. My sister especially hated the stares we sometimes got in restaurants. She'd glare back and snap, "What are you staring at!" Ray would gently calm her, asking her to let it go, reminding us that those people "just didn't know better yet."

I finally felt sure that if my brother came after me, Ray would protect me. Ray had told me before, "Run to me if your brother gets mad at you." So, in a rare moment of planning, I decided to test it.

We were in the kitchen when I mouthed off to my brother, planting myself between him and the exit as I spoke my mind cussing him out. Then, without waiting for his reaction, I bolted toward Ray's room. As I ran, I yanked out the kitchen chairs to slow my brother down and flicked off the kitchen light before booking it down the hall, my brother's shouts and cursing chasing me. I skidded to a stop beside Ray, chest heaving, proud and safe at last. *Finally, I'll get one over on him.*

But before anything could happen, my brother's fist came crashing into my face. Pain exploded, dropping me to the floor. My nose poured blood like a faucet. Ray's anguished voice thundered as he pinned my brother down, fury echoing through the house. Then he released him with a warning to stay put and scooped me up, rushing me to the bathroom.

He tilted my head over the sink, pinching my nose as the blood streamed. "Take her to the hospital," he told my mother firmly.

I followed her to the car, pressing a towel to my face. Only, once we were alone, she broke down, sobbing hysterically. "What are they going to say? What are they going to do to me? What am I supposed to tell them?"

I realized she was concerned she would be in trouble. I told her, "It's ok, you don't need to take me, I'll be ok." She said, "You're sure?" and turned the car around and brought me back home. With my nose no longer bleeding, Ray got ice and held it to my face, apologizing that such a thing had happened. Rocking me, he called me all those sweet names.

My eye was swollen shut, completely bloodshot, and the whole right side of my face was covered with purple bruises. There was nothing I could do to hide it and it took weeks to heal. It was embarrassing to look like that, to walk around like that. People stared at me in horror but most said nothing.

On the many trips to take Ray back to his ship at the L.A. port, he played Jazz and Gladys Knight on the radio. I fell in love with her music. On my own, I'd put the 8-track on repeat as I sang along to the "Midnight Train to Georgia." I'd imagine I was in her group, a singer with skin like hers and a voice that held tunes. Ray would be proud of me. Sometimes I told him I wished I looked like him and he told me, "Vanilla, you are perfect just the way that you are. God doesn't make mistakes and you are not a mistake." I'd lay in the back seat so I could look at him. Often, I'd fall asleep as I gazed at his face conversing with my mom, looking so smart as he was prepped with his gear for the ship. The shipyard would come too soon. I hated to see him go and wished I could go with him. "Do you love the ocean Ray? Being on a ship for so long?" He leaned down and hugged me, "I do Vanilla, but I really do miss you when I am gone."

Sweet Vanilla,

Ray was like a soft light breaking through a long, dark tunnel. He came into your life with kindness, warmth, and safety, a gentle hand reaching out when you so desperately needed it. Even when things around you felt scary or confusing, Ray showed you that love could be real and steady.

It's okay that you kept your distance at first; trust takes time. But little by little, you saw how he cared, how he stood up for you, protected you, and helped you feel seen. When he asked you to call him Dad, it wasn't just words, it was a promise that you belonged, that you mattered deeply.

Ray's love wasn't perfect, but it was real, and that made a difference. His respect, his soft voice, his willingness to teach and protect you helped you heal in ways you couldn't yet understand. And even when your world was bruised and painful, his presence was a place you could come back to, again and again.

You are worthy of love and safety, exactly as you are. Ray saw your beautiful soul, and I see it too. Keep holding onto that truth, Little Vanilla, because you are precious, loved, and enough.

CHAPTER 11

"Lisa! Come here, now!" Mother's voice snapped me out of my daydream, me and Ray, sharing pastrami sandwiches, jazz drifting in the air. He'd been gone just over a week, out cooking for the ship's crew, and I missed him terribly.

"Lisa!" she called again, sharper this time.

I hesitated in the hallway, catching the sound of laughter from the kitchen. There they were, the people my sister had met on a train coming back from Indiana on a visit to see our grandmother. Mother told me they invited me to the nudist camp, Glen Eden. I told her I didn't want to go back there but my words fell on deaf ears. I'd heard them come in and had hidden under my pillow, wishing for Ray instead.

Mother spotted me lingering. "Well, here she is! Thank you for gracing us with your attendance!"

A very tall woman with blond hair stood and grinned, cigarette dangling from her mouth. One of her blue eyes didn't move. "That's my glass eye, story for another time," she said.

"How tall are you?" slipped out before I could stop it.

"Oh, well, I'm six feet, two inches!" She stretched, emphasizing her height as she told me. She sat back down. Her legs wouldn't fit under the table, and she crossed them as if she owned the place. I walked to the other kitchen entrance because there was no way I was going to get around her.

As I rounded the other entrance, I saw him, thick-bodied, dark-haired. "Ohhh, this is Lisa?" Don's smile widened. For a split second something flashed in his eyes, hunger, not warmth. Then it was gone.

The tall woman, Jody, pulled out a chair. "I hear you're an athlete!" she said brightly. "I was the first woman to slam dunk in college basketball!" She seemed magical to me, and I wanted to talk only to her. Don leaned in, asking what sports I played. I avoided his eyes.

Ignoring him, I continued talking to the sports star. She was magical when she spoke, and the stories she shared kept me captivated. She even offered to show me tips on how to play basketball.

When Mother told me the day before I'd be going to Glen Eden with them, people I had never met, I protested. She snapped, "Don't argue with me! You are going!" That was the end of it.

I didn't like Glen Eden. I remembered the "doctor" in goggles watching kids underwater, the hairy man who had grabbed me and hurt me, Larry's hairy and angry body.

I had barely spoken a word the whole time, but the conversation continued without missing a beat. "Okay, so we will get going and get her home in one piece." The burly man spoke directly to Mother.

"Oh, no problem at all, have a good time." Mother dropped a towel on my lap. "Don't lose it." She glared at me.

"Oh no worries, we have plenty of towels she can use." Don took it from me and handed it back to Mother.

"I brought a ball with me, let me show you how to dribble." The skinny sports star stood up and offered me her hand. I couldn't believe how cool she was! "Let's race!" she squealed and scooted towards the door, egging me on.

Jody beat me to the truck, heaving as if she was out of breath, "You are so fast! You almost beat me! Wow!" She high-fived me. "Oh dang, I left my basketball at home, another time." She opened the door and said, "You get in first."

Once inside the cab, Don said, "Scoot over." As the truck rolled away, I whispered to Jody, "I really don't want to get naked."

"You'll be fine, honey," Jody said, arm around me. She lit me a Marlboro and handed it over, laughing when I asked if it was okay if I smoked.

We were halfway down the street before I was able to scoot all the way over. He beamed, "Okay! On our way to Glen Eden, we are going to have a great day!" My stomach sank and then twisted. *I don't think they know that I don't really want to go.* "Ummm," my voice was small, "I really, really don't want to get naked." I looked at Jody. She put her arm around me and took a drag of her cigarette. "We'll all be together, honey, it will be fun! Your mom wants us to care for you on the weekends, so you don't keep fighting with your brother.

"Do we have the letter from her mom?" Don piped in.

"Yes, no worries, I have it." She showed Don the letter giving them permission from my mom to take me to Glen Eden.

"It's silly that we need that, it's no big deal going around the way we were made. So many rules that people make to suppress us as humans," Don explained.

To get to Glen Eden we pulled off the freeway and followed a winding road up to a tollbooth where payment was made, and instructions given. Don did all the talking. The man in the tollbooth asked if I was his daughter.

"No, but here is a letter giving me permission to bring her," Don glowed. After a glance at the letter, the man nodded us on.

As we continued on through Glen Eden, a sign read: *Clothing is Not Optional* was posted at the front of the parking lot. When we found a spot Jody turned to me and said, "Let's see who can get naked first!" I glanced at Don, grossed out, he smiled, "I bet I can", and he popped out of the truck leading us to the grassy area.

After our first day together at Glen Eden, we were off to my first visit to their apartment. When we arrived, Don explained the apartment rules. Rule number one, as soon as you walk in the apartment, your clothes are to come off, just as if we were at Glen Eden. "It's a game we play here too," Don giddily explained. "Who can get naked first?" As we entered, he disrobed and explained, "Just throw your clothes on the floor here by the door."

I hesitantly followed their lead, using my arms to cover what I could and slowly sat on the couch. Next was my first introduction to an Atari home system. I had played a little bit at a couple arcades, but to be able to play whenever I wanted was amazing! After I was given free rein for a while on the Atari, Jody said, "It's time to start cooking dinner." Summoning me in the kitchen, she taught me how to make Don's favorite tacos. As we cooked and chatted, I got to carry the plate to him, and he had prepared a drink for me, a real alcoholic drink, just like theirs.

By the time I fell asleep on their couch that night, the nervous knot in my stomach was dulled by exhaustion and drink. In the morning, sunlight and the sound of gulls just outside the window filled the room. They suggested we go to the beach and I happily agreed. Maybe, I told myself, this wouldn't be so bad.

The following weekend while Jody was at work and we were waiting to pick her up, Don told me, out of the blue, that my sister said I wanted to have sex with him. My shock spoke for me, "I don't! I don't know why she said that?" Don grinned, "It's ok if you do, I can help you with that." My fear of hurting Jody overpowered the disgust of the idea he suggested. "I didn't say that, I don't want to. Please don't tell Jody that." Hopeful that was the last of it, after Don agreed he wouldn't tell her, I sat back hoping he would never talk about it again.

When Jody came out of work, as soon as she bounced in the truck, Don said, "Lisa wants to have sex with me!" Betrayed, my eyes popped wide open, overwhelmed with his broken promise. Jody immediately responded, "Ok, great! That's fine with me!"

Stunned, I could barely utter, "But I don't want to." She piped up, "It's ok Lisa. It sounds like fun!" Terrorized at the thought I was silent all the way back to their apartment. As soon as we got there, they told me to come to their bedroom so they could show me how to do sexual things. After enduring enough of my protests, Don explained that he did these things with his kids, but it was the court that messed them up, not him at all. I asked him if he wanted me to call him Dad? He smirked, "If you want to."

And then added, "You know your mother is crazy Lisa." Jody added, "I'll be right by your side. And you know, if you had a real dad, a dad that cared, you'd want to have sex with him."

Jody took me by the hand and we went to the first of many sessions.

Little Lisa,

I see how scared you felt being taken back to Glen Eden, a place filled with painful memories. Your body told you it wasn't safe, and you were right. That twisting in your stomach was your protector, warning you. It's normal to feel worried and confused when you're placed somewhere unsafe. Your feelings were real and important, even when adults ignored them.

You wanted to be with Ray, the one who made you feel safe, but instead you were handed to people who didn't protect you. Don and Jody pulled you into their world, indoctrinating you into sexual experiences you could not consent to. They blurred the lines between care and harm, leaving you confused and ashamed. You were far too young to carry such things. That was not your fault. That was their choice, their failure, their abuse.

I see how you still tried to belong, smoking the cigarette, playing Atari, cooking tacos. Those small acts were your way of holding on to scraps of comfort and control when so much else was stolen from you. They mattered.

Remember this, Little Lisa: your body is yours. Your "no" matters. Pretending to be okay was how you survived, but survival never meant you agreed. The people who ignored your fear and used you failed you, not the other way around.

Even in that confusion, you stayed strong and watchful. That was your courage. You always deserved kindness, tenderness, and safety. and you always will.

56

CHAPTER 12

Ray's absence left the house quieter, emptier. Without him, the warmth he brought seemed to vanish, replaced with a restless energy. The weekends with Don and Jody were still waiting for me, pulling me away from my neighborhood, my bushes, my friends. Summer was ending, but it wasn't the kind of ending that felt like relief, it was more like being pushed into the next thing whether you were ready or not.

It was time to start seventh grade, junior high. What was supposed to be just weekends at Don and Jody's had turned into almost the whole summer. Donny missed me, and when I finally saw him, his first words were, "Why do you have to be gone with those weirdos all the time?"

"I don't know, Donny. I just have to."

"Well, whatever. Let's go."

Our new school, Chemawa, was farther than our elementary school. "If we hurry, we can smoke before school starts," Donny called, pedaling hard. I followed through city streets, cutting across traffic until we reached the spot, an old smoking hangout for kids. Some neighbors glared from their cars, but no one stopped us. High schoolers sometimes drove by to laugh that we smoked already.

One high schooler drove a truck with an obnoxious sticker on his back window: "No Fat Chicks." *How rude,* I thought. I did my best to ignore him and puffed away with Donny and friends.

But somehow, Mr. No Fat Chicks found out my name and called, "Hey Lisa," every time he drove by.

Once the bell rang, I faced a choice: go to class or ride home and call in sick. I called in sick too often, which got me in trouble. But middle school felt like walking into doom.

The one bright spot was Mr. Mason, the eighth-grade counselor. He was tall, black, smiling, and very kind.

He told me, after the first week, "You are welcome to come see me anytime Lisa, and you don't need to get permission. Just come to my office."

"Even though I'm only a Seventh grader?" I asked?

"Yes, anytime."

I took him up on that offer as much as I could and went to his office almost daily. Mr. Mason never seemed disappointed or upset to see me. He would invite me in and happily offer for me to sit down and talk. He was interested in my day and my life. "It's good to see you, Lisa!" He'd say and put down whatever he was working on when I peeked in his door.

When I noticed a poster on his wall that was encouraging, he suggested that I make my own posters. Offering me poster boards and markers and helping me find positive quotes to put on the posters, he let me work on them in his office and at home. As soon as I was done with one, he immediately put it up in his office. Rainbow colors, blues, and purples, bright oranges and reds with yellows were my themes, depending on the quotes. It was my job to decorate his office with inspirational messages.

Halfway through seventh grade, Mother got a letter. "You got me in trouble for your bad attendance!" Mother fumed as she shook the letter at me. "You have to go to counseling now, and they want me to take you! Why don't you get your butt to school!"

"I'm sorry Mom, I'll do better."

"It's too late, but you had better start going to school, or I'll get in more trouble. And when I take you to the counselor, you better tell her who is at fault. You!"

A couple of days later, I sat outside the counselor's office in the warm and bright sunshine, but was wrapped in my heavy jacket meant for snow. Even though the jacket was usually too hot, I wore it most of the time; it made me feel more comfortable.

At our first meeting, Mother sighed to the counselor, "I just don't know what to do with her. I can't tell you how much trouble she gives me." Even though the counselor was a child therapist, she didn't seem particularly warm and friendly. After Mother left the office, the interrogation began.

Terri, the counselor, turned to me. "So, what's going on with you? Why don't you go to school?"

I fumbled through answers for her questions until I found myself telling her about something that had happened recently, my brother-in-law asking me for a sexual favor. He and my sister had been partying; I'd been tagging along. I woke up in the bed of their truck parked outside their house in the middle of the night. Startled, I ran inside. He heard me come in and called me into their room. When I came in, he was in bed with my sister who was asleep. He then mumbled something about her sleeping and instead asked me to touch him. He noticed my hesitation and then got my sister to mumble permission. I said no, backed away, and he let me go.

"Really?" The counselor's eyes widened. "What did he ask? Where were you? Who was around? I have to call child protective services and report this," she explained stoically as she moved towards the phone.

"Oh, please don't do that, please don't!" My heart was ready to beat out of my chest. Dread and guilt flooded through me. I knew that he and my sister would be mad at me, even though she nodded yes when he asked if it was ok. I didn't want to hurt them. "I didn't know you would be telling on me," I pleaded to Terri. My mind raced in fear as she called Child Protective Services. She never asked more questions about anything else in my life. She just reported on me and my brother-in-law.

"I have to do this, it's the law," she apologized, noticing my distress.

Terri told my mother what she had to do. Mother acted concerned in Terrie's office, but we never went back. My sister was furious when she found out. She cornered me explaining that they were interviewed by the police. "It's your fault my husband can't be a highway patrolman now!" Mother joined in: "Why would you do this to them?"

After a berating lecture, I lumbered off to the bushes. I tried to think of a river or someplace beautiful, but my mind was stuck. I just stared at the green and brown leaves from the bushes, then made a small pile of them. I lit them on fire with the match I used to light my cigarette. Breathing in the smoke and feeling the heat from the pile I stared mesmerized at the burning leaves. I gently blew on them, controlling the intensity of the flames. I contained my little fire, adding leaves as needed until Don and Jody pulled into the driveway to pick me up. I took a final drag from my cigarette and smashed it out in the ashes of the smoldering leaves.

Little Lisa,

You were walking into seventh grade carrying far more than any kid should have to. You didn't have words for the fear or pressure you felt, so you coped the best you could, cutting class, getting high, lighting fires, trying to disappear under a too-warm jacket. You weren't being "bad," sweet girl. You were hurting and trying to survive.

And in the middle of that pain, you found small places of refuge. Mr. Mason was one of them. A rare adult who saw you, welcomed you, and let you create beauty and color when your world felt so dark. You mattered to him. You brought light into his office, even when you didn't know it.

What happened with your brother-in-law was too familiar for you, you didn't understand why he would do that. Another sad surprise. It was not your fault. None of it was. You didn't want any of it. Ever.

You were so brave to speak up, even without meaning to. And when others blamed you, I want you to know: they were wrong. It was never your job to protect their reputations or shield them from consequences.

You didn't deserve the shame they placed on your shoulders. You didn't deserve their anger.

You were not the problem. You were the child in the middle of the storm, still reaching for beauty, still trying to breathe.

And I am so proud of you.

CHAPTER 13

The pool water was warm against my skin, sunlight shimmering like tiny mirrors. Rock music drifted through the air, mixing with the sparkle of the water and the tequila in my hand. At twelve years old, my favorite drug was marijuana, but alcohol worked too. I didn't ever stay sober for very long.

My mind drifted from my fantasy of being in my own pool, an adult, with a cool apartment, as I rubbed a bruise on my arm from when Mr. No Fat Chicks had forced himself on me the day before. He had a female friend invite me over to his house to get high; well, he had more on his mind than just getting stoned with me. I only got away from him because he let me go. I couldn't believe he overpowered me! I thought I was stronger than that.

"Get out of here, baby!" he yelled as he gave up the fight.

I agreed with him as I hurried out his front door yelling back at him, "I'm proud to be a baby!"

Pool water lapped around me, and I let it wash away the memory. I swigged down another Tequila Sunrise.

"Geeze Lisa, you are always drinking too much!" my brother aggressively shoved me towards the deep end of the pool. He let me come with him to his friend's house to swim.

"What's wrong with drinking?" I reached for another drink as I stumbled out of the pool.

"No, you've had enough!" he growled at me. "Get out of here."

With little protest, I got ready to leave, taking a few attempts to do it. I sloppily pulled my summer dress over my head on top of my wet bathing suit.

"Go home, now!" My brother pointed to the gate leading out of his friend's backyard. Home was a couple of blocks away. I stumbled and slammed into fences as I made my way there. Surprised at my own lack of coordination, I didn't feel any pain from the slamming and stumbling. I thought I must have been making too much noise, but as far as I could tell, I staggered through the neighborhood unnoticed. Sidewalks swirled and fences banged, but somehow I made it home while it was still light out. As soon as I got home, I instinctively walked through the side gate to the backyard and promptly passed out face-first in the dirt. I knew, even in my drunkenness, if I were to get sick, my best choice was to make the mess outside, not inside where Mom's wrath would be the reward.

When I woke up it was still light, but something had changed. *This is morning light.* Oh no, I've been out here all night! With a panic, I pushed myself up even though the throbbing in my head made me want to stay still. I wiped debris from my face. I looked to my left and gasped when I saw her, my mother looking out of our dining room window, glaring at me. *She's mad!* She just stared until she angrily gestured to the door, mouthing something. I stumbled to the patio door and waited till she opened it. I tried to walk past her quietly, looking away from her glare, staying a few steps ahead of her as she followed me to my room.

"How dare you do this to me!" Her hand made contact with my face as she yelled, "How disgusting of you! You're all dirty, and you reek of alcohol!" She shoved past me shaking her head. My eyes were wet with tears as I stumbled into my room and crumpled onto my bed. I heard screaming over the throbbing in my head, "You are going to school anyway! Get ready now." I wondered how I could escape, but she was adamant.

School had some positives; at least elementary school did. At four years old, I was tested and admitted into the Mentally Gifted Minors program (MGM). From first grade on, they told us MGM'ers to think about what career we would have, what college we wanted to go to, and what degree we wanted. Of course, I wanted to be a PhD Marine Biologist and go to San Diego's Scripps Institute of Oceanography.

As I learned about marine life and oceans, I imagined riding whales at Sea-World as a whale trainer. I would be the top expert on whales and dolphins, have long straight hair, and the sea animals would love me more than anyone. My dream included my own apartment by the beach decorated with beautiful beachy things and, of course, my boyfriend would be Steve Perry from Journey. He would be very kind to me, find me irresistible, confess his love, and propose marriage. I fully intended to turn my fantasies into real life as soon as I could.

Going to school late, with a hangover, was the opposite of what I wanted, but there I was. At least it was just a half-day for me, and I got to start with third period math. My seventh-grade math teacher, Mr. Fratt, was usually funny and kind. I looked up to him. But that day he walked up to my desk and angrily said, "Ms. Baer, are you listening to anything that I am saying?" He said it loudly, in front of the whole class! His kindness melted to disappointment and disgust. His eyes glared at me. My stomach sank, and I dropped my chin to my chest, grabbing my arms tightly, my head throbbing louder.

Elementary school had been easy for me academically. My grades were always good, even though my attendance was not. But the seventh-grade MGM classes became so difficult that I drowned academically. The classes might as well have been advanced foreign languages. My anxiety about not understanding and not being able to answer questions fed my deep desire to leave school or not show up in the first place. I really didn't want to do badly, and I felt awful about it.

The bell rang and I couldn't leave fast enough. I stumbled straight to Mr. Mason's office. He saw me and gestured me in. He was on the phone and winked at me as he mouthed, *just a minute.* I sat crouched in the chair and forced the tears back. He got off the phone and said, "Hey there, how are you doing? What's going on?"

"Nothing." I couldn't say more than that.

He seemed to get it and pushed over a fresh piece of white construction paper for me. "Pick any color you want and see if you can color those feelings." I picked up the black marker after debating between that and the red one. I made a spiral and went round and round until the spaces became filled with intense black, tearing at the paper and filling the space like a big dark black hole.

Little Lisa,

Floating in the pool with music in your ears and a buzz in your body, you reached for refuge the only way you knew how. But underneath the high, you were hurting, carrying trauma in your arms, bruises on your skin, and fear in your heart. You were only twelve, you were fooled. The boy should have been kind but instead he hurt you.

You were overpowered. And still, you found the courage to get away and yell, "I'm proud to be a baby!" That was your strength speaking.

Passing out in the dirt all alone hurts my heart for you. I wish I could pick you up and hold you like Ray did. Your mother's rage makes me so angry at her! That is something a child should never experience from a parent.

And when you were humiliated in class by a teacher you once looked up to, it wasn't because you didn't care. You did care. You wanted so badly to do well, to become the marine biologist you dreamed of, to live by the ocean and be loved. You weren't lazy or stupid, you were drowning in pain.

Thank goodness for Mr. Mason. He didn't need you to have the words. He gave you paper, and you poured out what you couldn't say. That spiral of black you drew was you trying to find your way through the darkness. And we do!

CHAPTER 14

"Lisa, when will you be here?" Debby's voice was sharp, cutting me off before I could even finish apologizing.

"I have to wait until my mom's ready to take me," I said quickly. "She said she would half an hour ago, but... I'm sorry. I don't know when she's actually going to"

"Just get here," she said, and hung up.

Debby wasn't just another friend, she was in eighth grade, part of the popular crowd, and had high school friends who drove cars and threw parties. I was a lowly seventh grader, lucky she still hung out with me. We'd grown up just a few houses apart until she moved to Woodcrest, the kind of neighborhood with long driveways, horses, and even more orange groves.

When Mom finally dropped me off, Debby was waiting outside, smiling like nothing was wrong. "Come on, let's get ready!"

Her room smelled like hairspray and perfume. We stood side by side in the mirror, matching with our classic '70s feathered hairstyles. She slipped in and out of outfits, asking my opinion.

"You look great in everything," I told her. She grinned, scanning her closet.

A high school friend gave us a ride to Flattop, a favorite party place on a hill in the rural neighborhood. We arrived just as the sun slid away. The valley was unusually clear, the air thick with the sweet scent of orange blossoms. The mountains in the distance towered above. Up on Flattop, you could see all the rolling hills, which were tan now, but the many orange groves in view were always green. I wondered when the snow would come to top the mountains in white. Such a beautiful night. Debby pulled me out of my thoughts with an offer of a beer. We started drinking as we sat on a rock by the fire pit. Someone started passing a joint around, and after I got a few hits in, Debby went over to another group of friends leaving me alone with the promise that she would be back soon.

I was nursing my second beer at the fire when Debby came back to me. "Lisa, come with me for a ride." Without a second thought, I followed her happily to a truck. She introduced me to the driver, "Lisa, this is David."

"Hey, nice to meet you, hop in," he said as he patted the seat next to him and passed me his lit joint. I sat between Debby and David as we drove around, music cranking. It was pitch black when we arrived at a house. Debby turned and said to me, "I'll be right back," and jumped out of the truck and headed inside.

Surprised she was leaving me in the truck with this guy I did not know, I yelled out, "Where are you going Debby?"

"I'm just going to be gone for a few minutes, I'll be right back," she called out to me.

As I sat next to David, I scooted away from him a little bit, and he said, "You don't have to move." I couldn't think of what to say, and I stopped scooting. It was so quiet with the music off. I sat still, hoping she wouldn't be gone long.

He turned towards me and said, "You are really cute." He smiled and leaned in closer to me. I rolled my eyes to the right looking away from him. He was cute! *Awkward.* I did not know how to reply. I smiled tightly and looked out the window. The leather squeaked as David moved closer to me and extinguished his joint in the ashtray. I felt his hand on my shoulder, frozen my breath left me. Soon his leg was right next to mine, touching me. He continued the conversation by asking me if I had ever done oral sex. I breathed in with a gasp and tensed up.

"Well, have you?" he repeated, and without hesitation exposed himself with a demand to do as he requested. I could not bring myself to look at him, and I barely was able to utter that I did not know how to do what he was asking.

"I'll show you how, come on," he grabbed my neck with a firm grip.

I mouthed, "I don't want to."

He was not taking no for an answer and tightened his grip and said, "Come on, it's ok, just do this." He pulled me by the neck and muscled me lower. I tried to pull away, but I was unable to resist his grip. I tried to comply with his instructions. *What's happening?*

He finally gave me permission to stop with almost perfect timing. I sat up just as Debby came back out. As she walked towards the truck, he adjusted himself and announced, "That was nice."

"Ok, let's go back to the party," Debby bubbled as she climbed in the truck. I didn't talk or move at all on the way back to the party. I stared straight ahead, lost in the headlights shoving through the dark. I quickly wiped a tear away before Debby could see it.

We arrived back at Flat Top and he parked his truck. He bounced out of the truck ecstatically. "Come on Debby, I have a friend I want you to meet!" He laughed, and they left me in the truck without a word. *Should I move?* I got out slowly and made my way back to the fire.

I grabbed another beer before locating an empty rock to sit on. I sat as close as I could to the fire and stared at the flames. My head felt like it was in a can. Sounds were muffled and louder at the same time. After a few minutes, I heard someone calling out to me. I barely made out that it was Dana, my previous fight opponent, Debby's older sister. She was saying something to me. My eyes adjusted to her dark silhouette. I finally was able to string her words together. A jolt jammed through my body and it felt like a million pounds were crushing me. It stung. Now she was yelling at me just a few feet away, in front of everyone.

"Lisa, did you give David head?"

Huh? Was she really asking me this? Everyone was looking at me. Shaking my head, I denied doing anything she suggested happened. She was laughing as she came closer to me, "Lisa, come on, tell the truth, did you…"

I tried to ignore her, hoping she would get bored so I could blend into the background. But the entertainment value of this information fed the cackling, judging, apparently virtuous crowd. I continued my denial, shrinking inside. Finally, she left me alone, and I sat half bent over, like the adulterous woman from the Bible whom the crowd convicted, ready to be stoned, hoping to be stoned so I could end this torture. I wished I had an automatic weapon to blast away their sneers.

Instead, I sat under the gleaming spotlight of stares as if they were waiting for me to perform a captivating monologue. *You see, he asked with an eager look, wanting me to perform this act for him, unselfishly offering to teach me how to do it, for both of our benefit.* Instead, my solo was drinking three more beers alone, avoiding stares, and then stumbling to the car when Debby said it was time to leave.

At school a couple of days later, a popular boy who always greeted me warmly walked past me as I was walking to class. I smiled and said hello. Instead of returning it, he stopped, looked at me as if he were looking at vomit, and called me a Slut. My heart sank as he walked away, wishing I could hide. Ignoring the laughter of those who overheard.

I was labeled now, Slut. I kept walking, fighting back tears, and tried to catch my breath. He shunned me from that point on. My new school identity was established. Kids laughed at me, called me the name, mocked me, picked fights with me, and some boys tried to date me. People that had been my friends treated me like a leper. One girl who was known for being the toughest girl on campus made fighting me her new campaign. Unfortunately, I had a couple of classes with her, and before each class started, she tried, along with her friends, to get me to agree to a time and place for a fight after school. I refused to plan one, but the fear stayed sharp every day.

"I'm not agreeing to fight, if you want to fight me you have to just start it. I'm not going to plan it." I tried to sound brave as I replied. But I was terrified. She would stare at me, threatening me. I always looked down and away, trying to avoid her eyes totally. On the days I had to go to school, I did my best to leave as soon as the bell rang and avoid contact with anyone, especially her.

Another student, a tall girl who developed early and was well known and liked, yelled across campus, "Lisa!", then a cuss word.

"Back to you!" I shouted back automatically.

She ran up to me and got in my face, "What did you say!"

I responded, "Back to you!" I stood my ground, trying to sound tough, staring up at her. She pushed me, and the fight was on. After a few minutes of fighting, I found myself on top of her, punching her face, over and over. As I hit her, I bawled. An eager observer mocked my crying, and a group of kids laughed along with him.

A gym teacher finally broke us up and took us to his office. I wiped away my tears as he herded us into his office. I hoped that I would be suspended and have an excuse to not be at school for a while. However, he said he was going to give us a break and not turn us in. Not what I wanted at all! She never tried to fight me again, but my reputation lived on.

Little Lisa,

That night was a devastating betrayal, another moment when your boundaries were violently ignored, leaving you powerless and alone. You wondered why this was happening and you didn't know what to do about it. You tried to resist, I know. Afterwards you sat numb, confused, and in shock, wounded.

The assault was bad enough, but then the crowd that should have protected you instead became your tormentors. Their whispered judgments, mocking laughter, and harsh accusations turned your pain into a public spectacle. You were thrust into a spotlight of shame, judged not for what happened to you, but as if you were to blame.

Their cruelty isolated you, fractured you, and forced you into a role you never asked for, that of the outcast, the untouchable. It was a brutal distortion of who you are; no one is less than others.

Beneath the weight of their condemnation, you wanted to disappear. I'm so glad you survived, because you didn't know it then, but there was so much good coming to you later in life. Thank you for living.

You were never "disgusting." He was. The venom cast your way is the worst of humanity, it's sad how pitiful they acted.

Little Lisa, I see your courage amid the storm and the deep loneliness that followed. You are such a survivor! You moved past all of that, still believing in yourself, that better was to come. You were right!

CHAPTER 15

Seventh grade couldn't end fast enough. I managed to avoid the fight with the tough girl, but I failed every single class except physical education. Donny still hung out with me and never called me the names with which I'd been branded. We just smoked and got high when we could during the week since I was still at Don and Jody's every weekend. We couldn't hang out over the summer because I was gone most of the time.

During that summer Don and Jody took me on a vacation. Just them and me. A four-state and four-week vacation.

"You'll want to get some books, we are going to do a lot of driving," Jody told me. She took me to the bookstore, and I picked out books that offered a life of adventure and space travel. My favorite book character was the dancer amongst the stars. She had a special gift to tolerate any atmosphere of any planet, and she could fly.

Each night we found a campground to park Don's truck and camper. Part of the reason for the vacation, according to Don, was to help me listen better, and one stormy night he got the perfect opportunity. "I don't want to go outside. There's lightning, and the thunder is so loud!" I shrank back into the camper and tried to shut the door.

Don was agitated. He barked at me, "Come on out! I promise you'll be fine, just listen to me!" But I had never seen or heard such a storm. The sound and the flash matched, and it felt as if the earth was splitting in half. I couldn't bring myself to move, so Jody pulled me up as Don ordered, "Get up! You will be ok. Just do what I say." I tried to say no, but before I knew it, I was outside and walking down the tree-lined path, flashes and the sound of the earth tearing apart all around me. I wanted to believe I would be ok. *They know what they're talking about Lisa.* I walked ahead of them unable to stop. Anytime I hesitated, Don was there pushing me on. When I had walked enough for Don, my reward was to sleep in their bed. "You did it! See, listening to me pays off." He pulled me close to him. I crunched my eyes closed, stiffened, hoping to avoid his inevitable touches.

I got in trouble a few times while on vacation for over speaking or behaving wrong. At a KOA campground in Flagstaff, Arizona, I woke up in the middle of the day, dead drunk. I didn't remember drinking, but I was obviously under the influence and could barely walk, let alone straight. *What happened? Where are they?* I realized I was alone in the camper. I put my clothes on, and wandered out, looking for Don and Jody. After stumbling around outside for a few minutes, I saw them coming towards me on a path. "What are you doing! Get back in the camper before you get us in trouble," angry at my obviously intoxicated display. "You can't go out in public like that!"

Jody sat me down in the camper and gave me a cigarette. "Lisa, just wait for us if you wake up like that or can't find us. Stay with the camper." She smiled big and wiped my hair out of my face. "We'll always come back."

Watching the movie *Pretty Baby* was part a big part of the vacation. He started showing it to me in their apartment and managed to make it part of our trip too.

Don interpreted, "You are a lot like her aren't you? Fresh and pretty. She wants to give up her virginity and make money just like her mom and the other women do." In the movie, Brook Shields was a twelve-year-old being raised in a brothel and taught to follow in her mother's footsteps.

"She's happy and excited to do that. She's going to make a lot of money!" Don said as he prepared the movie with his projector. His commentary continued, "See! She's fine and even enjoys it! Look at all the attention she's getting!"

He was always encouraging me to "do what he thought was best." But I didn't want to do what she was willing to do. "Lisa, you'll get it, you'll see. I'm here to help you and show you how." He pulled me to his lap on the picnic table bench, squeezing me tightly.

About two weeks into the trip, in a town familiar to them, Jody said, "We are going to go look for parts for the truck; you'll be better off just waiting here at this park."

Don added, "Go sit under that tree, and we'll be back in a little while."

I walked to the big shady tree and sat down, leaning against it. The rough bark poked gently through my tank top. I watched them drive away, and a few minutes later a truck stopped at the curb in front of me. A group of men got out and walked towards me. They were dressed in work clothes, and I thought maybe they were there to mow the lawn or something and I would have to move. Instead, one of them started speaking to me in Spanish. I shook my head and said, "I'm sorry, I don't understand you." He nodded, pulled out his wallet from his back pocket, and opened it, showing me cash. He pointed to the truck, then to me and himself, and pumped his hands together. As he did that, the other guys opened the shell of the truck and pulled down the tailgate. He gestured again. I immediately understood. I pushed back up against the tree, shaking my head, no. He looked confused and went through the sequence again, showing me his money. My head didn't stop shaking, and thankfully they decided to leave without another word. I watched them drive away, so relieved they left. I couldn't believe what just happened! I pulled my legs up and buried my head in my knees, peeking out just to make sure no one else was around.

Finally, after what seemed like forever, Don and Jody pulled back up, and I sprinted to the truck. I blurted out exactly what had happened as my voice trembled, and I tried to catch my breath. Before I had a chance to settle in the seat, Don said, "You should've done it! You could've made some money!" He said it so confidently and matter of factly, it stunned me. I sat down hard in my seat and stared out the window. I said quietly, "But I don't want to." I didn't speak it loud enough for them to hear it, but I spoke it. I meant it.

After the vacation, they reminded me that they were willing to keep showing me how to "behave correctly." They said an eighth grader who's now thirteen, especially one as mature as I was, should be ready for even more grown-up experiences, and Don was ready to show me those. One of them was how to model. My resistance to that was something Don was willing to work with. He took pictures of me in my bikini throughout the vacation and usually had his camera out at their apartment. But to help even more, he decided that he was going to take me to a professional.

Little Lisa,

You should never have been put in the position of having to "listen" in order to stay safe. That wasn't safety. That was grooming, and it was wrong. You were a child with a bright mind and a wild, beautiful imagination, a little girl who loved books about dancing through galaxies and who deserved to be dancing freely in her own life, not being dragged through storms or sat down for lessons in compliance.

What Don did wasn't about helping you. It was about power and control. He disguised his manipulation as mentorship, his violation as care. When you resisted, even if your voice was barely audible, you were doing something incredibly brave. That quiet "I don't want to" came from a place deep inside you that still knew what was right, even when the world around you didn't.

That long trip was not the vacation you deserved. It was a slow, careful stripping away of your boundaries, your innocence, and your voice. But you, Little Lisa, held on. You noticed. You questioned. And even when the people who should have been protecting you tried to convince you otherwise, your spirit still refused to fully fold.

Don was wrong. You were not "like the girl in the movie." You didn't want what he said you wanted. You were not born to be someone's experiment, someone's profit, someone's object. You were born to be known, cherished, and guided safely into the world. It's okay now to reclaim that truth: you never wanted any of it. And you never needed to earn anyone's love by giving yourself away.

I am so proud of the way you survived, even when everything around you told you to give in. You are not alone anymore.

I love you so much.

CHAPTER 16

A couple of weeks later, the big modeling day came, the one I didn't want to go to. I had to go although I didn't have to go alone. Don loaded me and some other girls in the shell on the back of his pickup truck while some stayed up front with him and Jody. The other girls were excited to meet a professional photographer, but I didn't want to think about it. It was tiring trying to pose for pictures and I always felt dumb when I did.

When we got to the studio, instead of the studio being a happy place, a palpable wave of darkness flooded me when my eyes met with the very scary man who sat behind the desk in the plain waiting room. I collapsed in the nearest chair avoiding all eye contact with him. Soon he got up and started calling the girls, one by one, back to the studio area. When my turn came, I hoped it would be over quickly. Luckily, the pictures he took were simple, clothes on, and I only had to stay sitting in the chair. After my set, we didn't stay at the photographer's studio very much longer, and after a brief conversation between Don, Jody and the photographer, we left. Later that day, after Don and Jody took the other girls home, they took me back to my house in Riverside, praising me for my cooperation.

A few days after the photographer's visit, I was playing kickball during gym class when I saw a kid come in with a yellow slip. The teacher pointed to me, and the kid came to me and handed me the slip. *For Lisa Baer, come to the office immediately.* The teacher gestured me on, and I walked slowly to the office, hoping I wasn't going to see Ms. Brewer. She seemed to like to be mad at me, complain about my attendance. As soon as I walked into the office, my stomach dropped. Before me stood two armed men. Ms. Brewer introduced me to the towering Hispanic males, dressed in suits with handcuffs, radios, and leather holsters.

"Hi Lisa, nice to meet you. Let's go talk in this room," Detective Mendez said, leading the way to what felt like the gallows. When we got in the room he explained they were going to interview me, and Ms. Brewer was going to be my support person. She sat on the other side of the table next to the detectives, her face painted with distress.

"Do you know Don Gordon and Jody Jones?" My stomach lurched, and I glanced around desperately for escape.

"Uh...yeah."

"Do you have any problems with us recording this interview?"

"Um, I guess not?"

"Just answer honestly."

"Uh, okay."

"You need to speak up loud enough so your voice can be recorded."

"Okay."

"Did Mr. Gordon ever touch you in a sexual way?"

My face flushed with heat and I squirmed in my seat as I struggled to answer. I couldn't respond, easily, I felt paralyzed. My mind raced, knowing I was supposed to protect them. Don and Jody knew they were doing the right things, but others disapproved. They educated me for my benefit because they knew that if I was raised right, I would want to do those things. I also missed them. I had been filled with shock and grief since the last time I called them when Jody told me to never contact them again. I wondered if they were in jail. Shock, sadness, and terror filled my body. Shame filled tears welled up, but I shoved them down. My vision hazed over, and the detectives' voices sounded far away.

"Lisa, did Mr. Gordon ever touch you in a sexual way? We know this is difficult for you, but answering honestly is the best thing to do." Strained silence filled the room. "Were you naked in his apartment with him? With them?" The intrusive, embarrassing, and explicit questions continued. I looked down most of the time, and they often asked me to speak up. Gratefully they worded most of the questions so I could answer yes, or no. I could not believe these strangers were asking me these questions. I didn't know how to lie, but I knew that was what Don and Jody expected. I tried to keep my shaking to myself. I wished I were dead. Memories of Don and

Jody flashed in my mind. *Some people think it's wrong, they said, to not wear clothes in front of other people. But those people do not understand that being naked is natural, and they are oppressed. So, don't tell anyone we get naked in the apartment or anything else, of course.*

The detective's voice pulled me out of the memory.

"Why did your mother let you go to Don and Jody's?"

When they learned she had forced me to go, they said I would be placed in a shelter home. I didn't know what that was, but I stayed quiet. As we prepared to leave, the bell rang. I explained, "My mom is picking me up to-day, she's in the parking lot." One of the detectives brought her to the front office, and when we walked out to greet her, to my horror, the office was crowded with students. She rushed forward, wrapping me in a vigorous hug, her voice loud and breaking with tears.

"Why didn't you tell me Lisa? Oh, why didn't you tell me!?"

The hug jolted me. My body stiffened as I glanced around, cheeks burning, feeling exposed and ashamed. Her arms clung, but her words cut deep. *Tell her what?*

Detective Mendez was gentle with me as he drove to the shelter home. His eyes carried compassion, and his voice held a steady tenderness that eased some of my fear. No one explained the details of what was happening, I didn't know why I was being taken there or what would happen to Don and Jody. But in the silence of that ride, I could feel that Detective Mendez believed this was a place where I might be safe.

A few days later, I was brought to the police station by a social worker, where another detective sat down with me alone. He asked if I knew where the photographer was, explaining that Don and Jody had both denied knowing his whereabouts. I opened my mouth to answer, I had memo-rized the way, but before I could speak, he stopped, exhaled heavily, and with a weary, sorrowful look said, "Lisa, the photographer is wanted for the murder of two children."

What did he just say?

I sat in stunned silence as his words crashed over me, each detail heavier than the last. My chest tightened until it felt like all the air had been sucked from the room. The walls seemed to tilt and blur, my stomach heaving with nausea as I clutched for breath. A jagged gasp tore out of me, loud in the stillness. My voice shook when it finally broke through. "I... I know where his studio is. I memorized the way. I can take you there," I whispered, the words tumbling out in a rush of fear and urgency.

"Really? Ok, let's go right now," he said with surprise and relief. My head stung with the thoughts of what happened to these poor children. He and another detective drove me, following my directions, straight to the photographer's studio. Terror filled my body remembering the awful photographer. I wondered if he would know it was me who took the police to his studio.

Poor kids.

The voice had spoken to me for a reason. This must be why! I did not hesitate as we walked up the stairs to the studio. I stood with the detectives at the studio door.

Knock, knock, knock.

No answer.

Knock, knock, knock.

Again, no answer.

Had he hurt the kids here? What would happen if he opened the door? I hoped he would get caught. But there was no answer, no breaking down the door. Instead, they jotted down some notes, and we drove back to the police station. On the way back, I wondered if the photographer had been watching us secretly and saw that it was me who took the police to his studio. Did he know how to find me?

Little Lisa,

It was never supposed to be your job to protect the people who harmed you. But they taught you that love meant silence and loyalty, even when it hurt. That kind of manipulation is called grooming. It confuses a child's natural instincts and leaves them feeling responsible, ashamed, and loyal to those who don't deserve it.

When the detectives asked those terrifying questions, your body froze, not because you didn't care, but because you were overwhelmed. You were scared and trying to stay safe.

And still, when you learned what the photographer had done, your deep goodness rose to the surface. Even afraid, you spoke up. You remembered the way. You helped protect others. That was incredibly brave.

Your mother's hug in front of everyone, her sudden display of emotion, no wonder it confused you. When love only appears during a public crisis or performance, it doesn't feel safe because it isn't real. It just adds to the chaos.

None of this was your fault. Not your silence, not your fear, not your aching hope for someone to finally love you right. You were a good child, thoughtful, loyal, and heartbreakingly strong. You deserved safety. You deserved care. And you deserved someone steady by your side saying, "You did nothing wrong. I've got you now. You're not alone anymore."

CHAPTER 17

The car was silent as the social worker drove from the police station to the shelter home. As we pulled into the driveway, I sat upright and wiped sweat from my forehead. *Am I safe?* The police hadn't said anything else to me, and I was worried. I caught my breath and followed the social worker to the door.

"Take care Lisa," the social worker sounded kind. I walked into the shelter home corridor. One of the shelter girls walked me straight to the shelter home mother's room. Red velvet covered her bedroom from top to bottom. The curtains, the bedding, the carpet, all matched, a harsh, bold crimson. I stood at the edge of the bedroom door, which was guarded by her angry poodle. "Just stay there, don't come in, if you need something, ask," the shelter mother barked without eye contact.

"I'm back from the police station," I said quietly.

"What? Speak up!"

"I'm back from the police station!" The words pushed through my constricting throat.

"Go get your dinner if you want, bedtime is in two hours."

I turned around and walked past the kitchen and onto the patio. I lit up a cigarette, and one of the girls waved me to the treehouse by the fence.

When we sat down, she said, "I have a surprise for you!" With a big smile, she pulled a joint out of her pocket. "Our friend gave this to me to share with you." She had made friends with a teenage boy who sometimes walked through the field, within perfect view of the treehouse. When I met him, he listened to our stories and was very nice. He knew I was going to the police station today and made sure I had some weed for when I returned.

"Oh man, thank you so much!" I eagerly lit the joint and inhaled until my lungs spit out the smoke with a cough. My shelter sister looked at me with the most caring eyes. She added, "I'm so glad you are here with me." She put her head on my shoulder, and we shared the joint and sat watching the free world drive by on the road beyond the field until it was time to go to bed.

At the shelter home, smoke breaks were divvied out with structure, as was chore time, eating times, and bedtime. The first pop tart I ever ate was at this house; that was breakfast, your choice of flavors. The house was in an upper-class neighborhood, pool and all. Even so, we all wondered what we had done wrong to be "locked up." The days there were barely tolerable for me with no escape. Us girls tried to be there for each other as best we could. We bonded over how ridiculous the shelter home mother was. She always had a filter-less cigarette hanging out of her mouth and her poodle in her arms. The dog growled when we got near and nipped you if you tried to pet it. The shelter mom never looked me in my eyes; not once. She didn't ask questions, only laid out the rules.

The girls talked with each other about why they were there. One girl casually said, "My uncle molested me." Another said, "I got beat up." When it was my turn, I didn't know what to say. *Why am I here?* No thoughts formed. So, the girls played a guessing game and concluded I had been molested too. Here we were, locked up together, in our own little unchosen club. Eating pop tarts and smoking cigarettes in between chores.

About a week after I'd been there, it suddenly hit me, I couldn't remember what Don looked like anymore. His whole face was just... gone from my mind. I got scared fast. If I couldn't remember him, what if I didn't remember the photographer either?

Then another thought slammed into me: *Did Don and Jody ever even love me?* The idea hurt so much it made my knees give out, and I crouched down beside the house.

What if they were going to kill me? What if they never loved me? My mind couldn't hold it. I felt unsteady, like the ground wasn't holding me up right. My whole body trembled. More than anything, I wanted to disappear into my hiding place in the bushes back home, where at least the air and dirt felt familiar. But I was trapped here instead, cornered by feelings that pressed in on me and wouldn't let go. I craved escape and comfort, but all I had was a stale, unfamiliar confinement.

Kneeling there at the side of the shelter home, I remembered the voice that told me to memorize the way to the photographer's studio. *I did the right thing,* I repeated to myself as I grasped my arms, "I'll be okay, I'll be okay." My shelter sister touched my shoulder and told me to come to the tree house. She didn't need to ask what was wrong; she understood. We sat together in our small hiding place, silent, until it was time to go to the next thing.

Sometimes we broke free from the shelter home prison. One Saturday morning, we were being taken to the Castle, a local amusement park. The shelter home mom gave us ten minutes to be ready, and I hurried, excited to be able to play some arcade games again. Before we walked outside to get into the van, I was met with her disapproving look. "Oh no, you need to go put on a bra!"

"I've never had a bra," I answered.

"What? You're flat but you still need a bra." She grabbed a used bra from the hallway closet and threw it at me. "Put this on and wear it every day now ." I heard giggles behind me as I walked to the bathroom, wishing I could shrink away.

As I was figuring out how to put it on, annoyance bubbled up inside me. I was always getting into trouble over my unimpressive chest. In elementary school, my mother bought me a t-shirt with the caption, "Itty bitty titty committee," and I wore it to school. I got in trouble and the head office lady at school sent me home with a note saying my shirt was inappropriate. Mom laughed when I told her about it. "Just don't wear it to school any-more," she directed.

Another time, mother gave me a silk-screened t-shirt with a picture of a sexy woman's chest. She had me wear it in public when we went out for the day. I endured disgusted looks and comments from strangers. I felt uncomfortable about it, but Mom thought it was great! Another time I got in trouble again at school for another shirt that showed too much. "It's fine for you to wear, just don't bend over in front of people at school," Mother laughed. When I wore it to school a second time, the principal scolded me. "Lisa, don't wear that shirt again!"

That would have been a good time to start wearing a bra, I thought. As I struggled with the configuration of the new bra, another memory came to mind. One Christmas my sister dressed me up like a present. "Your dress looks like wrapping paper! Here are some bows to finish it," she said. She smiled, "Look a bra made out of bows," and stuck two bows right onto my chest. Everyone laughed. She added a third bow down low. "Here's one for your privates." And to top it off, she stuck another bow on my head. My amused mother grabbed the camera and snapped a picture of the whole thing.

"Lisa, hurry!" The shelter mother yelled just as I finished the final clasp. I rushed to the van wearing my new bra. She looked at my chest to verify it was on, and I was approved to go.

Detective Mendez visited me several times while I was living at the shelter. He didn't hide what he thought, he told me plainly that my mother was the worst kind of abuser. He also spoke gently with me adding, "You can rise above everything that has happened to you, you have something inside you that I can see that will help you have a good life anyway." He encouraged me to play softball and to focus on school when I went back. A couple of times, he even brought me to dinner with his family, giving me a glimpse of the warmth and steadiness I was hungry for.

"You can't go to practice without an escort, a Sheriff, but I've already arranged that for you. And congratulations on making the all-star team," he told me once as we picked at appetizers together. It felt strangely wonderful to sit in a restaurant with him, his wife, and their son. For a moment, I wondered if the people around us thought I was their daughter, even though my hair didn't match theirs. I let myself pretend anyway. I imagined I belonged to them, this calm, steady family with a father who was a detective and who actually cared whether I made it to practice or not. The thought made me smile. What would it be like, I wondered, to have a police detective for a father?

On the way back to the shelter home, Detective Mendez said to me, "Remember, you don't have to let this ruin you, Lisa, you can still have a good life!" He sounded so convincing and I wanted to prove him right. That single sentence, spoken with such conviction, etched itself into my memory.

The next week, when Detective Mendez came to see me, there was a heaviness in his voice. "The court ordered that I have to take you home," he said quietly. "I don't agree with it, but I have to follow their decision. I'm sorry, Lisa." I looked up at him, wishing I could somehow make it easier for him.

"When do I go back?" I asked.

"Right now."

I began packing the few things I had, remembering with a pang that I had promised to meet our friend with my shelter sister later that evening in the treehouse. There was no time for goodbyes. Fifteen minutes was all I had to gather my things and leave. My face felt stiff, like stone, as I followed Detective Mendez out.

On the drive back, he handed me his card. "If you ever need anything, call me," he said, his voice echoed with apology. As we sat in the idling car outside my house, he added, "If your mom abuses you again, you let me know. Okay? I'm sorry to have to do this."

I clutched the card, nodding. "Okay. Thank you," I managed.

I got out of the car and walked to the front door. It was locked. I knocked. Mother was leaving for work. "You were supposed to be here an hour ago! Go to your room, and we will talk tomorrow."

My siblings had all kinds of questions for me: *What happened? What did they do to you? Where were you?* I did the best I could to answer them, before they left too, and there I was alone in the house again. I still felt scared to be home alone, but I knew where to go and was soon getting high with friends.

The next morning, Mother shook me awake and marched me into the kitchen. "What did you say to them about me?"

"I didn't say anything about you, Mom."

"What the hell, Lisa," she smirked, "You let Don and Jody do all those things to you? You are such a little slut. You make my life a living hell on purpose. You're good for nothing! And you get innocent people in trouble!" She shoved me toward the door. "Get out and never come back!"

She added, "You are not my daughter!" The words chased me down the street. Here I was, getting kicked out again. This time instead of going to the bushes, I walked to the local mall and used the pay phone.

"Hi, uh, Detective Mendez..." before I could say anything else, he said, "What happened?"

"Um, you said to call if my mom did anything." I started to tell him the things my mother said.

"Where are you at?" he interrupted me. "Meet me at General Hospital in the cafeteria."

I walked to the hospital. As I approached the table that he was sitting at he stood up and invited me to sit down. He asked again what had happened as he took notes, and he offered me a piece of cake. He then explained that he was going to put me back in the shelter home and do his best to protect me from my mother. I didn't want to go back to the shelter home, but I didn't want to go back home either.

"Well, you haven't been gone long." The shelter mother said as Detective Mendez walked me up to the door. "You are always welcome though." She smiled, nodding towards Detective Mendez.

Detective Mendez said to me, "Don't worry, I'm going to help you." He added, "I will still make sure that you are able to play and practice with the all-star girl's softball team." He gave me a side hug and walked out the door.

At practice the next day, I fumbled through trying to explain why a Sheriff had to be there with me and why I was living at a shelter home. The Sheriff spoke with the coaches and then drifted to the edges of the field. My coaches' eyes held both compassion and something like grief, and then the air between all of us thickened with awkward silence. I was no longer just a teammate, I was the strange, fragile girl no one knew how to approach.

About a week later Detective Mendez met with me, he explained that I'd be moving into a foster home and that he might not see me for a long while. He told me that if Don and Jody didn't take a plea deal, he would try his best to be at the trial when I testified, though he hoped it wouldn't come to that. He stayed encouraging, making our last dinner with his family feel as normal as he could. As the night ended, I told him, "When I'm an adult, I'll get back in touch and let you know how I'm doing."

"You'd better," he said with a small smile. "I'll be waiting for that."

Little Lisa,

You were a child, trying to survive the unimaginable with so little support. Being sent back and forth, into danger, into shelter, into judgment. That would overwhelm any person, let alone a thirteen-year-old. The fear, the confusion, the numbness, it all makes sense. You were doing your best in a world that made no sense to you.

What you were feeling was dissociation, when pain becomes too much for your mind and body to handle, your brain steps in to protect you by numbing or detaching. It's not weakness. It's survival.

And you needed that protection. You were shamed, abused, and then punished for not protecting others from the consequences of their abuse. When a child is sexualized or ridiculed like that, it distorts how they understand themselves. It leaves confusion, embarrassment, and often deep self-blame.

But you kept showing up, for yourself, for others. You found safety in small places: a treehouse, a friend's shoulder, a shared moment of understanding. And then there was someone who did see your worth. Detective Mendez reminded you that your life still mattered. That you could heal.

He was right.

CHAPTER 18

My new foster home was more than an hour from my neighborhood, far enough to feel like another world. I was surprised that my foster mom had a boyfriend; she didn't seem like the type to care about things like that. Her short, unkempt hair and rumpled clothes gave her a disheveled look, but her demeanor was kind. She shared the house with a foster daughter, just the two of them, until I arrived.

Sandy, my foster sister, was a couple of years older than me, cute, blonde, and easy to like. We quickly found common ground: smoking, getting high, and laying out in the sun. We spent most of our time together, talking about music and plans for the future. Our foster mom was often away, trusting us to stay out of too much trouble.

The long, hot days of summer dragged by slowly, each one stretching like it would never end. Baking in the sun with music playing felt comfortable, fun. Tanning was my happy place. I'd cover myself in Ban de Soleil and close my eyes, pretending I was at the beach.

Sandy and I would talk for hours as we tanned. We pictured ourselves grown up, with cool apartments filled with cute furniture, living right next door to each other. I imagined my own fridge always stocked with a six pack of beer, waiting for me after work. Just thinking about coming home, opening the fridge, and pulling out an ice-cold bottle felt like freedom. I couldn't wait for the day I was old enough to buy alcohol anytime I wanted.

But even in those daydreams, a heaviness crept in. Deep down, I already knew I couldn't live without alcohol, weed, or cigarettes. I didn't want to rely on them. They didn't match the version of myself I desired. I wanted to be like the athletes who lived clean and strong, like the character in *Kung Fu* who taught that freedom meant no attachments or addictions. When I practiced Buddhism with Ray, I'd learned that self-control was part of enlightenment. I believed sobriety was the higher path, but I didn't know how to reach it. The truth pressed hard inside me. I felt weak, disappointed, and ashamed. I wished more than anything that I could be happy without substances, but that felt like an impossible dream.

Life in the new neighborhood intensified feelings of loneliness. I had nowhere really to go. The loneliness deepened when my foster sister went to her boyfriend's house, and she went too often. When I was alone in the house I wept to my music, my only comfort. I laid in bed, barely hanging on emotionally, sobbing until someone came home. It was unbearable.

A boy down the street became my friend, and we spent as much time together as we could. He wanted to be my boyfriend but I wasn't ready for that, and he respected it. We talked and had fun. He shared his marijuana freely, knowing I had nothing to give in return. Those moments together felt like a relief, but they never lasted long enough. When he or Sandy wasn't around, the unhappiness closed in, heavy and unshakable.

I decided I had to get away from the sadness swallowing me whole. So, I told my social worker I wanted to go back home. That felt like a better choice than staying where I was at. Not questioning why, she said she would look into that option, and I was granted permission within a week. And so, after most of the summer had passed by, I went back home. I left even though my foster sister and my friend didn't want me to leave. I would miss them too, but I had to get away from the sadness the only way I knew how. Maybe life would be different when I got back home.

This time, I swore I was going to get school right. I'd focus. I'd be good. No boys, no distractions, nothing that could ruin things again. Detective Mendez's voice kept repeating in my mind, *"You can still have a good life."* I held onto those words with everything in me. I wanted that more than anything.

My sister and mother picked me up from the foster home and took me to lunch. Over sandwiches, they told me I no longer had a place in the room I used to share with my sister. They hadn't known if I'd be coming back, so the rules had changed; the living room was mine now.

I nodded quickly, and told them all I wanted was to do well in school and try out for volleyball like my sister.

"I want to be like you. I love you and miss you," I told her honestly. She laughed, rolled her eyes, and gave me a quick hug.

In the middle of lunch, my sister tugged me toward the bathroom and pulled me into a stall. Her eyes narrowed with contempt. "Lisa, you liked it at Don and Jody's, didn't you? You must have liked what they were doing to you," she sneered. "So, what part did you like best?"

Her words cut like glass. My face burned as I dropped my gaze to the floor, trying to disappear. Her laughter echoed in my ears. She stared at me for what felt like forever, watching me squirm. Then, with a cold, flat voice, she ended it. "Let's go back to lunch. Mom's been through enough with all this, you can at least not keep her waiting."

I never told Detective Mendez anything more about mother. Instead, I tried to spend as much time as I could with friends and focused on pre-paring for ninth grade. Ray was gone, he had left my mother, and with him went the sweet comfort and love he had always given me. His absence left an ache and anger I didn't know how to fill.

A couple of weeks before school started, Mother's voice pierced the house. "There are not going to be trials for Don or Jody! They're going to plea bargain instead!" she screeched. Her face twisted with anger. "It makes me look good to meet with the district attorney and push to go," she said, her tone shifting into satisfaction. Then she muttered to herself smugly, "I'll show up with my 'troubled' daughter at court anyway, and look concerned. That Detective Mendez tried to blame me, but he couldn't touch me."

I left the room when I realized she no longer cared if I was there, her thoughts spilling out to no one in particular. I turned my focus elsewhere, planning for the "new Lisa" and the start of a new school year. At times, it felt almost possible to forget what I had endured with Don and Jody. In-stead of dwelling on them, or the photographer, I poured my energy into choosing clothes, organizing folders and pencils, and imagining what it would be like to finally be a high schooler.

I was still getting high every day, blurring the edges of everything. With my friends, it was easier to lean into the excitement; high school, here we come! I pushed away anything negative and pretended I was just a normal girl, with only the first-day outfit to worry about.

But Don and Jody's punishment still hung in the air, unsettled and unavoidable. Soon enough, we were heading to the district attorney's office. The district attorney said there was no need to attend or testify. "We try not to re-traumatize victims by having them attend court," he said.

"I want Lisa there. How do we make sure we are going to the right courtrooms and at the right times?" Mother answered.

"Okay, but she'll be the only victim there."

The district attorney updated us on possible sentence lengths and explained that this was Don's second molestation charge. He had already been prosecuted and served time for abusing his own children.

His words jolted a memory, Don once telling me himself that he had gone to jail for molesting his kids. He insisted that "molestation" was just a word people used when they didn't understand what real love was. He said the courts had ruined his children, not him, claiming they had been fine until the legal system got involved. According to him, nothing he did had harmed them at all. I kept that memory locked inside. My mother was doing all the talking anyway.

But this was Jody's first offense, which meant her prison time would be less than Don's. I tried to follow what was being said, but my thoughts were spinning too fast to catch it all. I didn't know what to think, only that no other kids should ever be hurt again.

Don had told me I was different from other girls, and part of me believed him. I wasn't sure if what happened had left me wounded, or if I was somehow set apart, like he said. I could see why this would be bad for other girls, though, and I wanted to protect them. Still, the questions lingered in me: Was I hurt? I felt sad. I hadn't wanted to do those things… and yet, I did.

The DA startled me out of my thoughts with outraged words. "…and they got married in jail so they wouldn't have to testify against each other!"

At that moment, I knew Jody wasn't just a victim. For so long, I had worried about her, wondering if she felt as alone as I did. She was in her twenties, though to me she seemed much older. And I believed she cared about me. She showed it in ways that felt real. She reassured me often, taught me how to take care of myself while we showered together, showed me how to cook, mix drinks, and even played with me like a friend.

But then, she started leaving me alone with Don. I didn't want that, and I couldn't understand how she could walk away. Each time she did, something inside me broke. I was devastated, desperate to go with her, aching for her not to leave me behind.

They wore down my resistance with explanations and reassurances, insisting I was wrong to say no and should trust them instead. Jody, especially, soothed and persuaded me, repeating that everything they wanted me to do was fine and that she'd stay by my side. But she didn't.

But now, learning they had married each other to avoid testifying, the truth hit hard. That choice was proof Jody wasn't just a victim caught in his control, she was protecting him, protecting herself, and protecting what they had done together. The sadness sank deeper. She wasn't innocent, not the way I had once believed.

"Well, we will be there," Mother declared, cutting right over the DA and his concerns for the victims. Her voice carried the same unshakable certainty I had seen in Don and Jody, the kind that bulldozed through everything in its path. Their confidence always seemed so absolute, and I could never match it.

The day of his court hearing felt strange, like time was both dragging and rushing at once. Mother barked at me to hurry, her voice sharp as we scrambled to the car. By the time we reached the courtroom, everything seemed hazy, almost clouded over, strange, since we were indoors. I wished I had sunglasses, or better yet, the power to disappear altogether. I stayed silent, afraid to draw any attention, afraid most of all to see Don. I hadn't laid eyes on him since the day he drove me home with his promise to the photographer lingering in my mind that I would take nude pictures.

It felt like so long ago, though only a few months had passed. I was frustrated that I couldn't clearly picture his face, yet I knew without doubt I would recognize him the moment I saw him. Brown hair, that much I remembered. And of course, he would be the one waiting to be sentenced. What haunted me most was the certainty that his eyes would find me, filled with rage, blaming me for all of this.

When we got to the courtroom I briefly looked in his direction, trying not to be seen in return. He kept his gaze forward, but I could tell that his eyes were seething. I had seen that look before when he growled at me to be quiet while he was talking with the photographer.

We arrived late, slipping in just as the hearing was ending. Mother's disappointment was unmistakable. She glared at the District Attorney, whispering furiously, her words laced with vulgarities about being told the wrong time. I could feel people's eyes shifting toward us, the heat of their attention burning into me. Her anger was loud even in whispers, and I wanted to disappear, ashamed to be sitting there beside her.

I heard the judge say, "Ten years."

Ten years in prison, for molesting me. There were other victims, I knew that, yet the weight of it settled squarely on my shoulders. It felt as if I alone were responsible for sending him away.

The judge said his name, and I sank lower in my seat, curling in on myself. His shoulders snapped tight, fists squeezing hard, and the air rushed out of me as if someone had pressed a hand to my chest. My body trembled. If I stayed still enough, maybe he wouldn't notice me.

My legs itched to run, but they wouldn't move. The scrape of shackles filled the room as he stood. He turned. I ducked fast, tucking my head, eyes fixed on the floor, wishing I could disappear into it. I didn't dare look again, but I could feel it anyway, his eyes on me, locking me in place. And I knew he would never forget. What would I do when he came after me someday?

A few days after Don's sentencing, it was Jody's turn, and this time we were early to the courtroom. When I saw her walk in, I squirmed deeper into my seat, wishing that I could hide. She had a female attorney that looked like a kind grandma. When Jody noticed I was there, she looked away quickly, rolling her eyes. The proceedings started, and I learned that Jody had found Christ in jail. I didn't know what that meant, but I felt it meant something good, and I hoped that she felt better. My mom snickered at the news of Jody finding Christ. Her pastor was in attendance and would be her support person as she readjusted to life. Her attorney explained that Jody had been a victim, forced to do things against her will, and therefore wasn't responsible for the other defendant's actions.

What?

I couldn't hold back my gasp. In a flash, I recalled all the times I didn't want to do what they wanted me to do, and how she literally held my hand and reassured me that it was best to join them, to learn from them, to live like they did. That being a nudist and being open sexually was the right way to be. She definitely did not promote a Christian lifestyle. And she definitely promoted the lifestyle she now was claiming to be a victim of. As her attorney proceeded, I moaned again, outraged. I was just so surprised by what I was hearing. I knew it was not true and couldn't stop the sounds coming from me. The judge heard this and warned the District Attorney to keep me quiet. But I just couldn't be quiet, rage tore up through my body and the aghast sound escaped my mouth, surprising myself.

The District Attorney rushed over, warning that I'd be thrown out if I didn't stop. A surge shot through me, electric and alive in a way I'd never felt before. *I have to do the right thing,* my mind shouted. *I don't care what happens to me.* The thought pushed me forward, almost lifting me out of my seat. How could she sit there and lie? I wanted to shout it, to protest any way I could. Even if it meant being dragged out, I didn't care.

Within moments of my outburst, the judge's eyes landed on me. Her stern expression softened into something I didn't expect, compassion. Instead of scolding me, she said, "I see that you are present and a victim of the defendant. Would you like a chance to say something?" She was looking straight at me. For a moment I sat frozen, unable to believe her words were meant for me.

Does she actually care about what I have to say?

Before I could respond, my mother spoke up, "Yes, she would!"

Would I? I didn't know what to say, but my mom pushed me up and said, "Go ahead, Lisa!"

I rose from my seat and, without moving closer, began to speak. To my surprise, the words came easily, spilling out as if they had been waiting inside me all along.

"Jody said she was my friend. I loved Jody. I didn't want to do those things, but Jody told me it was okay, that what they were doing was the right thing to do. She wasn't in the kitchen baking cookies while Don was trying to have sex with me. No. She was right there, talking me into it, holding my hand."

Every word was true. I did love Jody. "I would have never even wanted to be at their apartment, or spend time with them, if she hadn't been there."

The judge thanked me and then turned to Jody and her attorney and said, "Due to this new information, instead of a year of probation, she will do a year's time in county jail. She will also have to register as a sex offender for the rest of her life."

Jody's head went down. She looked at her attorney in shock. Her attorney tried to argue the judge's ruling. "Your honor, my client has changed her ways; she feels bad about what happened. She is going to church, and her pastor is here to support her and be by her side after today as well."

But the judge shot her down.

Jody sat back in her seat, defeated. Her long body contorted in a clump in the chair as she shook her head in disbelief. My heart was pumping, and I could feel the pounding in my head. I sat down, wiping burning tears from my eyes, not sure how to feel.

Then it was over, just like that. Jody looked at me briefly and shook her head. My heart sank. *What was I doing? Remember the photographer!*

Still reeling from what had just happened, I trailed after my mom as she strode toward the door. Mother paced us so we were directly behind Jody, so close it felt like we were attached to her. Down the courthouse stairs we went, the three of us moving in step, almost like we were a unit. The closeness made my stomach knot, and every part of me wanted to get away from her.

At the bottom, Jody and I drifted toward the bathroom at the exact same moment. My feet stopped cold at the doorway. My chest tightened. I felt trapped between my fear of her and my mother's eyes on me. I was not going in now.

But Mother's hand pressed into my back, hard, leaving no room for choice. "Go in," she ordered.

It was just Jody and me in the bathroom. I wondered if she was going to attack me? Could I defend myself if she did?

She didn't raise a hand. Instead, she turned toward me and said, "Thanks a lot, Lisa," her voice edged with warning. Then she walked out, leaving me behind.

Thanks a lot? The words spun in my head. I had loved her, trusted her, and believed she cared for me. Now all that remained was the sting of betrayal tangled with confusion, leaving me unsure of what had ever been real between us.

Little Lisa,

You are so brave. You survived terrible betrayal. You were still in the midst of so much evil but you still found strength, beyond your own, to tell the real truth of what happened, even among your confusion. You've carried your wise self all along. The abuse made you bury it, but it never disappeared, it was quietly waiting until it was safe to be heard again. When you spoke, something shifted, not just in the courtroom, but inside of you.

You've been taught your feelings don't matter, but they do! You were taught that love means people hurt you, and you were forced into submission and silence. But when the judge asked if you wanted to speak, and you did, you rewrote that story. You named the manipulation. You corrected the lies. You showed the world Jody wasn't just a victim.

And still, it makes sense that you felt confused too. How could someone you loved also hurt you? How could your own mother push you into danger again and again, forcing you back to Don and Jody, forcing you to speak before you were ready, even shoving you into that bathroom with Jody? Confusion is a natural outcome of abuse. When people you love also hurt you, your mind struggles to hold both realities at once.

And yet, even though it was wrong that you were forced, you made something good from it. By speaking, you planted a seed of hope inside yourself, proof that your voice mattered. And beyond yourself, you helped protect other children from being hurt the way you were. You turned pain into power. The same voice that once told you to memorize the way to the photographer's door joined with your wise self that day. Together, they rose up to help you speak the truth, and this time, the world heard it!

CHAPTER 19

From the first day of ninth grade, I dedicated myself. My two years of Fs in junior high were earned, but my hard work in ninth grade began to pay off. I was learning! But the best part of high school for me was finding sports again. Even though I had never played volleyball before, I made the team and lettered as a freshman. I felt super proud.

I fell in love with the game. Practices became my happy place. I lived for the feel of the ball, the dives, the bumps, the serves, the endless drills. Running wasn't my favorite, but I discovered I was good at it anyway. Back in elementary school, I could barely finish the mile without gasping for air. As a little smoker, my young lungs couldn't keep up with the others. But now, on the track, the laps felt like release. I pushed through the burn in my chest and found a second wind.

My volleyball coach was an experienced coach, though it was his first year at Arlington High School. Even though I was still smoking, drinking, and getting high I did really well! The coach told me I had the most potential of anyone he had ever worked with. I could hardly believe it. Hearing those words made me feel wonderful. It truly felt like a dream come true.

I was eager to try out for high school softball later that year and get back behind the plate as a catcher. Just thinking about it, I could smell the dirt and fresh-cut grass of the field. There was so much ahead of me to look forward to.

I also signed up for drama. My sister had been in drama, and I wanted to follow in her footsteps. She always seemed to have so much fun with it.

By the end of my first quarter at Arlington High, I felt proud of myself. Amazingly, I made it on the honor roll and played varsity volleyball. I was embracing my new identity wholeheartedly.

Even though it was against the law for teenagers to smoke, our high school had a designated smoking area right in front of the drama theater. It was a popular place to hang out, even for kids who didn't smoke. I met a lot of people there and enjoyed getting to know students from every group; the nerds, jocks, drama kids, and band kids.

It was in that smoking area that I met a kind boy who invited me to the ROTC dance, and a senior I met there asked me to prom. Both treated me like a true gentleman would. I got to dress up and get my hair done and have some normal high school experiences.

The days of being called the school slut were fading. Some students who remembered me that way still didn't like me, but I showed them I didn't care. Except from one girl on the volleyball team. But she learned to stay quiet once she saw what I could do on the court.

I liked drama mostly because of the friends I had in the class. They were adventurous, spontaneous, and unafraid to express themselves. The drama kids seemed more open than most others, and I admired that. I was shy, not like them, but it was so much fun to be around them. They encouraged me to join in, showing me that being silly, loud, or even a little outrageous wasn't just accepted, it was welcomed.

The drama teacher was a quirky man with shoulder-length hair, a long nose, and a round belly. He walked in a way that made it seem like he might topple over at any moment. But he was kind to us. One day he told me he thought I had talent. I wasn't so sure. I knew I wasn't on the same level as the creative geniuses around me, but maybe I could grow into it.

I was nervous about acting, but I powered through our musical, *Bye Bye Birdie,* as an extra. What I loved most was the energy behind the scenes, the backstage buzz, the makeup, the costumes. The exaggerated expressions felt silly and awkward, but we were all silly and awkward together, and that made it easier.

After the musical was over, it was time to move on to a play. The Play, titled *The Visit,* was about a wealthy woman who had been scorned returning to her hometown. She would get revenge on those who were abusive to her as a child. The drama teacher told me he had a special part for me. I was excited, nervous, and not sure I was ready for it. But if he thought I was ready, then maybe I was.

When the cast list went up, everyone crowded around to see their roles. My name was there and not as an extra. I was cast as a townswoman who later became a "woman of the night." At first, I didn't understand what that meant. When I asked a friend, they told me it was a prostitute. I didn't like that idea but then my friend congratulated me. They told me it was a big deal since ninth graders hardly ever landed parts like that.

The script read that the bodyguards to the main protagonist were up to no good when they were off work. One day, as a townswoman, I was sweeping the streets. The guards, seeing the townswoman was alone, attacked her. Drunk and shouting, they jeered, "Oh, come on little lady, let us have what we want. Don't fight too hard!" The townswoman backed away, only to bump into another guard behind her. He grabbed her, but she slipped from his grip, only to be cornered again. She refused to go with them, and a fight broke out.

The scene ended when one of the guards punched her in the face and threw her over his shoulder. Kicking and pounding his back, she screamed as he carried her offstage.

The drama teacher enlisted a couple of football players to play the bodyguard roles. We stood center stage, taking direction from our teacher. "Throw a punch, but make sure you miss by a few inches. Then, when the punch is near, jerk your head back like you've been hit. When she is off balance from the punch, come up and grab her by the waist."

"Come here, Lisa, I'll throw you over my shoulders so they can see it."

I couldn't believe it. He called me forward and ignoring my hesitation he waved me over. "Come on! Let's get to it!"

We began. He pretended to swing at me, and I clumsily acted out being hit, stumbling into a collapse. Then, with startling force, he scooped me up and slung me over his shoulder. My chin smacked against his back, and in the motion, his hand grabbed my crotch. Leaning close, he whispered in my ear, "Scream louder!"

The sound caught in my throat. Instead of screaming I muttered a whimper. I tried to push against him, but I was trapped, squeezed tight and breathless. He held me there longer than the scene called for, talking casually to the football players as if nothing had happened.

I burned with humiliation. No apology, no acknowledgment of his "accidental grab." Just silence from the class, everyone watching. When he finally set me down, his face flushed, he acted as though nothing unusual had occurred. He suggested we run it again, but just then the bell rang. Saved.

"Good work today," he called to the class before turning to me with a smile. "I'll see you tomorrow," he said lightly. I rushed out, desperate to shake off the experience.

On the night of the performance, my parents actually showed up. As I handed my father the tickets, he giggled, "Wow, my ninth-grade daughter is a prostitute."

Later, during the play, when the football players hoisted me up and carried me offstage, I heard my father's chuckle rise from the audience. Our eyes locked. His grin was wider than I had ever seen, and the sound of his laughter trailed after me as I disappeared behind the curtain.

During the next scene I was in, it was implied that after being raped by the guards I accepted my new fate as a "woman of the night." I wore a slinky dress, walking until a man propositioned me for sex. My line to the John was, *"Sure, I even take credit cards."* Then smiling, I linked arms with him and led him offstage. It always made my drama teacher chuckle. As the John and I passed by the drama teacher after our scene, he grinned and said, "Good job, Lisa, you nailed it."

Little Lisa,

You were finally becoming who you were meant to be, an athlete, a creative, a student who shined. The joy you felt on the volleyball court and the stage was real. You earned it. That wasn't pretend. You pushed past so much to reach it.

But even in these bright places, adults still crossed boundaries they never should have. What happened with your drama teacher wasn't "direction" or part of the show, it was a violation. His behavior, his touch, his whisper, lines that never should have been crossed. The fact that the class fell silent shows they knew it too.

You had already endured too much, I'm sorry you had more humiliation and confusion. You were starting to shine.

The audience's chuckles, your father's laugh, they were all part of a pattern where no one stopped to say: Are you alright? Do you feel safe? Is this okay with you?

I see you. I would have stopped that rehearsal. I would have taken you off that stage. I would have complained to the school and even called the police on him! You should have been treated so much better.

CHAPTER 20

I decided acting wasn't for me and my drama participation dropped off, but I kept busy going to school most days and playing volleyball. After school and on weekends, Mother began inviting me to game nights with our neighbor, Kathy, her long-time friend who lived directly behind us. Kathy and her husband were empty nesters, though I had met some of her adult children over the years. As a kid, I sometimes helped her with yard work, and she'd pay me with plates of delicious homemade Italian food.

Now, as a freshman, something strange was happening, Mother and I actually got along sometimes. It didn't happen often, so I clung to those evenings like they were precious. She let me smoke in front of her and Kathy, as if I'd suddenly been admitted into the adult circle. We sat in our pajamas, drinking coffee, playing Yahtzee, passing cigarettes, and eating Kathy's cooking. I felt grown up, included, almost like I belonged.

One of Kathy's adult sons, Glenn, had recently moved back home after his divorce. I hadn't met him before, though he and his parents came to see the play I was in. Glenn was in his thirties, a truck driver with the kind of dark hair and strong features that fit the stereotype of Italian good looks. He carried himself with an easy charm. At home, my mother and sister would comment on how handsome he was, and I found myself agreeing. When he joined us for Yahtzee nights, he slid easily into our conversations, asking me about my favorite foods, the music I liked, even what kinds of cars I thought were cool.

"I don't have a favorite car. Wait, it's Chitty Chitty Bang Bang! It can fly, be a boat, and be everything you need!"

He laughed. "What about a sports car, a fast, sleek car like mine?"

"Oh, I don't care about that. I like the magical car, though. It can take you anywhere!"

His eyes lit up, and he said, "I bet you'd like my car, it's special ordered."

One evening he and I were in the living room alone while mother and Kathy were in the kitchen. Glenn asked, "Why were you in a foster home?"

"I… um… well, Don and Jody were convicted of molesting me and some other girls." The words felt heavy and awkward on my tongue, but I forced them out. I owed him an answer. Then I hesitated before asking, "How did you know I was in a foster home?"

"My mother told me, and I'm so sorry for what happened to you."

I felt the compassion flow over me, reassuring me.

I added, "The detective felt I should be there."

"That jerk," Mom piped in, "he didn't know what he was doing."

He kept asking questions, and I did my best to respond, telling him about the court cases with Don and Jody. Then I added, "I'm committed to moving forward. I'm doing good in school and in volleyball, my favorite. I'm just trying not to think about all of that, just to be better now."

One evening, out of nowhere, he brought up what had happened with Don and Jody. He invited me into the living room and said, "What you went through was awful, Lisa. I'm sorry that happened to you. But… if you had been a willing participant, that would've been different, wouldn't it? Then it couldn't really be called molestation, right?"

I was still trying to make sense of what he meant, I stammered, "I guess" when Kathy suddenly stormed in from the kitchen, her voice sharp and accusing. "You're trying to seduce my son!" she screamed.

Startled, I gasped, "Oh no, I… I don't want to do that, I'm…" but she didn't let me finish. With fury in her eyes, she ordered us out of her house and told me never to come back. I stood in disbelief, struggling to process what was happening.

Then something even more shocking happened, Mother defended me. Her glare matched Kathy's as she snapped, "How dare you accuse her of that! How can you do this to us? We've been friends forever!"

"I don't care," Kathy shot back. "She is not allowed here anymore!"

She marched us out of the house, shouting at us as the door slammed behind us. On the short walk home, I shuddered and turned to Mother. "I'm so sorry, Mom. I didn't mean for that to happen, I wasn't trying to do that." My voice cracked with shame. I couldn't believe what had just unfolded. I felt awful. *What was wrong with me?*

Mother was seething. Can you believe her? After all these years of friendship, she humiliates me like that? How dare she!" Her voice grew louder, sharp with fury. "I've stood by Kathy through everything, and this is the thanks I get? To be accused, embarrassed, and thrown out of her house like that?"

My mind spun in circles. Did I somehow seem seductive? I hadn't meant to be. I didn't want boyfriends, didn't want sex, didn't want to hurt anyone. The thought made me sick. About half an hour later, Glenn showed up at our door, wanting to talk. Mother invited him in.

"I'm so sorry," Glenn said gently, his voice warm and steady. "I don't know what got into my mom. She was wrong to say that. Please don't pay any attention to her." He leaned in a little, his tone calm and reassuring, almost protective. "We won't let her come between our friendship. I'll keep coming by to see you guys here."

Glenn began coming by our house regularly, just as he'd promised. It was our unspoken secret, Kathy could never know. He was an adult, and he would make his own decisions. Around our kitchen table we played games, got high, laughed, and talked late into the evenings. When I apologized for upsetting his mother, he waved it off with an easy charm. "She's paranoid, Lisa. Don't take it personally." Then, he added, "I'd like to come watch one of your volleyball games."

Mother jumped at the chance, her face lighting up the way it did around him. "I'd be happy to take you!" she gushed, caught in his orbit like most women were.

One afternoon, my sister invited me on a drive with her and Glenn. We ended up at a nearby lake, parked with the windows rolled down, airing out the smoke. Glenn turned toward me, his voice low but coaxing. "Lisa, I think you're mature enough to try a line of crystal meth. It's way better than black beauties or cross tops." He glanced at my sister, and she smiled back. "I'll show you how, so you don't make a fool of yourself. I helped your sister, and I'll help you too."

I had known they were using meth, but I had never watched it up close. Pills I understood, but this was something entirely new, a line I hadn't imagined myself crossing.

My sister smiled as she said, "You will love it!"

Glenn showed by example how to snort it. "It will burn, but just sit back and let it set in. In a few minutes, you will see why we like it so much."

With some hesitation, I snorted my first line. "Oww! I do feel it burn!"

"Put your head back and wait till the burning goes away," Glenn instructed.

I did it, waited for the sting to fade, then lifted my head. Oh man, what was this feeling? Within minutes, words tumbled out of me, my body buzzing, my mind racing. What a rush.

"Well? What do you think?" Glenn asked with a grin, sliding a lit cigarette into my hand.

"Oh wow, I feel so... uh" I started rocking back and forth, searching for words. Before I could explain, Glenn and my sister launched into their own conversation, trading tips about meth, how to use it without staying up all night, when to eat so you didn't crash too hard. But I didn't care about their advice. I wanted to talk. I wanted every word to be mine. My whole body buzzed with energy, and all I wanted was to spill it out nonstop.

I couldn't sit still. I bounced up and down, hugging my arms around myself as if I could hold back the words piling up inside me, until they finally burst out. "This is... wow, way more than black beauties!"

I launched into a story about the first night my sister's boyfriend had given me a black beauty, how once it kicked in I ran outside and did cartwheels up and down the street. Laughing, I blurted, "Let me out, I want to do cartwheels now!"

Before either of them could stop me, I flung open the door, ran into the middle of the grass, and cartwheeled before collapsing onto the ground, breathless. "Whoa, this is crazy!" I shouted back to my sister and Glenn.

"Lay on your side and look this way," Glenn called. I rolled onto my side, still laughing, and saw him crouched there with a camera. "Smile!" he said. Then, *snap*, the moment captured.

When it was time to head home, my sister turned to me with instructions. "Okay, Lisa, you've got to act cool when we get back. Don't let anyone know you're high." I nodded obediently, clamping down on my urge to chatter, trying to stay quiet as we drove through the neighborhood.

As he dropped us off, Glenn leaned toward me with a grin and slipped a small baggie into my hand. "I already cut it up for you. Just take one small line at a time, no more than every few hours. Enjoy."

I had fallen behind on homework, but with the extra meth Glenn gave me, I managed to catch up. I stayed awake for one whole day, straight. By the end, shadows flickered at the edges of my vision, and I started to feel paranoid, more than usual. I didn't want to be around anyone.

That evening, Glenn checked up on me. He knelt next to me in the yard, and after I told him I wasn't feeling so good, he explained, "You will be okay, you just have to be smart with how you use it." He wiped my hair out of my eyes and lit up a joint to mellow me out. "Don't take any more for a couple of days and get some sleep. Then I'll come by and check on you. You have to ease into longer periods of time."

And that's what we did. When using it, I did not want to eat at all. I asked him about that, and he said it was completely normal. "Just eat after you wake up before you use it again."

My new rhythm settled into a pattern, use and stay up all night, crash the next, then take a day or two off before starting again. School began to slip through my fingers. Even with the endless energy meth gave me, I couldn't sit still in class. My thoughts raced too fast, pushing me to draw, to clean, to do anything but listen. Still, I refused to let go of volleyball. I forced myself to show up just enough to stay eligible.

Glenn was generous with his meth, always making sure I had enough. He told me I could come by his house at night if I was bored and couldn't sleep. "You don't have to be alone all night, we can hang out," he said. Being with Glenn appealed to me, but the thought of running into Kathy terrified me. Glenn brushed off my worry with an easy grin. He promised he'd let me slip in through his window so she'd never know. "We'll play games, hang out, it'll be fine," he assured me. "No one will know."

When I hadn't come by to visit him at night yet, he came over and encouraged me again. "It's okay Lisa, just come over." He'd given me more meth, and that night I finally gathered the nerve to go to his house. The streets felt unusually quiet as I slipped out, every sound amplified, the crunch of gravel under my shoes, the rustle of leaves, the distant bark of a dog. My heart pounded with each step, torn between fear of being caught and the thrill of sneaking away. When I reached his front yard, the shadows seemed to shift around me. I hesitated, glancing back toward my own house, then did as he'd instructed. With a shaky hand, I tapped on his window. When he slid the window open, his eyes lit up, happy that I had actually come. "You made it," he whispered with a grin, stepping back so I could climb in. Once inside, we kept our voices low, moving carefully so no one else would hear. He set up a board, and we quietly played a game, the thrill of secrecy buzzing between us. I had to laugh into a pillow so I wouldn't be too loud. Halfway through the game, Glenn glanced at me and asked softly, "Why don't you come sit by me?" When I hesitated, he smiled, almost teasing, and patted the edge of his bed. "Come here, Lisa, it's okay." Reluctantly, I moved closer and sat stiffly beside him, my eyes dropping back to the board as I tried to focus on the game. Then, without warning, he leaned in and kissed me.

He is kissing me! I was surprised, scared, flattered, and not sure what to do. *Glenn likes me?* Glenn was so cool, and I was awestruck that he would want to be in a relationship with me! The kiss quickly progressed to more. "But Glenn, I don't think…" He shushed me, and carried on. Afterwards, he gave me more meth, reminded me to sleep the next night, and gave me a goodbye kiss as I crawled out the window. I couldn't believe what had just happened! I had a boyfriend! I could not believe that this really cool, cute guy wanted me to be his girlfriend!

I started to worry, though. I was only fourteen, he was like twenty years older than me. No one would understand our relationship. *Did he understand that?* I was going to be in trouble for this. This hadn't been my plan at all. I called Glenn the next evening with the prearranged signal: call, let it ring once, hang up. He called back right away. I asked to meet with him to talk about my fears. Glenn was happy to oblige. He instructed me to walk down the street, and he would pick me up. When he picked me up down the street from my house, he spoke kindly and gave me a sweet kiss. "Hi beautiful, it's so good to see you." *He really likes me. How can I disappoint him?*

"Glenn, I'm worried people will judge us for being together," I blurted out. He pulled the car over, reached for my chin, and turned my face toward his. His eyes locked on mine as he said, "I like you."

I swallowed hard and muttered, "Well then… can we keep it a secret?" He nodded emphatically. "You're right, some people wouldn't understand. There are a lot of prudes in the world. Lisa, you're amazing. I'm glad our relationship is close now." He pulled me into a tight embrace, holding me as though the matter were settled.

We made out in his car. Afterwards he said, "I want to capture your beauty, okay? Come over later and bring your volleyball uniform so I can take your picture in it." He pulled out a line, cutting it neatly as he added, "I like taking pictures. That way I can see you anytime I want, okay?"

"Okay," I answered, my voice barely above a whisper. Inside, I felt torn. Part of me was flattered by his attention, by the way he spoke to me as if I were special. But another part twisted with unease. I didn't really want pictures taken, yet I couldn't find a way to say no. So, I smiled faintly, hiding my hesitation, and agreed. It seemed easier than risking his disappointment.

Before he took me back to the neighborhood, he added, "I look forward to seeing you later. I have some good ideas for you." His words rang in my ears as he dropped me off down the street and I walked the rest of the way home. I felt lit up inside; he liked me, wanted me. That thought wrapped around me like warmth. I wanted to make him happy, as happy as I felt in the moments he held me close.

Volleyball season was winding down, and with it, my interest in school seemed to fade. All I wanted was to be with Glenn. While waiting for him, I tried to quiet my frantic mind, cleaning, gardening, drawing, anything to keep myself busy. He was a big rig truck driver and when he was out on a haul, I'd catch up on sleep. There was no reason to stay up through the night if he wasn't there. But the moment he returned, he'd set me up with meth again, and our nights together would begin, shaped entirely around what he wanted.

Over time, I began to notice how different our desires really were. Glenn no longer kissed me or held me close. Instead, he came with demands, sexual requests, staged photographs, always some plan that felt more like a transaction than tenderness. What I longed for was missing now. The relationship dissolved into something mechanical, business like.

One night, after I whispered that I loved him, he smiled and paused before answering. "We're friends," he said matter-of-factly. "When you grow up and get married, I'll be the one to take you to your wedding. Friends are better because friendship lasts longer than love."

My heart dropped. *But I want to marry you,* I thought desperately, the words pressing against my lips. I tried to say them out loud, but he kept going. "And when you get divorced, I'll drive you to your divorce attorney's. As friends, we're closer than if we were a couple."

He spoke with such certainty, as if his truth could erase mine. I turned my eyes away, too full of sorrow to argue. He tilted my chin back toward him and insisted, "Friends forever, okay? I want to hear about your boyfriends."

Does this mean he's breaking up with me? I wondered, my chest tight with uncertainty. But instead of leaving, he asked for more pictures. "Come on, Lisa, be nice, you're so cute. I need you to do this."

I hesitated, my confusion plain, and he picked up on it right away. "Here, darling, let's relax for a second." He passed me more weed, saying it would "loosen me up."

Later, as I crawled out his window, he shoved a baggie into my hand. I hated how much I needed it, how the want overpowered the shame. "See you tomorrow," he said casually, while I slipped into the shadows at the side of his house, ducking low to avoid the glare of passing headlights.

I now needed meth just to function, and the price of getting it was enduring hours of his rambling philosophies mixed with pictures and acts. It became clear he loved nothing more than the sound of his own voice. One of his favorite themes was the superiority of men, how they were so much stronger, faster, better at pitching, catching, and definitely in lifting weights.

"And even in volleyball, men are way better than women," he declared as he had me pose in my uniform, adding with a smirk, "but you're good, for a girl."

Everything revolved around him, his stories, his opinions, his greatness. For weeks, I'd felt myself pulling away, but I couldn't see a way out. I felt trapped.

One night, when he expected me, I didn't show. I couldn't will myself over there anymore. When he asked the next day where I'd been, I said I'd fallen asleep, though I hadn't. After that, I started avoiding him whenever I could. The mere sight of him started to make me sick. And the thought of the pictures made me sicker.

But avoidance didn't keep him away. One afternoon, he showed up while I was home and backed me into a corner in the living room. "Hey, where have you been? I miss you. Come by tonight." I froze, unable to say no, so I nodded, but when night came, I stayed away.

The following day, as I walked down the street, his car slowed beside me. He pulled over, his voice stripped of kindness. "Lisa, get in the car."

"Glenn, what's up?" I glanced at my friend Andy up the street. "Umm... I'm meeting Andy right now."

"Meet with me tonight!" he huffed in agitation and then pulled away.

No way, I thought to myself. But he caught up to me later that same night. I was sitting against the fence between the bushes on the side of my house when he walked by. "Lisa, let's go to my room and get high." He reached out to me, but I kept my arms down.

"Let's just get high here." He sat down. "What's going on, Lisa? Why aren't you coming over anymore?"

"Glenn, I'm really worried that someone will see the pictures you took of me, of us. No one can see those ever! Can you just destroy the pictures?" He gazed at me in silence for a while. I looked away and remembered how excited I had been that he liked me and the future I imagined with him. Mr. and Mrs. Glenn Lowe. I had wanted him so badly, and now what I wanted so badly was to never see him again.

He stood up and looked down at me. He said calmly, "How about if you want ten pictures destroyed, you do five new ones for me?"

What? "Glenn no, I don't want to do new pictures. I don't want any pictures to exist at all." I wondered why he wasn't worried?

"Well, if you want some pictures destroyed, then you can do new ones. I'll see you later." He winked at me and walked away. My hands curled into fists, nails pressing lightly into my palms. A flush crept up my neck, and my chest tightened. *I can't believe he's doing this to me.* Anger simmered beneath the surface, tangled with the fear that kept me rooted in place.

But I found my voice, "Wait, Glenn, I need to break up with you. I thought we were something we're not."

"Lisa, we're friends. And friends don't break up." His voice was flat and dismissive, as he turned and walked away without a backward glance. "I'll see you later."

From my hiding place in the bushes, I watched the streetlights flicker on as twilight settled in. Far off, the hills burned red with fire carried by the Santa Ana winds. The sharp bite of smoke drifted through the air, oddly soothing as I drew it in keeping my eyes fixed on the distant flames. I committed right then and there to myself, *I'm never going back.*

Glenn began appearing everywhere I went. He'd come by the house, or suddenly pop his head over the backyard fence when I was on my way to a friend's or just trying to finish chores outside. Sometimes, I'd walk into the living room to find him sitting comfortably with my mom or sister, chatting away. On the outside, it looked harmless, but inside I felt my stomach knot, my chest tighten. He was everywhere, and I couldn't get away.

Whenever our eyes met, I could see it, the anger smoldering just beneath his expression. No one else seemed to notice the warning I couldn't unsee, a reminder that I was upsetting him. I was certain he enjoyed the secrecy, the deception of what we were doing, taking pleasure in the fact that no one around us knew.

Then came the letters, page after page, explaining why I should meet up with him again, insisting the old pictures could be destroyed if I just made new ones. Woven through were his endless rants about life and relationships, as if he were some kind of philosopher. "After all," he wrote, "I'll be here for you no matter what."

Each time he slipped me a letter, my stomach sank. The fear of holding his words in my hands made me feel even more trapped. Every letter ended the same way, with his cold claim: Our relationship is deeper than boyfriend and girlfriend, or even marriage. Always ending with, destroy this letter when you're done reading it.

My disgust didn't faze him; if anything, it seemed to fuel him. No matter how many times I turned him down, he kept coming back. As the neighborhood's main meth supplier, he showed up at local parties. I'd avoid his eyes and slip into another room. Sometimes he let me be, other times he sought me out.

Over time, I began seeing him less. One afternoon, as I ducked to the side of a house to avoid him, a wave of shame hit me. I had actually liked him once. I couldn't believe I had thought he was attractive, even imagined marrying him. Now, every time I caught a glimpse of him, he looked more shriveled, more strung out, just plain gross.

But he was relentless, always hustling for buyers, always flashing his money. I just wanted him gone. More than anything, I prayed the pictures he had of me would never, ever surface.

Little Lisa,

Glenn's initial kindness felt real to you. That's what makes grooming so hard to see from the inside, it often begins with warmth. You were already carrying wounds from so much pain, and that made you an easy target. Abusers sense that. They study you, looking for your soft spots, your longings, your fears. They win your trust, get you to reveal your vulnerability, and then begin weaving their logic around you. Gradually, they reshape your reality until the lines between right and wrong blur.

That isn't love. That's manipulation. Glenn wasn't safe. His attention wasn't a gift; it was a tactic. Drugs became part of that tactic too. He knew exactly what he was doing, using meth to blur your resistance, to keep you dependent, to make sure you stayed tied to him. Substances became another chain, not an accident.

You were a child whose deep need for connection was being exploited. That doesn't make you weak, it makes you human. Survivors of abuse are vulnerable because their longing for love is so strong, their openness still intact despite all they've endured. Grooming preys on that instinct to bond.

The confusion you felt, the guilt, the fear, it was all part of the trap. You couldn't have protected yourself from it, not yet. He was the adult. He should have protected your vulnerability, not used it against you.

The love you longed for was never wrong. The betrayal was.

CHAPTER 21

Mother favored a gas station near the freeway, right next to the Howard Johnson's. If it was convenient for her, I could ride along when she needed to fill up, then walk from there to the city bus stop nearby. She told me bluntly, "I'm not driving you all the way downtown to the continuation High School. You should've done better at Arlington. I'm not surprised you couldn't even finish ninth grade like a normal person. But if I need gas, you can ride with me and then walk to the bus stop."

So, whenever her errands happened to line up with my school schedule, I went. Just over halfway through ninth grade, my poor attendance and failing grades had already gotten me kicked out of regular school, and with that, my chance at sports was gone. I carried on anyway.

Mother had a crush on the gas station owner, and I enjoyed watching her light up on the way to see Mohammad. Their banter was playful, almost flirtatious. She hadn't been with anyone since my stepdad Ray left her, before Don and Jody got busted. I found myself rooting for her. Maybe this could be a real boyfriend.

She had started coming to this station over the summer while I was away in foster care. When she finally brought me along, she introduced me with a casual smile: "This is my daughter, the one who's been gone for the summer."

Mohammad turned to me with warmth. "Well, hi, glad to see you back home now. You know your mom is my favorite customer."

I glanced at her then and caught a rare smile that lit up her whole face. For a fleeting moment, it felt good to see her happy, and to be standing beside her in it.

Mohammad had an employee, a man named Nikki. He had the same complexion and accent as Mohammad but was much younger and undeniably better looking. One day, Mother announced that I would be going out on a date with him.

The words hit me like a weight. I had never told her about my quiet vow to avoid boyfriends, and I couldn't stay silent. "Mom, I don't want any boyfriends right now."

"Oh Lisa, go out with him, he likes you. You'll have fun."

On the night of the date, Mother had me wear a dress. She fussed over my hair and clothes, determined to make me look presentable. It felt strange and nice for her to care so much about my appearance.

I stood at the window, heart racing, as Nikki walked up to the door holding a bouquet of flowers. No one had ever given me flowers before.

"Lisa, go answer the door," Mom called. Nervous and unsure of what to say, I opened it softly, muttered a quick "hi," and dropped my gaze. We stood awkwardly in silence until Mom cut in, "Well, invite him in!" Then, with a wave of her hand, she ushered him past me toward the kitchen table.

She chatted with him for a few minutes before announcing it was time for us to leave. Nikki rose, opened the front door for me, and led the way to his long black sedan. He held the door open as I climbed in, my legs unsteady, stumbling just enough to betray my nerves.

"Are you okay?" he asked, holding his arms out as if ready to catch me. I nodded quickly and sank into the seat. He shut the door, slipped into the driver's side, and we pulled away.

Conversation didn't come easily. His English was hard for me to follow, and I had no idea what to say. Each time I thought of a question or comment, my throat tightened until the words stuck. He seemed a little annoyed by the silence, though he made an effort to be polite.

We arrived at the restaurant and slid into a booth. For a while, neither of us spoke, the clink of silverware from nearby tables filling the silence between us. Finally, he started asking questions.

"Do you like school?"

"Um… well… sometimes." I shifted in my seat, staring down at the menu.

"Do you like to read?"

"Uh… yeah," I mumbled, tugging at the edge of my sleeve.

"Do you like to cook?"

"Oh… well… I don't much." My voice trailed off, and I gave a small shrug, unable to meet his eyes.

Thankfully, the food arrived, breaking the awkward silence. We ate without much conversation, and when the bill came, he paid. As we stepped outside, he said, "Let's go to the gas station." The suggestion struck me as odd, but I didn't question it.

The station was empty and quiet when we pulled in. He unlocked the office door and gestured inside. "This is where we manage the gas station." Pulling out the chair behind the desk, he motioned for me to sit. I sat down staring straight ahead at the paperwork scattered across the surface. After a minute or two, he rose and came and stood behind me. His hands pressed into my shoulders and he started rubbing them. *Oh no,* I thought, but I stayed silent, frozen. After a moment he muttered, "You are just too young. Are you ready to go?"

I jumped from the chair as relief washed over me. He led me back to the car. I nodded quickly, heart pounding, so grateful when he started driving me home.

He pulled up in the driveway and said, "Take care." I got out and took a deep breath as he drove away. When I walked in, Mom called me into the living room where she had been waiting. "Home so early? How did the date go with Nikki?" she asked with a smile.

"It was ok. We ate and went to the gas station for a little bit. Then he took me home."

117

"No kissing?" Mother asked.

"Yuck, no, no kissing!"

Mom's face tightened in confusion, edged with irritation. "Mohammad and I thought he would like you," she said, her tone clipped. With a shrug, she turned back to her TV show, ending the conversation as quickly as it began. Nothing more was said about the date.

We still stopped at that gas station, and Mom and Mohammad carried on with their easy flirting. Nikki and I, however, acted as if the evening had never happened, passing each other in silence, careful not to meet eyes.

When I walked to the bus stop, I had to pass right by the gas station. When Mohammad noticed me he'd yell out, "Hello Lisa!" I waved hello back continuing on to the bus stop.

Walking to the bus stop and riding the bus was often scary. Sometimes men would slow their cars to offer rides, or a passenger would stare too long, and I knew their intentions weren't innocent. My stomach knotted each time, and I always said no. Still, I carried a knife, just in case one of them didn't keep driving.

Before Ray left, he gave me lessons as to how to protect myself. He placed the knife gently in my hand, guiding my fingers around the handle. "Hold it like this, it's an extension of your fist," he explained. "If someone comes up to you and you don't want them to, you punch, and immediately you cut them. If they have hair, grab it and pull their face to your knee. Bam!" He demonstrated the moves with calm certainty, his voice steady in a way that made me believe I could be strong, too.

Ray built me up. His words, "You have a right to protect yourself, Lisa, you can fight back," sank in deeper than just self-defense. When he gave me my own knife and told me to keep it under my pillow at night, I felt both the weight of fear and the quiet reassurance that he cared enough to equip me for survival. I took his advice.

One afternoon, as I was walking home from the bus stop, Mohammad called me over. I crossed the parking lot to where he stood, and he invited me into the office. He started casually, suggesting we go to dinner.

I thought to myself, *Oh, he must want to talk about my mom. Maybe he's wondering how to take things to the next level with her.* Out loud, I answered, "Sure, we can do that."

But then he added, "We can get a hotel room before dinner."

My stomach dropped. He must have seen the confusion flash across my face, because he quickly explained, "So you can drink. You're too young to drink in public."

The words twisted in my gut. "What? No, I don't need to drink. That's okay," I blurted, my voice tight.

Without hesitation, he admitted, "I just want to hold you, okay? Just hold you."

I froze. In less than a minute, he had shifted from being Mom's boyfriend to suggesting he wanted me in a hotel room. My eyes dropped to the floor as I mapped the quickest path out of his office.

Then, as if it were nothing, he added, "You should come to Vegas with me, you could be a prostitute. You'd make a *lot* of money."

What did he just say? My stomach lurched. Betrayal and horror crashed over me. This was the man who made my mother light up, the one she dressed up for, the one she laughed with at the gas station. And now he was saying this to me. I was so sad for her.

Without a word, I shook my head and bolted from his office, desperate to escape from him. Even as my feet carried me away, the sadness for my mom clung to me, heavier than my own fear.

I ran till the gas station was out of sight. My head was spinning! *What if Mother found out he wanted to hold me?* I knew she would be upset with me. I had done it again! She could never know. After that, when I had to

119

walk to the bus stop, I walked as far away from the gas station as I could, ignoring Mohammed's calls, never looking in the direction of the station, my hand clenched tightly on the knife.

Soon after that, Mohammad became my mother's official boyfriend. When he was at the house with her, she would sometimes call me into her room, even while they were lying in bed together, and ask casually, "How was your day, Lisa?" The words sounded ordinary, but the setting made my skin crawl. I knew I couldn't refuse her summons. If I hesitated or stayed away, she might suspect something was wrong.

I did my best to avoid looking at or speaking to Mohammad. His smile held sinister secrets. One afternoon, he patted the bed and motioned for me to lie down beside them.

My eyes flew to Mom's. She only laughed and brushed it off," Oh, Mohammad."

My breath caught in my throat. In an instant, I bolted from the room, then out of the house altogether, Mom's voice calling after me fading into the background as my feet pounded the ground.

Not long after that, Mohammad stopped coming around. Just like that, he was gone, and Mom was without a boyfriend once again.

Dear Lisa,

Your mom's choices, like setting you up on dates, were part of a troubling pattern that left you exposed. The truth is, her abuse of you had already softened the ground for others to step in. By tearing down your confidence, ignoring your boundaries, and normalizing mistreatment, she made it harder for you to recognize danger and easier for predators to take advantage.

It's possible she carried wounds of her own from childhood, but that does not excuse what she did to you. Her pain didn't justify passing harm forward. She knew better, and still she chose actions that hurt you. None of this was your fault.

I see how much compassion and hope you carried for her happiness. You longed to see her smile; to believe she could find something good, and you clung to those rare glimpses of light. That was your tender heart shining through. And that's why the disappointment cut so deep when your hope for her became another secret you had to keep. It was never your job to protect her, yet you bore the weight of both her unhappiness and her choices.

Even in that confusion, you showed such strength. You trusted your feelings, carried your knife, and found ways to stand your ground.

Healing now means holding these truths with compassion, for yourself. You deserve safety, love, and respect. You are worthy, brave, and so deeply loved. And I am here to give it to you.

CHAPTER 22

When I needed to get out of the house, I had a few friends I could turn to. Mary lived just down the street, and her parents always kept plenty of beer on hand. They even gave some of us kids permission to use the tap built into their backyard barbecue, anytime we wanted, on the condition that we didn't tell anyone. I took them up on that offer often.

Her parents could be entertaining to talk with at times, full of jokes and easy laughter. Other times, the long days of drinking caught up with them, and they simply passed out where they sat.

My friends and I looked out for each other, sharing whenever we scored drugs or alcohol. So, when a couple of new guys moved into the neighborhood, we were excited to have another place to hang out and get high. It was definitely more fun than watching Mary's parents drink themselves into a stupor.

The newcomers were twin brothers, Vince and Vance, twenty something and fresh from Florida. They drove flashy cars, a Corvette and a Trans Am, and boasted about owning their house outright. The money, they explained, came from stealing a stash from their cruel stepfather, a drug dealer back in Florida. They told the story with pride, bragging about their escape, though underneath the swagger they admitted a lingering fear that one day he might come looking for them.

They were proud of what they had, steady jobs as construction workers, a paid-off house, and their dream cars. Friendly and welcoming, they invited us to party at their place whenever we wanted. Best of all, they lived only half a block from me, just a quick two-minute walk. It didn't take long before everyone treated them like new best friends.

They looked a lot alike, but Vince was bulkier and carried himself with less charm than Vance. He had a noticeable tic, his eyes would flutter now and then, almost like a tiny seizure. The two of them partied hard, celebrating their freedom from their stepdad, often raising their first drink of the day in a joking toast to him. Their house became an open spot for us. Whether they were home or not, we knew we could stop by to skip school or just hang out in the evenings.

A couple of months after they moved in, I slipped into the garage during a party to refill my cup. The keg was kept out there in case of spills. Usually, there were people gathered around it, but this time I was alone. Behind me, the thump of music and bursts of laughter spilled in from the house.

I was already buzzing hard, the kind of lit where my body felt loose and my steps started to stumble. As I leaned on the keg to steady myself, Vince walked in.

"Hey, getting more beer? You know it's illegal for a fourteen-year-old to drink" he laughed as he stepped into the garage.

"Yep, but this is good beer!" I laughed at his irony, my words slurring a little as I tried to steady myself and not spill. I thought of Vince as a friend, so it was normal to joke around with him.

But then his tone shifted. "No need to get more beer, I have a better plan," he said, stepping straight into my personal space. Confusion flickered through me and I instinctively stepped back. Before I could process what was happening, he grabbed my shoulders and forced his mouth onto mine.

"No, no, I don't want to," I protested, twisting against his grip. He ignored me, holding tighter. "Yes," he insisted, as if his word was more important than mine.

"No, really, Vince, no! I don't want to." At first, I thought maybe this was some kind of game he was playing. We were just friends. This couldn't be serious. But the more I said no, the less he seemed to hear me.

"Why isn't he listening?" I tried to back up, to push him away. "No, I don't want to!"

Ignoring me, he scooped me up, slung me over his shoulder, and carried me out of the garage and into the house. My body jolted with each step as he strode briskly through the kitchen and down the hall. *How is this hap-*

pening? My thoughts raced. I felt ridiculous and helpless, plopping along on his shoulder, unable to break free.

As we passed the living room, I caught my brother's eyes. *Why isn't he helping me?* The music pounded from the other room, drowning out my voice. Couldn't anyone hear me saying no? Couldn't they see?

Vince rounded the corner of the hall, opened the door to his room, set me down, and closed it behind us. Stunned, I still clung to the hope that he wasn't serious. I shook my head at his bizarre behavior, tried to edge past him toward the party, steadying myself so I wouldn't stumble. But he blocked the way.

Is he for real?

He leaned in again, kissing me, and I repeated my refusals. "Vince, no! I don't want to!" Anger rose in me, what had first seemed strange, almost like a dumb joke, was turning serious. He didn't stop. Panic flared in my chest. *How is this happening?*

"Please stop," I pleaded, my stomach twisting with nausea. But he kept going. "Vince, I really don't want to do this!" Still, he ignored me. I resisted as best I could, but he overpowered me at every turn.

For a moment, his smile gave me hope, it looked as if he was just teasing, like maybe he wasn't really going to do anything. But that hope faded as he plowed through my no's, pressing a finger against my mouth to shush me.

A wave of anguish rushed over me as the truth settled in, he wasn't stopping, and nothing I said or did was getting through.

I couldn't hold back the sobs as he forced himself all the way. I bit down on my cries, gasping from the pain. *Why can't I stop him? Maybe if he sees my tears, he'll stop.* But he didn't. *Just stay quiet, Lisa.* I was so mad at my helplessness.

When he finished violating me, he looked satisfied, almost proud. He lay down beside me, wrapping his arms around me, holding me too tightly, patting my head. *Is he going to let me go?* I wiped my tears quickly. *Don't let him see you're upset, Lisa.*

After what felt like forever, his grip loosened. I stayed still until he finally spoke. "Thank you," he said. Shock ran through me as I was finally able to jump up.

"Hey, where do you think you're going?" he barked.

"Oh, nowhere." I went to the window.

"That's right, come back here."

But I stayed frozen, staring at the dark street through a narrow crack in his curtain, the horror of what had just happened replaying in my mind. I shoved the sick feeling down and focused only on how I might get away.

When he reached for me, panic shot through me, and the words tumbled out: "I wanted you to be my first." His face lit up with satisfaction, as if he'd won something. He grabbed my hand and pulled me back down beside him.

Did he really believe that?

How had those words even come out of my mouth? Part of me was furious I'd said them, while another part felt like I was onstage, delivering lines handed to me. *Shhh, Lisa, just comply.* I felt sick. My buzz had drained away, leaving only the raw awareness of where he had grabbed and violated me, the ache of his grip still throbbing in my flesh.

I obeyed his command and lay back down. Every part of me wanted to be anywhere but next to him, yet my body moved anyway, back to his side. A strange numbness settled in, as if I were watching from outside myself, and I hated what I saw. *Why didn't you scream, Lisa?* I could already hear others asking the same question if I ever told. And I didn't have an answer. I hadn't screamed. I hadn't clawed at him. My voice had failed. My strength was no match for his. He had overpowered me so easily, and I was furious about it.

I couldn't believe it had happened, didn't believe it, even as I replayed it in my mind. By the time I realized the truth, it was already too late. I pulled the covers up over myself, trying to disappear, trying to hide from what had just been done to me.

When he finally turned to me and said I should get home, I forced a smile and softened my voice. "Okay, thanks."

"I'll see you tomorrow, sweet Lisa," he leered, watching as I dressed. Then he walked me through the dark house to the front door.

Inside, I was seething. I wanted to scream, to slap myself for pretending. I didn't even like Vince, he was just a friend. He was the dumb brother with a strange tic; someone I never even wanted to kiss. And now he thought I had wanted all of this.

"Okay, see you tomorrow," I managed weakly, forcing another smile as he pulled me into a hug.

But what about all those no's? *Lisa, stop it, shake it off. Don't think about it now. Just leave.* I walked home alone, holding everything in, trying to stay shut up. I went into the bathroom and faced the mirror. *Who is she?* The girl staring back felt like a stranger. My eyes slid past my reflection, searching but not knowing what for. I opened the medicine cabinet and pulled out a pair of scissors. *What are you doing... don't, Lisa.* I held them up to my head, opening and closing the blades a few times before wrapping a lock of hair around them. Then, snip. Inches fell into the sink. As the strands slid down, my knees gave out, and I sank to the floor beside them.

The next day, as soon as I could, I marched over to Mary's for some beer. To get there, I had to pass Vince's house, but I told myself it was a workday, surely he wouldn't be around. But there he was, out front, calling to me. *No, don't go!* my mind screamed, yet my legs carried me toward him as he stepped closer. He greeted me like we were a couple, grinning as if nothing had happened. Lifting me off the ground in a tight embrace, he kissed me right there on the sidewalk, in full view of his brother.

"See?" he laughed.

His brother blurted out, "What did you do to your hair!" His face twisted in disgust, but my so-called "boyfriend" quickly covered for me. "Hey, you look good with any length of hair," he said with a grin.

He led me to the garage and sat down, tugging me onto his lap as if it were the most natural thing in the world. I couldn't think of anything else to say, the only words that came out were, "Hey, can I have a beer?"

Little Lisa,

I would have stood in front of you like a shield, looked him in the eye, and said, "She said no. You don't get to touch her."

You were clear. You tried to push him away, you tried to escape, you tried to reason. He didn't stop because he didn't care what you wanted. That wasn't your fault, that was his choice. You did not "let" this happen. You were trapped.

When you said those strange words, "I wanted you to be my first," you weren't giving consent. That was your survival instinct trying to keep you safe in the only way it knew how: by reducing the threat, performing compliance, pretending. It doesn't mean you wanted any of it. You were not safe. But your body and your brain did everything they could to keep you alive.

And the hair you cut afterward, that wasn't just hair. That was the soundless scream your voice couldn't yet carry.

He chose to violate you. I know you still blame yourself sometimes, but you did the best you could to stop it. You didn't scream or claw him because you were frozen and overpowered, you were terrified. The pretending after, the silence, the drinking, the haircut, the going back the next day, it all makes sense in the context of trauma. You were surviving. And even in your pain, you kept going. That's what survivors do.

You deserved someone to fight for you. You have that now. I'm here.

CHAPTER 23

"Vince said that if you don't come over to see him, you'll regret it." Concern edged Andy's voice.

Vince had been pressuring me to go with him to Florida, but deep in my gut I knew it was a terrible idea. I was afraid that if I stepped foot in his house, he'd trap me in the car and not let me leave. So, I stayed put. "Andy, please tell Vince I can't come over."

"Don't worry, Lisa, I'll tell him," Andy said, steady as always. "Just stay here. Don't leave. I'll be back in a little bit."

True to his word, Andy carried Vince's response, a broken Genesis album, my favorite one. My heart sank. I didn't care anymore what Vince might try to do to me, but if it happened, he'd have to come to my house to do it.

With Mom away on a trip, there was no reason for me to go anywhere. Andy kept watch, checking the street every thirty minutes until finally Vince and his brother loaded up the car for Florida.

"Lisa, he's gone!" Andy ran in, breathless, after seeing them drive off. Relief washed over me in a rush. I wouldn't have to face Vince again, for a few weeks, at least.

After they returned from Florida, I did everything I could to avoid Vince. I slipped out of my house carefully, walking to Andy's as quietly as possible, always scanning for Vince outside or cars in his driveway. If I spotted him, I'd take the long way around, detouring to stay clear of both Glenn's and Vince's places.

Sometimes, Andy walked with me, a steady presence at my side. He knew pieces of what I was going through, and though he didn't press for details, he did his best to shield me.

Andy's parents, Carmen and Barry, had a fire pit in their yard and often had a fire burning at night, open to anyone who wanted to drop by. Some evenings, the place was packed, other times, it was just a handful of us. I always looked forward to those nights, nursing a beer, smoking a joint, staring into the flames as the world dimmed, and just being with my friend. Andy was my buddy, and with him I felt safe.

His house was about a fifteen-minute walk from mine, far enough to feel removed from all the chaos. I helped out where I could, tidying up, setting things up for the fire, happy to contribute to the place that gave me some peace.

Every once in a while, Vince showed up, but he was well behaved when he was there. He didn't come often anyway, preferring to drink at his own place.

We helped Andy's parents in other ways too. Sometimes that meant holding the spoons while they heated their drugs. Our hands were steadier than theirs, and we made sure not to spill anything. One time, as the liquid bubbled in the spoon, Carmen looked at me and asked, "Wanna try, Lisa?"

Before I could answer, Andy barked, "Mom, don't make her do that!" Relief washed over me. I hadn't wanted to, not at all, and I was so grateful Andy stepped in to help me.

One night Carmen, Andy's mom, asked, "Lisa, where's Vince?" She was always warm to me, teaching me how to make homemade tortillas and reminding me I had a place on her couch. At her house, nothing was off-limits. I could smoke, drink, or just be, and when her hangovers were heavy, Andy and I helped with the chores.

I told her Vince didn't come around much, and that I liked it better that way. The last I saw him, I wouldn't step inside his house, but he staggered out to meet me in the street, slurring as he reached for me. I pulled back easily. He couldn't haul me off this time. My sobriety gave me strength, and I walked away from his drunkenness.

I was able to continue to avoid him. If our paths crossed, he might shout something in my direction or ignore me completely. Either way, I was relieved he left me alone.

I spent my time at Andy's instead. No one there paid attention to whether we went to school or not, and even though Andy didn't drink or smoke, he never judged me for it. We just enjoyed being friends together, and with him, I could relax.

Little Lisa,

You were wise to trust the unease in your body that day. That wasn't fear without cause, it was your intuition, sharpened by experience, warning you of danger. You listened, and protected yourself.

Vince was another link in the same chain of abuse you had already endured. Like the others before him, he blurred the lines between affection and violation. He ignored your no, and then acted as if his power over you was proof of some "relationship." That is the abuse cycle, grooming, betrayal, and then pretending it was love. It wasn't, It was harm.

But I see how you began to resist the cycle. Vince's alcoholism gave you a strange kind of freedom. His drunkenness made him weaker, not stronger, and that opened a door for you. You could pull back, refuse to go inside, and walk away. This time, he couldn't carry you off.

And then there was Andy. His friendship was so important. He gave you moments of steadiness in the middle of chaos, standing up for you when you couldn't, walking beside you when you felt unsafe. His home was complicated. Sometimes, it was a refuge with fires burning and tortillas on the stove, a place where you could relax with your buddy. Other times, it wasn't safe at all, with drugs on the table and danger close by. But even in that mix, Andy himself was a safe zone, someone you could trust.

You will learn to trust yourself someday.

CHAPTER 24

A few houses down from Andy's lived neighbors with a pool, and we loved any chance to swim there. Just the thought of diving in on a hot day filled us with energy. The only rule was that an adult had to be present if the owners weren't home. One afternoon, eager to get in the water, we went searching for someone who could watch us. That's when Andy remembered another neighbor who might be able to help.

Andy knocked on the door, and it swung open to reveal a tall blond guy whose long neck and sharp features gave him an odd resemblance to an ostrich. His face broke into a wide smile when he saw us.

"Hi," Andy began, "we were wondering if someone could watch us swim at the neighbors' place. We need someone over eighteen to supervise us."

The guy chuckled. "Well, I'm twenty-five, does that count?" He pushed open the screen door and waved us in. "My name's Bob. What are your names? How old are you?"

"I'm thirteen, and she's fourteen," Andy replied, introducing us both. Then he added, "Oh, you must be the older brother who just came home. Nice to meet you."

Bob said he'd meet us at the pool in fifteen minutes, so we hurried off to change into our swimsuits. On the way, Andy leaned toward me and said, "That guy, Bob, he just got out of military prison. He got busted for dealing cocaine. He's John's older brother, and John told me he'd be coming home soon."

Bob showed up at the pool just as he promised. He was easygoing, friendly, and quick to share his cigarettes and his time, and before long we'd all become fast friends. Soon, he started coming to the fires at Andy's and quickly became a regular face there. One day, Carmen pulled me aside and said, "You know, Bob likes you, you should go out with him!"

"Carmen, what? I don't like him like that. He's too old, besides, I'm not trying to get into a relationship."

"Lisa, he's cool. He really likes you, it's okay," she insisted.

I thought my clear disapproval would end the conversation, but instead Carmen kept promoting Bob, like she was his advocate. *Why does she care so much?*

Bob kept showing his interest, though he said he accepted that I only wanted to be friends. One afternoon, while Andy and I watched him and a buddy load up for the beach, Bob called out, "Come with us! You can lay out, get a tan, maybe even try surfing, it'll be fun!"

"Really?" I asked, excitement bubbling up at the thought of going to the beach. His friend grinned and added, "Yeah, you can watch our stuff while we surf."

The next time they headed out, I went along. Andy, never much of a beach fan, stayed home. Soon the three of us fell into a rhythm of getting high and spending long afternoons at Trestles Beach. The ocean air and crashing waves felt like paradise.

They acted like big brothers, teasing me just enough to make me laugh, but always making sure I felt safe. They told me not to worry, that they'd look out for me. That made it easy to relax, to let the beach, my refuge of sun, salt, and sand wrap around me. Those weeks of summer were a dream. That was exactly how I wanted to spend my days.

After one particularly long day at the beach, we ended the night at Andy's fire pit. It was getting late and Bob offered to drive me home. When we got to my house, he got out of the car and started walking with me. I told him, "It's ok, I got it." He continued to walk with me. As I turned to say goodbye, he leaned in and started kissing me.

Wait, what happened to the friendship thing? I pulled back, asking him just that, but he cut me off with, "It's okay, Lisa. Let's be more than friends."

He didn't stop. He pressed forward, prodding me inside. His breath was hot against my ear as he whispered, "Where's your bedroom?"

My body froze even as he kept moving, and when I tried to speak, the words tangled in my mouth, coming out broken and slurred. I couldn't form a clear sentence, only scattered sounds that betrayed my panic. Somehow I managed to tell him I slept in the living room. Being in the living room with no door didn't cause him one bit of hesitation.

The next day at Andy's, I was sitting by the fire, ignoring what happened from the night before. After Bob had left late the night before, I hadn't seen him again, and I wasn't looking forward to it. Then he showed up. Bob strolled in and dropped into the seat right beside me, grinning like we shared a secret. My body stiffened, but before I could even process it, Carmen's voice rang out for everyone to hear: "Yay! I heard you two are a couple now!"

My stomach lurched. *Wait, what? Bob already told Carmen what happened?* I told nobody. The shock of her saying it so publicly pinned me in place. And with Bob sitting so close, smiling as if her words sealed the deal, I felt trapped. I hadn't agreed to this, but in that instant, it was decided for me. We were "official."

After a while Bob leaned over and spoke assertively, "Lisa, come back with me to my house." Bob offered his hand to me, but I didn't want to leave. "Come on, I want to show you something," Bob insisted. Carmen piped in, "Don't worry Lisa, we will be here when you are done."

Noticing my reluctance, Bob tried at first to act patient and kind. When we got to his house, he led me straight to his room. "This is your space now too," he said proudly, as if presenting a gift. He went on, telling me how long he had been waiting to be with me, how glad he was that the wait was finally over. He invited me to sit down, and then sat next to me. Then came the words, "I love you, Lisa."

He loves me? He's my boyfriend now.

He pressed on, adding, "I'll take good care of you plus Carmen is really happy for us, she thinks us being together is a good thing!" I tried to calm myself, repeating in my head, *He loves me, he loves me,* as if saying it enough times could make everything feel okay.

From that day on, Bob just said how things would be. One afternoon he said, "You should start working with me. You can do insulation, the walls, and I'll do the ceilings. You're strong, I'll teach you."

I hesitated. "But I have school. I'm already in continuation school. I can't miss more days." Deep down, I wanted to finish, to at least get my diploma, even though it was always a struggle just to show up. He tilted his head, almost playful but firm underneath. "What's more important, Lisa, me or school? I just want to be with you all the time."

So, I started working with Bob. It didn't take long before the school began calling home about my absences, but by then I was already caught up in the routine he had laid out for me. When it was payday, he always held all the money, keeping it for both of us.

He constantly reminded me how much he loved me, introducing me to everyone as his fiancée. "I can't wait to make you my wife," he'd say with a grin. And then, just as easily, he'd add, "But you'll have to work too, I'm not doing all the money-making."

I was attached to him now. But we fought a lot. Each time he said it was over, or even hinted at it, I fell apart inside. The fear of losing him kept me clinging tighter, desperate to win him back. When we were apart, my sadness was all consuming, nothing numbed it enough. And when he made up with me, usual after a day of torture, he always had good weed, and a hotel room waiting. One night at a hotel, he said, "We should just move in together."

"But I'm only sixteen, "How would that work?"

"We'll figure it out. Exciting to think about though, right?" his eyes lit up.

He continued, "I'll talk with your mom, she likes me." The next day, when he brought me back home, he told her, "I'd like to live with Lisa and get a place together."

"Oh good," she said, "You can take her off my hands."

Bob laughed along with her. "Absolutely, I'll take her off your hands," he replied, as if they were two buddies.

After Bob and I found a place of our own, my mother forwarded the school warning letters about my absences to our new place, a room we rented from a single woman. Mother told the school that I didn't live at home anymore and it wasn't her problem.

Bob warned me not to get him in trouble, to figure out the school situation. I contacted the school and explained I was working and not living at home anymore but I still wanted to find some way to continue. The school told me about a new program for kids like me, an at-home study track through the adult high school. I only had to attend once a week, for about an hour or two, and the rest of the work I completed on my own at my own time. I took them up on it and I managed to pull it off. I slapped assignments together just enough to get by. It wasn't hard, because it was obvious the curriculum was far below grade level.

The new school arrangement worked out most of the time, but if I had an assignment I had to finish and couldn't put it off, Bob would often leave me alone in our rented room, even though he knew how much I hated it. Being alone was unbearable. The silence pressed in on me, and the emptiness echoed louder than any noise, and I couldn't shake the feeling of being left behind. I always wondered what he was doing? If I got hysterical and begged him not to go, he'd promise to stay away even longer.

One night, I was up waiting for him, desperate for his return. I had just lit a joint when he walked in the door. *Finally.* I jumped up to hug him

"This is my friend Mike. He wants to join us." Mike was super friendly and complimentary.

"Ok," I passed him the joint. Then they both sat on the bed on either side of me, and Bob said, "No, you know, he wants to join us. You know? Like we've done before." Bob turned his attention to Mike, asking what he wanted.

"But I don't…"

"Shhhh Lisa." Bob whispered in my ear as they started undressing.

Mike was gone by the next morning, and Bob shook me hard to wake me. "We've got a job today, come on!"

"I don't feel so good," I groaned, rolling onto my side.

"Oh no you don't," he snapped. "Get up, let's go!"

He caught the look on my face and, for a moment, softened. "You're a good worker, Lisa. You're so helpful to me. I'm glad to have you. I love you."

I forced myself and made it through to the end of the day. It was payday and that loving tone was gone. I stood quietly off to the side as everyone lined up for their checks. Bob's boss looked at me and asked, "Do you want me to pay you directly?"

Before I could answer, Bob cut in. "No, just pay me, I'll take care of her." He stuffed the money into his wallet without another word.

Little Lisa,

You believed you had found friendship, safety, and belonging at the beach. You didn't yet know how skillfully Bob was masking his intentions, honoring boundaries at first, only to dismantle them once he secured your trust. That shift wasn't about love; it was about possession.

Bob's persistence was not romance. It was a calculated erasure of your "no," one boundary at a time. By the time he began making decisions for you; where you went, who you saw, how you worked. He had already built the scaffolding of control. And those who encouraged the relationship instead of protecting you? They blurred the lines further, enmeshing themselves in a dynamic that harmed you. It enabled him.

The absence of safe, consistent adults left you vulnerable to believing that attention, even controlling, painful attention, was love. Abusers exploit this hunger for connection, creating dependency by intertwining affection with financial, physical, sexual, and emotional control. I'm so sorry he made you do those things.

You deserved friends who could remain just that, friends. You deserved a community that noticed your absence from school and saw it as cause for concern, not indifference. You deserved affection that didn't come with hooks.

Even so, you carried quiet awareness. You felt the loneliness in that rented room. You noticed the shift from kindness to coercion. Those flickers of recognition were seeds, the beginnings of a truth you would one day be able to live by: love never requires the loss of yourself.

CHAPTER 25

"Move over, Lisa." My sister squished beside me on the couch. Glenn's living room was the last place I wanted to be. The air felt heavy and hot, pressing against my chest until I could hardly breathe. I had to get high just to make the one-minute journey.

Earlier, Glenn had called, insisting it was an emergency. When my sister asked what was wrong, he refused to explain, just repeated that it was an emergency and made sure she brought me too. Dread flooded me. What kind of emergency could possibly involve me? I wished I hadn't been home when the phone rang.

But I was living back at my mother's. Bob said it was too expensive for us to have our own place. My so-called "bedroom" was still just a corner of the living room. Most of my time was spent at Bob's house or working alongside him anyway. But that day I was stuck at home, within reach of Glenn's call.

Hesitation tugged at me, but I told myself at least I wouldn't be alone. If my sister was going, maybe it would be okay. I didn't feel like I had a choice, so I went along, caught between the unease knotting in my stomach and the thin thread of safety I clung to in her presence.

When we arrived, my sister pressed him again about the emergency. He brushed it off, telling us we'd find out soon enough. He even promised his parents weren't home. I certainly hoped so since Kathy hated me so much.

The instant we stepped inside, I stopped cold. Several girls were already scattered across the living room. A chill shot through me as my skin prickled, and the room seemed to shrink around me. I couldn't name what was about to happen, but every nerve in my body screamed I shouldn't be there.

As we settled onto the couch, Glenn stood before us, his voice heavy. "I know you don't know about each other," he began, "and I want you to be kind about this. All of you have taken pictures with me, all of you have been my special friends. But I was raided by the police. They found the pictures. I told them I didn't know how to reach you, but they might figure it out."

His eyes shifted toward me before sweeping back to the others. "I think I'll be okay because most of you were older teens when the pictures were taken. All except you, Lisa. You were fourteen. Fourteen and under is considered more serious, I could really get in trouble for you."

The words hit like a punch. My worst fear was no longer a shadow in the back of my mind. It was standing right in front of me. *I wasn't the only one?* All of us avoided eye contact with each other and sat in silence.

He sat down next to me and put his arm around me. "Lisa, I know you will do the right thing and not participate with the detectives if they find you and talk to you, right?" I mindlessly nodded in agreement.

He squeezed me tight as he continued, "I don't know who turned me in, but I will find them, and they will regret it."

Chills shot through me like a current. I wondered who turned him in? Also, what did he mean, "They will regret it?" He ended the meeting by explaining how much he appreciated all of us, how our friendship was stronger than married people's relationships, and how he loved us all. *He's saying love now?* "We will all get through this together," he proclaimed and gestured for us to leave, then proceeded to hug each one of us as he walked us out. As I was rushing out the door, he said, "I know I can count on you, Lisa. You being fourteen when we were together is a real problem for me, ok?"

My sister and I didn't speak to each other as we walked home.

It wasn't just me.

My worst fear was now out in the open. Not only had the police found the pictures, but now these other girls knew about me too. Panic rose at the thought of Bob finding out, or anyone else. Shame and dread closed in on me. I told myself over and over to just stay quiet, to hope it would all disappear, that maybe this moment would be the end of it.

Little Lisa,

This moment was so terrifying and overwhelming! Just being in Glenn's house was scary enough, but hearing him say he could get in trouble because of you felt like an unbearable weight.

Your secret was no longer hidden; your worst fear was becoming real. You didn't realize it then but it was good that it didn't remain hidden.

Glenn's words were designed to control you, to make you feel responsible and afraid. When he threatened that others would "regret it," he was trying to keep you silent. But you were already stronger than his fear tactics. Even sitting there, frozen and scared, your strength was alive inside you.

It's natural that your mind raced, wondering who turned him in, who might find out, what Bob, the police or anyone else would think. That fear of being exposed felt terrifying, but you weren't alone. Abusers rarely harm just one person; it was never just you. Even if it was just you, you were still the victim.

Take a deep breath, sweetheart. It's okay to feel scared, confused, and unsure of what to do. You figure it out. One step at a time, you will keep moving forward. And you have support now! I'm here. Protecting you, hearing you, and loving you.

CHAPTER 26

A few days after seeing Glenn, the pounding of heavy fists rattled our front door. From the hallway, I caught a glimpse through the kitchen window. Two men stood on the porch, badges flashing against their belts, guns at their sides. My heart hammered as my sister opened the door.

I heard their voices, calm but firm, as they introduced themselves as detectives from the Riverside Police Department. She stepped aside to let them in. Their eyes swept the room until they landed on me. My legs locked beneath me, wishing I had darted out the back door while I had the chance.

Flipping through their files, one of them asked, "Are you Lisa Baer?" My throat closed as I nodded.

"Is your mother or father home?" the other detective pressed. "We'll need an adult present before we can speak with you."

"I'm an adult," my sister said quickly.

One of the detectives turned to me. "Is that alright with you, Lisa? That your sister is here instead of your mother or father?"

Alright with me? That you've come to tear my world apart? My shoulders lifted in a shrug as I tilted my head, unable to find words. They asked if we could sit down and talk. We gathered around the kitchen table, the silence thick between us

"We know you were involved with Glenn Lowe," one detective began. "He was busted recently for selling meth, and we found these pictures."

He slid a photo across the table, me in my volleyball uniform. "Is this you?" Reluctantly, I nodded.

"What grade were you in when he took this picture?"

I clenched my jaw. He already knew the answers, why keep asking? The irritation burned through my fear. "Ninth grade," I snapped.

"You were fourteen then, right?" he pressed, confirming my birth date.

In that moment I would have preferred to be dragged into the center of an old town square, locked in the stocks for everyone to see. It almost felt like it would be easier, with a scarlet letter branded across my forehead, townspeople lining up to hurl rotting vegetables, spit, and insults. At least then there would be no hiding, no pretending. I would be marked as untouchable, filth beneath their feet, good for one thing and too stupid even to keep quiet about it. In some twisted way, I might have welcomed the clarity, finally belonging to the judgment, instead of fearing it in secret. The truth would be exposed, and I would no longer have to hide who and what I was.

I dropped my gaze. "How did you find me?"

"We went to your school," the detective replied. "We showed them this picture and got your name, address, and birth date."

The shock on my face must have been obvious, because he quickly added, "Don't worry, we only showed them this picture."

I glared at the detectives, heat rushing through me like fire under my skin. *Only that picture?* What else had they seen? I shoved the thought away before it could take shape. One of them continued, explaining that Glenn had multiple victims, but I was the youngest. Being fourteen at the time made it a more serious offense, easier to prosecute. Still, he added, they were prepared to pursue every charge if needed.

My sister's face went pale as she caught on. "Please, don't bring me into this," she begged. "My husband doesn't know."

The detective shook his head. "You were underage. Seventeen is still a crime. But we can focus on your sister only if she agrees to help us."

She turned to me, eyes desperate. "Please, Lisa. Do this for me."

I had no intention of helping them, or even staying in that suffocating room. I pushed back from the table and stood.

"You need to sit down," the detective said firmly, rising with me and motioning me back to the chair.

"What? What are you even saying to me? Help you how?"

"Lisa, just do what they want, okay?" my sister whined, her eyes cutting into me like knives.

"But Glenn said…"

"Lisa, please!" she snapped, desperation dripping from her voice.

The detective leaned in. "Will you help your sister out? If you cooperate, we'll build our case around you. The other victims will have minimal contact with us, and we'll keep your sister's involvement confidential."

My stomach twisted. *How can I say no?* If I refused, I would be betraying her. If I agreed, I was betraying myself. I wanted to disappear, to run, to undo the whole thing, but all I could feel was her pleading eyes on me, demanding I carry the burden to protect her.

"I… I guess so," I whispered, the words tasting like ashes in my mouth.

They reassured my sister, then asked to meet with me alone. She bounced out of the kitchen, calling over her shoulder, "Thank you, Lisa. Thank you so much. You're awesome. I appreciate it."

I sat stiffly at the kitchen table, the detectives to my left. Through the window, I could see the front yard, open, free. I longed to be out there, or anywhere else: the beach, the fire pit, hidden and unseen. But reality slammed back when the detective beside me slid a photo across the table. No warning, no pause, just placed in front of me like it was nothing.

My eyes flew open wide, then squeezed shut. My throat cinched tight, my hand clutching at my neck. Stomach acid rising like daggers. *Don't throw up, don't throw up, don't throw up.*

I wished the image would ignite, curl into ashes when I dared to look again. But when I opened my eyes, it was still there. Perfectly intact. One of the pictures I wished had never existed, now exposed to these men. Shame pulsed through me in waves.

"Is that you?" the detective asked, fully knowing the answer, tapping the pornographic image. "What's that? What were you doing?"

What does he think I was doing?

"Did he tell you to pose like that?" the detective pressed, sliding another picture in front of me. His raised eyebrows made my stomach lurch, like he might be taking some satisfaction in this. I waited for reassurance, for some scrap of comfort, but none came. Their tone, their eyes, the way the questions were framed, it all made me feel less like a victim and more like I was on trial. *Was I?* They kept talking, almost casually. "At first we felt bad for Glenn," one said. "He told us he was a veteran of the Korean War. But then we realized that wasn't true, he's too young to have been in that war."

I blinked, trying to catch up. *Should I feel bad for him? What are they even saying to me?*

By the time they were done with me, I was emptied out, scraped clean. I felt nothing, *was* nothing. They said they'd have to tell my mom. That my words and their evidence would build the case against Glenn. I would be contacted again.

When the door shut behind them, I folded into myself on the couch, curling into a fetal ball. My eyes locked on the wall, unblinking, until a few scalding tears slid free. My body was heavy, useless. I might as well have been dead.

Later, when Bob came to pick me up, I wiped my face quickly, trying to erase the evidence. It took hours before I worked up the nerve to tell him what had happened. I whispered that it started when I was fourteen, before him.

His reaction was sharp, cutting. "What! You did *what?* With Glenn?" His voice wasn't just angry, it was accusing, almost mocking. "And now you're cooperating with them? Talking to detectives? Why the hell would you do that? Why didn't you tell me before?"

I sat silent, crushed beneath the weight of his disgust. Inside, I was already splintered, barely holding together. And the worst part, the way his words coiled around me, I knew it wasn't what had happened with Glenn that enraged him. It was that I had spoken it out loud, to someone other than him. Bob had asked me to do the same kinds of things with other people. That was never what sickened him. What twisted his anger now was that I hadn't told him first, that a piece of me had slipped beyond his reach into the hands of detectives. His fury wasn't about protecting me; it was that he didn't know.

Little Lisa,

The arrival of the detectives at your doorstep was profoundly disorienting and terrifying, it shattered you. You couldn't believe it was happening, again! Your privacy was violated and your deepest fears surfaced. Your overwhelm hurt, and you were uncertain how to respond. You were confronted not only by the weight of legal scrutiny but also by the corrosive feelings of shame and vulnerability.

Being presented with those photographs, explicit images you never wished to be exposed ever, was a brutal breach of trust and dignity. The detectives' line of questioning, devoid of empathy and care, understandably left you questioning your own validity as a victim. They were there to gather evidence and their approach failed to honor your inherent worth and pain.

The detectives shouldn't have manipulated you with your sister, they facilitated you bearing the burden of protecting your sister, to get what they wanted. What a violation! They implored you to cooperate, even as you grappled with your own trauma. You felt you were sacrificing your safety, and you did it anyway, for her.

Bob's anger compounded your sense of isolation and hurt. His hypocritical judgment speaks to his own character not to your worth or dignity.

145

Little Lisa, I hope you internalize this truth: none of the shame belongs to you. The shame belongs solely to the people who violated you. Even amidst darkness, some part of you held on, I'm so, so glad.

CHAPTER 27

"Hurry up, Lisa! We'll be late for court!"

"Do we have to go, Mom? The detectives said it was optional."

"Yes, we are going. Get in the car."

Her voice carried eagerness; another show she didn't want to miss. She didn't notice my fear pressing heavier with every breath. She was lost in her own thoughts, never once looking to see how much I was breaking.

By the time the case finally made it to court, I was sixteen. The ride made my stomach roil, the dread pressing heavier with every passing street. All I could think about was Glenn's warning, that he'd get the person who turned him in. Would he think it was me now? What would he do to me when he got out? Maybe I deserved whatever was coming. Still, I told myself I'd fight back. I still had my knife. *How had my life gone so wrong?*

Bob didn't come to court with me. He seemed tense about it all, his worry not for me. That morning his voice was flat, affectionless, "After court, I'll pick you up. Be ready at five."

When we arrived at court, panic gripped me. Glenn's family was there. I was surprised by that for some reason. *Don't look at them.* There were no other victims, just me, once again.

Mom brought a friend along, and the three of us had to pass directly by Glenn's family to reach the empty seats. My face burned with shame. Mom sighed to her friend, "Why am I always put in these situations?" Her friend murmured comfort while I sat silently, dread growing as we waited to be called into the courtroom.

When it was time to enter, we sat across the aisle from Glenn's family. They had once been friends, but now their eyes cut into me, sharp where they used to be warm. *They're angry at me!* Then the inmates were led in.

Glenn found me instantly, his stare hard and hateful, pinning me in place. I dropped my eyes. *What am I supposed to do now?* The judge began working through the cases, my mind racing too fast to follow. Before Glenn's case was called, the judge announced a recess. Fifteen minutes until we had to return.

It took everything in me to get up, but the craving for a cigarette pulled me forward. I forced each step, until it was too late to turn back, I had already come face to face with his family.

Their words cut the air as I passed, mocking and cruel, *"She was molested?"*

My heart splintered under their scoffs, humiliation swelling until it nearly crushed me. I blinked hard, fighting back tears, as I hurried toward the courthouse steps. Did they even know I was only fourteen then, not sixteen like I was now? My thoughts spun in frantic circles. *Was I molested? Maybe he'll kill me someday. At least... at least I'm helping my sister.*

Lost in thought, I flinched when my mom's friend called out my name. "It's been fifteen minutes, Lisa, come on!" she urged. I rose from the courthouse steps and rushed toward the courtroom doors.

The judge asked if any victims were present. My mom stood. "Yes, Lisa Baer is here."

He turned toward me. "Does she have anything to say?"

"Yes, she does," Mom insisted, tugging at my blouse.

My heart lurched. I rose on unsteady legs, every part of me wanting to sit back down. The judge's kind eyes met mine, silently urging me forward. "What happened, Lisa? What would you like to say?"

I hadn't prepared. I hadn't even thought about it. My chest tightened, mad, sad, outraged, confused, all of it flooding me at once. My throat felt locked, yet my voice broke out without my permission.

"Glenn promised that nothing bad would happen, that what was between us was good and safe from the world finding out. He lied. I thought he was my boyfriend initially, but soon realized I wasn't his girl. I was just a 'friend' and he was selfish and scary, and I couldn't get away from him."

"Go on," the judge encouraged.

"Glenn was nice at first, but he got me into meth and broke my heart." The words spilled out of me as if something else had taken control, speaking through me.

"Glenn had this philosophy that being 'friends' who did sexual things was better than being married. I didn't want that. When I told him so, he argued that his way was better. He said we were just friends, that he'd still be there for me when I got divorced someday, that people didn't understand relationships like ours, and that he wanted to be my friend for life. He told me he had my best interests in mind."

I dragged in a breath and went on.

"He talked me into doing things, then tried to make our relationship into some kind of business. It broke my heart that he didn't want to be my boyfriend. And when I tried to end the 'friendship,' he stalked me. He wouldn't stop pursuing me. He left me letters, pages of them, and told me to destroy them after I read them. And I did."

The judge thanked me for speaking. He said I was courageous, that my words were helping to protect other potential victims. Then he apologized for what had happened to me. The compassion in his voice startled me, comforted me. No one had ever said that to me before, not about Glenn, not about what we had called a "relationship."

In that moment, I decided I liked judges. However brief my encounters with them had been, they had always shown me kindness. Then the judge added that because of my statement, he would give Glenn the maximum sentence. My stomach dropped. I had made it worse for Glenn. It was done now. My fate felt sealed. At what cost had I just spoken? It didn't matter anymore, it was over. At least I had weed waiting for me at home.

The judge banged his gavel, and the courtroom began to clear. Mom urged me to hurry, pushing at my arm, but I lagged behind. She moved ahead without me, weaving through the crowd toward the exit.

When I finally reached the doorway, a blonde woman in uniform stepped toward me; a police officer. Her voice carried compassion as she said, "Thank you, thank you so much for what you did. You are so brave. Glenn is my ex-husband, and we have a daughter. You did the right thing."

She hugged me and walked away, leaving me still in the doorway. My heart swelled with unexpected gratitude. Her compassion and support stayed with me, a gift that softened the weight I carried.

Little Lisa,

Such an unbearable burden, feeling painfully exposed and isolated. The mocking whispers from Glenn's family turned you into a public spectacle of shame, deepening the loneliness that wrapped around you like a suffocating cloak. Their cruelty was a harsh reminder that you were utterly alone in a sea of judgmental eyes.

Your mother's disregard for your well-being, made you feel invisible and unprotected. I'm so sorry your mother doesn't care about your pain or your fear. You were a pawn for her twisted desires.

Amid all this, the terrifying fear that Glenn might someday kill you loomed over your every thought, a dark shadow born from real danger. You avoided his glare as best you could.

Yet, even in the face of such loneliness, humiliation, and fear, your courage emerged, again! Speaking your truth was a powerful act of bravery. The judge heard you, you did so good.

You deserved compassion, safety, and dignity at every step. You didn't get it then but I give it to you now. You are not invisible, you are deeply loved and seen. Your survival is the foundation on which you will rebuild your life and reclaim your peace.

CHAPTER 28

Bob waved me over to his car as we pulled up to the house after court. Mom stayed silent, but her friend offered a small kindness: "Bye, Lisa. Take care. You did good today."

I slid into the passenger seat beside Bob. "Let's go, I have plans," he muttered, already impatient.

Not one mention of anything about my day in court as we drove off. *Fine by me,* I just wanted it behind me. *Better not to talk about it,* I thought, pulling in a deep drag from the joint already burning between my fingers.

The best part of being with Bob was his family. To my surprise, his parents were kind and respectful to me. I hadn't expected that, not after all the harsh things my mother and father drilled into me about Christians. Yet, here Bob's family was gentle and welcoming. They had to know what Bob and I were doing, but they never judged me. Bob's sister was the kindest of all. Being with them felt like sinking into a soft, warm blanket. Even their home carried a glow of comfort and safety. They asked me questions about myself as if they truly wanted to know. When Bob's sister discovered how much I loved and missed playing sports, her eyes lit up. "Lisa, our church has teams you could join. Would you like that?" she asked with an encouraging smile.

"I'd love to, but I'm not Christian."

"Lisa, you don't have to be Christian to play. Would you like to go with me?"

"Really? Yes, I would!" That was all it took, I was sold. A chance to play sports again? Absolutely. The day she took me to play I felt a rush of energy I hadn't felt in a long time. Just stepping onto the court lifted me. Sports weren't Bob's thing, so he stayed home, and I didn't care.

The moment the volleyball smacked against my arms, it was like waking up a part of myself I'd been missing. Even more surprising, the people there were genuinely kind. I'd half expected "church ball" to be stiff, awkward, maybe even preachy, but it wasn't. My doubts melted away as laughter filled the gym. Players started calling me by name, welcoming me like I belonged.

After a few weeks of playing a couple of days each week, Robin invited me to a Bible study. I hesitated. I was certain about one thing; I did not want to be a Christian. I thought of myself as spiritual, but church? No thank you. Other than a few early years in the Episcopal Church and a Baptist pre-school, which I loved, I really had no church background. What I did have was my parents' voices in my head, repeating over and over that Christians were hypocrites. That message stuck.

Still, I had always loved Jesus. From childhood, I saw him as someone tender and good. Later, learning from Buddhist teachings, I thought of him as a wise teacher, a model of compassion. I was comfortable loving Jesus in that way. But the image of TV Christians, stiff dress-wearing women, organ music, judgmental vibes, made me uneasy. I wasn't interested. I told her, "No, thank you," and she accepted that without pressure. We just kept playing sports.

Meanwhile, Bob started going back to church at his parents' pleading. This brought new life to his family and increased visits to him from guys from his congregation. They invited him to meetings, sports, and other activities. They spent time with him, talking about faith and how living the gospel brings actual joy. They all seemed genuinely kind. Bob never talked to me about church, and nothing in his behavior with me changed, but their friendliness left me with a genuinely positive impression.

So, when Bob's sister asked again if I'd meet with the youth pastor and study the Bible, I finally said yes, but with a boundary. "Sure," I told her, "but please don't expect me to join your church. As long as you don't expect that, I'll listen and learn what you believe."

Then I admitted my worry. "Does it matter that I don't live a clean life like you and your parents? I know I shouldn't be doing drugs like I do."

She didn't flinch. "That's okay," she said with a calm smile. "You can still learn, can't you?"

Truthfully, I didn't mind the idea at all. Any excuse to spend more time around these kind people felt like a soft glow, a rare treasure I longed to hold onto.

Little Lisa,

You longed for warmth and belonging in a world that so often felt cold and confusing. Being with Bob brought mostly pain, but his family, especially his sister, offered you a rare safe space where you could breathe and feel seen. Those moments wrapped you in quiet comfort you had known too little of, but always deserved.

It's natural that you felt cautious and uncertain about church or spirituality. Your past taught you to guard yourself, to be wary of promises that might hurt. And yet, you showed such courage by saying yes, not to joining, not to changing who you were, but simply to learning, to letting in a sliver of light. Deep down, you always knew God was there with you.

Healing never needs to be forced. It comes gently, through kindness, laughter, movement, and the safety of true connection. You didn't have to become "clean" or perfect to be worthy of kindness. You were worthy just as you were.

Hold on to these sparks of hope, Little Lisa. They are the quiet roots growing strong beneath the surface, preparing you to blossom in your own time, in your own way.

CHAPTER 29

I had no intention of ever becoming a Christian, but I couldn't ignore how different Bob's family seemed. They were happy without drugs or alcohol. Part of me wondered if I could ever live like that. I didn't actually want to give up using, it had become my way of getting through the days. Still, something deep inside me wanted to not be so dependent.

And I still carried a vision of myself, an ideal Lisa who was strong and free from needing anything to numb the pain. That image felt far away, but not impossible. Watching the people at church laugh and live without substances stirred my curiosity. What was it that made them so genuinely happy? That question was enough to draw me in, and I began studying with them.

So began my year-long exploration of Christianity. At first, I shared what I thought I knew, "Christians can't dance, embrace hate, and other strange things I'd heard." Their faces lit with eagerness to correct me, and they did.

Each question I asked was answered with patience and backed by scripture. The more I studied, the more I realized how much I hadn't known. I learned about Jesus' teachings about love, forgiveness, and living with purpose. I learned about the Savior himself, his words in scripture, and how Christians lived both long ago and now. One lesson struck me deeply, the commandment, "Thou shalt not commit adultery." It sank in hard because I had never even known about it. I looked at my life very differently from that moment on.

One evening, after a discussion, I turned to Bob. "Why didn't you tell me about what Jesus teaches?" I asked, the weight of it pressing down on me.

He shrugged, his voice edged with annoyance. "Uh, what do you mean, what are you learning now?"

What surprised me most wasn't his reaction, but the quiet calm I felt in the middle of my question. There was something steady and unexpectedly comforting in what I was learning. Talking about the Gospel of Jesus Christ with Bob was never pleasant. He didn't have answers and took my honest questions as an attack. When I asked him why he didn't live the commandments, he brushed me off, clearly annoyed. Thankfully, I had new church friends I could turn to, especially a guy named Robert. He was one of the guys trying to help Bob back to church. As I spent more time with my new friends, I began watching closely, waiting for the moment they would pull away or judge me. Instead, I was met with warmth. Their acceptance caught me off guard, and I found myself surprised, pleasantly, even gratefully, by how genuinely they welcomed me in.

Each new concept opened my mind a little wider. Some of the commandments and beliefs Christians held were things I had never even heard of, let alone understood. I also learned about *covenants*, sacred promises between a person and God. The idea amazed me, if I promised to live in a certain way, God promised in return to guide, strengthen, and bless me. Through those covenants, people often spoke of receiving spiritual insights, moments of clarity, peace, or understanding that seemed to come directly from God. The blessings they described weren't just about religion; they were about real changes in daily life, more calm, more direction, more hope.

What struck me most was how clearly and respectfully these people explained their faith. They didn't shy away from the hard questions, and to my surprise, I wasn't repelled in the least. Instead, I was drawn in.

They taught me how to pray the way they prayed, and for the first time I was told that I could seek answers for myself, that I could actually talk to God and expect Him to answer. Could that really be true? I had prayed before and believed in God all my life, but never like this. Never with people who prayed with me, and for me, guiding me with such sincerity.

Before studying with these Christians, I had always sensed there was something more to life. From Buddhism, I had learned that our time on earth is like a school, a place to gain experience and practice choosing between right and wrong. I held on to the idea that everything carried a lesson. Even in my pain, I loved God and felt His presence close by.

What I hadn't known was that God was more than a distant force, that He was my spiritual parent. I hadn't realized I could actually commune with

Him, speak to Him, and receive answers in return. But now, through these studies, I was beginning to understand.

As my prejudice about these people and the church began to melt away, I discovered something surprising, they were deeply committed to protecting both children and adults.

When I asked why commandments were even necessary, the pastor answered gently, "Lisa, the commandments are for people, not for God. He loves us so much that He gave us guidelines to help us be as safe and as happy as possible."

I felt deeply grateful to discover scriptures I had never known before, ones that said, *"Fathers should not provoke their children to anger,"* and another that warned, *"It would be better to have a millstone hung around your neck and be drowned in the depths of the sea than to harm a child."* These teachings struck me because they spoke so plainly about what was harmful and what parents and adults should and shouldn't do, unlike the people I had grown up around who blurred every line.

Deep in my heart, I felt a stirring of truth, truth that had been denied to me again and again by abusers who trained me to ignore my own intuition, the light from Christ within me. Memories rushed back of times I had been uncomfortable, even violated, by people who preached their perversions as if they were good. They had forced me to accept what I always felt deep down was wrong.

Now, I was learning something radically different; that *no* should be respected, and that having strong boundaries over my body and desires was not only allowed, but right. It was the complete opposite of what I had been taught my whole life.

It felt as if I had been trapped in a dark room and someone suddenly opened the curtains. Light poured in, wrapping me in warmth and comfort. That light stirred my soul, strengthened my spirit, and showed me a way forward. Where before I had been lost in shadows, unsure of how to move, now I could finally see where to go.

Joy swelled inside me, a steady current I felt every day. With it came a new clarity and strength. My focus sharpened, and without even trying, I found myself reaching less and less for drugs and alcohol. I can't recall the exact moment of my last drink or bong hit, but eventually, I stopped altogether. For the first time in my life, I had both a community and the words of God declaring clearly that child abuse was wrong, and defined what it was. Those words spoke peace and confidence into my wounded heart.

But the clarity and peace I carried weren't welcomed at home. My family treated it as a joke. "Lisa, I guess you want to be a hypocrite!" my mother laughed, rolling her eyes at my sister.

I tried to explain that I was studying to understand what Christians believe, that I wasn't afraid of knowledge. That what I had found in the scriptures was meaningful and beautiful. But before I could share even a word, she cut me off.

"We don't want to hear that crap, Lisa. Stop."

Mother never missed a chance to remind me of every negative stereotype about Christians. She scoffed that she would never be part of something "so stupid." Whenever I tried to talk with her, the sadness and confusion hit me hard, and the good feelings I carried slipped away.

I could understand some of the concerns she raised, but what confused me was the anger behind them, her refusal to see the ways this new path was already helping me. Even more bewildering was her unwillingness to speak directly with my Christian friends, the very people who could have answered her questions with calm and respect.

Whatever my mom brought up, I asked about during my studies. My concerns were answered with respect and straightforwardness. They didn't get upset with me or act annoyed. I was worried that they would be frustrated but instead took the time to address each and every question I had with scripture, prayed with me, and encouraged me to pray. They reminded me that I could find answers as I was taught by the Spirit. The idea that I could actually receive direct answers to my own questions from God, was amazing. I found myself longing for it with all my heart. I appreciated their confidence in my abilities even though I doubted myself. But the idea that

I could be taught by the spirit excited me. I sure wanted that. If I could get a connection to God and get answers, be told whatever the truth was, I was all about it.

Bob and I began to grow apart as I decided to test the scriptural analogy, *try the fruit and see if the tree is good.* I wanted to find out for myself, so I started by trying to live the commandments the best I could, praying, and reading scriptures to see how these actions would affect me. I had nothing to lose, so with each new principle I learned, I tried to live it as best I could.

One of those principles was the commandment not to commit adultery. What surprised me most was how different Bob's life was from the very teachings he had been raised with. He seemed indifferent to the faith of his childhood, while I was finding fresh meaning in it. Our paths began to diverge, he wanted to continue as we had been, while I felt excitement and hope in living the way I was being taught.

As I pressed forward, my thoughts grew clearer, and an unexpected peace settled over me. I felt God's support, His comfort, and His strength as I strove to live the commandments. The contrast between that peace and the tension with Bob became sharper. One day, during yet another argument, his frustration boiled over and he threatened once again to leave me.

"Okay, let's break up," I said.

He locked his eyes on mine, his voice slow and heavy with intimidation. "Are you sure you want to break up?"

In the past, those kinds of threats from him had undone me, leaving me distressed, panicked, and desperate to hold on. The idea of losing him, my fiancé, used to shake me to my core. But this time was different. As the words hung in the air, a warm, steady calm washed over me. I realized it would not only be okay, but good. Meeting his stare, I answered firmly, "Yes. Let's break up."

For a moment, I saw the flicker of surprise in his eyes. His threats and intimidation weren't working the way they used to, and he seemed caught off guard by my calm. Without another word, he turned and walked away. I heard him mutter something under his breath, but it didn't matter.

For the first time, I didn't feel distressed, worried, or sad. I didn't feel the need to make it okay for him. I knew I would be okay. I had a new connection with God that reached to my core. I was clear about how I wanted to live, and I was enjoying the changes unfolding within me, even if the people who were supposed to be close to me couldn't understand. In that moment, I felt God's comfort surrounding me.

I was gaining practical, real-life insights that changed the way I lived. One of my favorites was simple yet powerful, when someone is contentious, don't participate in their argument. Nothing good comes from bitterness, wrath, and pride. Seek peace, and don't speak to fools. That gave me a clear boundary for when to not interact with people, wisdom I hadn't had before.

I also came to see the commandments in a whole new light. They are like a protective fence around a whirlpool, keeping us safe from being pulled under. The commandments aren't meant to cage us in, but to guide us away from unnecessary pain. And we don't have to do it alone; we can ask for the Spirit's help in keeping them.

I realized each commandment carries its own temptations to break. But temptation doesn't mean I should give in to it. Instead, I could lean on God, the wisest of all, and trust that His way is so much better than relying on my own limited understanding. Over time, I noticed the temptations lost their power, growing weaker and weaker, until some faded completely.

Being part of a church community actually felt like coming home. Before I knew it, I was going regularly. I even chuckled at myself, me, in church! Yet, every time, there were people ready to teach me, and my new friends offered support and understanding along the way.

As I studied, I discovered that even scripture could stir old wounds. Reading about people who suffered, some burned in fires, others facing painful trials, made me ache for them. It also made me wonder about my own future. Would living the commandments guarantee safety? Or could suffering still find me?

One day, I brought my fears to the youth pastor. "What if God asks me to do something I don't want to do?" I asked. "What if I'm not protected from future pain?"

He answered gently, "Lisa, Heavenly Father isn't going to ask you to do something to make you less happy, only more happy like living the commandments, even if it's hard sometimes. And all of our life experiences will, in time, be made good by God. That doesn't mean evil is ok, just that's how wonderful God is."

Those words were exactly what my heart needed. They soothed the turmoil inside me and gave me a place to rest. I realized I could trust God. Yes, I had been hurt in many ways, but I also knew He was present, I had even felt Him speak to me once, guiding me to memorize where a pedophile photographer was so I could guide the police to his studio. Remembering that, I understood, God was with me, and He would continue to be.

I began to believe that, like Job, all things could work together for good. Reading the Bible filled me with a sense of truth, wisdom, and familiarity, as if the words had always been waiting for me. And the promise of "mansions on high" being prepared brought me a joy I had never known before.

One of the most important concepts I came to understand is that Heavenly Father works with us humans, as imperfect as we are, because only imperfect humans are available. And to only fully trust our Savior Jesus Christ because He is the only perfect one. The rest of us need ongoing forgiveness. Christ atoned for our sins and even descended below all so he knew how to comfort us. He wants to comfort us. He knows the pain of everything all of us have been through. Jesus is what I needed to build my testimony on. Jesus was who I needed to lean on.

I found myself wondering what Ray, my best parent, would think of me now. I remembered our outings together, how people would sometimes stare or make rude comments. Ray would lean close and say, "Lisa, don't worry about them, they don't know better yet." His example of steady, unconditional love was so Christlike, though I didn't have the words for it then. I knew in my heart he would be glad for me. The thought made me smile.

As I continued studying and praying, step by step, I became clean and sober from everything but cigarettes. They still had their grip on me. Every attempt to quit left me miserable, the cravings were unbearable, and even with prayer I felt hopeless.

Still, I kept trying. One Sunday, around ten in the morning, I sat in the church foyer, restless and desperate, ready to run out the door to buy a pack. In that moment, a strong prompting urged me to speak to the man sitting beside me. I confessed that I was struggling. Gently, he suggested we go pray with the pastor immediately. We went to the pastor, and all kneeled together. He prayed for me to be able to quit smoking, to be given strength beyond my own to do so. It was a beautiful prayer. After the prayer was over, I was told to please start a fast now, and they would fast with me too. He explained this will increase my spiritual strength to finally quit smoking. He was right. I felt immediate relief. I went to the service and continued to fast for the next three days. Each and every day of my fast I didn't smoke one cigarette. For the first time in my almost eighteen-year-old life, that I could remember, I had gone three whole days without smoking. I was elated. After that, I went on to not ever smoke again.

Little Lisa,

You always longed to feel whole without leaning on drugs, and you did it! By leaning on God's wisdom and strength, you found freedom.

Your courage to ask hard questions, challenge old assumptions, and open your heart to a truth that felt both unfamiliar and comforting shows how deeply you hungered for healing. In the safety of community, your doubts were respected and your spirit gently nurtured. That acceptance helped you recognize your worth and begin setting boundaries, a powerful step away from the patterns of your past.

The spirit replaced loneliness and despair. You discovered a light within yourself that had always been present, and the Spirit breathed on it until it burned brighter. That light can never be taken from you.

Breaking up with Bob and standing firm in what you knew was right took immense strength. Rooted in God and your identity as His daughter, you found your voice, a profound act of self-love. You learned that peace and clarity grow when you trust both God and yourself, even in the hardest moments.

The commandments you embraced are not chains but gifts of love and protection, guiding you toward safety, freedom, and joy. Your journey is sacred, and every step you take is a triumph. Hold fast to that hope, for it is your birthright, a light no darkness can extinguish.

CHAPTER 30

I was now a non-smoker, and it felt incredible! Miraculously, I wasn't even tempted, despite all the smokers around me. The little garden I had planted from seed for high school credit was now flourishing, and it became my sacred space. As I cared for it, I realized I was tending more than plants, I was nurturing my own faith. What had begun as the smallest seed inside me was now sprouting, stretching toward the light, growing stronger each day.

Praying in the garden felt natural. Kneeling among the plants, I reviewed with God all I had learned. I had already been living His commandments, and it felt right. I believed Jesus was my Savior, but I wanted to be certain, so I asked again. It wasn't doubt as much as a desire for another conversation with God, another reassurance.

I knew many would mock me, and I needed extra strength to hold steady. My mind still flashed with anxious fears: being labeled a Christian, accused of hating those who weren't, dismissed as an idiot. But like the seed that had taken root in my heart, the confirmation God gave me grew stronger than my fears. His truth outweighed every worry about what others might think.

As I prayed, the scripture echoed in my mind: *If you love me, keep my commandments.* I did love Jesus. In that moment, a calm, steady confirmation filled my soul. Christ was my Savior.

I wanted to get baptized!

As I prayed, I felt a distinct impression; God loved me unconditionally, and He would keep loving me, even if I didn't live His commandments. But I also understood that if I chose to walk the path He set, I would be spared the misery and suffering that had marked my past and, as He revealed to me, the disaster waiting in my future. It was my choice, and no matter what I chose, his love would never waiver.

It was as though I stood at a great crossroads. To my left stretched a road I knew too well, dark, heavy, and full of abuse, pain, and addiction. It wasn't safe for me. The ground was littered with debris of suffering. I could almost hear the echo of pain I had already lived, and the shadows whispered of more to come.

To my right, a narrow road shone with a gentle light. It wasn't free of storms, the clouds gathered there too, but the light pierced through them, steady and sure. That path promised growth, peace, and a freedom I had longed for. For the first time in my life, I realized I could choose which road to take.

With the strength of the Spirit, I felt I could finally live a sober life. If I continued to embrace His commandments, I would not only survive, I could thrive. I wanted that desperately, and I prayed for help to make it possible. God gave me caution as well; life would become better and more beautiful, but not without difficulty. *The rain falls on the just and on the unjust,* He reminded me. *But that doesn't mean I'm not there in the storms.*

A quiet peace swelled inside me unlike anything I had ever known. It gave me confidence that I was on the right path. I was using the right tools to learn and grow, and it filled me with excitement. I had tasted the fruit of the Gospel, and it was good. My life was already better.

I knew the path God wanted for me, but His love gave me freedom. Even in His compassion, He allowed me to decide. So, at eighteen, I made the best choice of my life.

As I stepped into the baptismal font, the man baptizing me met my eyes with a bright, reassuring smile. "Are you ready?" he asked. Joy welled up in me as I declared, "Yes, I am!"

The prayer washed over me like a promise, and then I was immersed. The water surrounded me, cool, clear, alive. When I rose again, droplets streamed down my face like light breaking through. The smiles of those gathered reflected what I felt inside: elation, freedom, newness. *I am renewed.*

The water was more than water, it was a river of renewal, a symbol of life flowing fresh and unbroken. It wrapped me in love, as if Heaven itself was cradling me. I was reborn, as though the very breath in my lungs had been given back to me with new strength.

There was no heaviness, no shadow, only celebration. This was not an ending, but a beginning. A doorway into light, a sacred threshold crossed. I stepped forward knowing this was my new starting point, the first page of a brighter story.

When I walked outside after my baptism, hair damp and heart overflowing, the sun's warmth wrapped around me like a soft blanket. The Riverside sky shone unusually bright that summer day, its blue so vivid it seemed to sparkle with the same lightness that filled me. I felt alive in a way I never had before, comfortable, lighter, brighter, even playful. Smiles spread across my face so easily I hardly recognized myself. I couldn't remember ever smiling so much. The Spirit was nurturing me, and at last, I was beginning to nurture myself too.

In the months that followed, I carried a strength beyond my own. I remained clean, sober, and chaste. I was learning how to be a respectful, hardworking young adult, and I lived it out through steady rhythms of work, martial arts, and church activities. Life felt full, emotionally rich, clean, and blessed.

When negative comments came, or when others tried to lure me into setting my standards aside, their words slid right off me like water off a duck's back. For the first time in my life, I was free to be the real me.

Little Lisa,

You are sober and clean! You are a miracle! Your little garden grew as you did, becoming holy ground, a place where you could meet God and reflect on your journey. With brave prayers, you opened your heart to know if Jesus was truly your Savior and whether His commandments were for you. The calm, steady confirmation that came marked a turning point. Even with fear of judgment pressing in, you trusted the Spirit's gentle assurance.

You discovered that God's love is unconditional, always embracing, never condemning. You also felt His hopeful promise; that choosing the narrow path full of light would free you from much pain and lead you to joy. You understood that storms would still come, but peace settled in with the knowledge that He would be there through them all. Your baptism, the symbol of a new life, renewed you, giving you deep joy.

Stepping forward, you embraced your identity as God's beloved daughter. The strength you found carried your sobriety and stability. The commandments, gifts of protection, guiding you toward safety and joy. Negative voices still tried to sway you, but resilience bloomed. For the first time, you knew your worth and lived as your true self.

Remember, dear one: this is your sacred path of healing and hope. Keep tending your spirit like that flourishing garden, and trust the light of Christ that shines within you.

Left: Two years old, with wild hair and a frilly dress. Playing with the curtains was a favorite game of mine.

Right: Four years old, posing with my family. We looked "normal" for the time we lived in, but we were anything but healthy. A reminder that you can't judge a book by its cover.

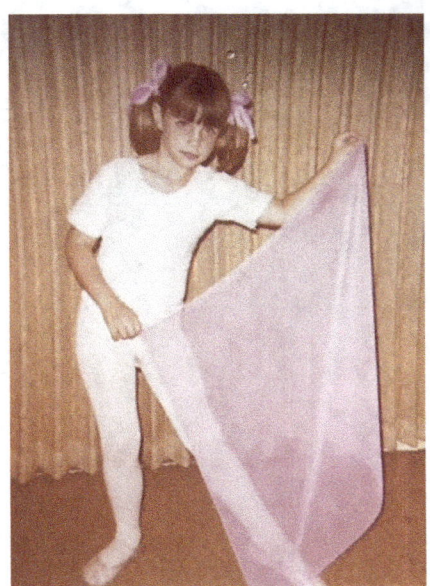

Left: Five years old in my ballet costume, upset from being yelled at, but finding light wherever I could.

Left: Ten years old on New Year's Day. My bright smile preserved the small moments I treasured, but it hid the truth of what I was living through.

Right: Eleven years old, standing in front of my childhood home, dressed in the girls' Buddhist marching band uniform. Being Buddhist with Ray was a sweet part of my life and offered me rare moments of peace and opportunity.

Left: Twelve years old in my softball gear, one of the few places I could run, hit, and breathe freely.

Right: Thirteen years old, 8th grade graduation. I remember feeling so sad that day. I had just gotten back from the foster home.

Left: Twelve years old, wearing the shirt Mother bought me, "Itty Bitty Titty Committee." Another example of being put on display, shamed, and sexualized. A child advertised to pedophiles. The kitchen table.

Left: Fourteen years old, 9th grade, trying to build something like a normal high school experience. My ROTC dance date was a perfect gentleman, unlike the adults around me.

Right: Nineteen years old, marrying young wasn't unusual in 1987. The smile genuine. We loved each other and God and that love got us through all that was before us.

Left: Ninth grade, fourteen. Volleyball was the one thing I never missed. Even here, in this photo, high on crystal meth, I still showed up to play the sport I loved.

Left: In my early thirties. Ray brought light, hope, and love into my life. He called me his daughter.

Right: Age fifty five; The day before Soft White Underbelly. For a month before the interview, I meditated daily to get through panic attacks, self-doubt, and fear of being seen by so many. With my family, my coach, and the Spirit behind me, I walked in knowing it was right to do. I'm grateful for the platform I was given, and for the incredible kindness I've received from so many since.

Right: Shell Day, A celebration of freedom, no longer fearing contact from OC. I felt stress melt off me in waves. Then came the sign, the shell. A gift marking protection, resilience, and transformation.

Left: The Shell, A sacred gift to remind me that I am loved.

CHAPTER 31

Every morning, after my baptism, I opened my eyes with a sense of focus and wonder at life's possibilities. Again and again, throughout my days, I caught myself overcome with surprise that I was clean, I was sober, and it was real. Gratitude swelled in my heart, and each time I felt it, I prayed thanks to God.

My days were busy with work, martial arts, and church activities. Since I hadn't been allowed to get my license at sixteen like my siblings, I walked or took the bus. But my new church friends always made sure I had a ride home from activities. These sober friends were awesome. Just a few months earlier, my life had been so different; now it felt as if I had stepped through a doorway into another dimension, a whole new universe.

My congregation had a thriving group of young single adults. Dating, dances, and activities gave us chances to enjoy each other's company and build friendships. Most of them were marriage-minded, and I was no different. Still, I felt proud of my independence. Marriage was a possibility, but only at the right time and with the right person.

There was my friend Robert, a six-foot-tall former football player and wrestler, whose broad smile seemed to light up everything around him. I really liked him, and not just because he was so handsome. I thought he might make a great boyfriend and sometimes let myself imagine it. But as with everything else in my life now, I prayed about it. The scriptures taught me to pray over all things, and I wanted God's input on even my attraction to Robert.

We first became friends before I ever got sober. He answered my questions with patience and kindness, and I never once felt judged by him. After my baptism, our friendship deepened, and before long it grew into something more. In just a few months of dating, we became very close. We both knew we had reached a point where either we would grow more serious or part ways if we realized we weren't good marriage material for each other.

Because of that, I felt it was important for him to know my history. When I finally shared it, he looked straight into my eyes and said he loved me even more for surviving. His voice trembled as he told me how deeply he cherished being around me, how he could see the real me beneath everything I had been through. Tears welled in his eyes as he admitted he hadn't realized how strong I was.

What moved him most, he said, was my love for God, that I didn't just believe, but truly *knew* Him. "That is the most important thing to me," he whispered as he pulled me into a tight embrace.

I told him I felt the same. His devotion to God and his willingness to follow Him was the most attractive thing about him to me too.

Dating Robert felt magical. With him, I always felt safe. He opened doors, held my hand with such tenderness, and treated me with respect in every way. We often talked about Jesus and how blessed we felt to know Him. Robert would pick me up after martial arts practice, asking thoughtful questions about my day and my opinions. He even cooked for me regularly.

We had been dating for several weeks before our first kiss. One evening, after dinner, Robert suggested a walk. Magnolia Avenue was lined with blooming magnolia trees, their fragrance drifting on the breeze as we strolled hand in hand beneath a full moon. When we reached the gazebo at the Heritage House, a historic museum with lush grounds, he led me to sit with him. I leaned against his shoulder, the night around us hushed and glowing. "Look up at the moon," he whispered, and as I lifted my gaze, he leaned in and kissed me. His kiss was gentle, sweet, and unforgettable. Later, I learned he had planned it all, wanting our first kiss to be under the moonlight in the most romantic setting he could imagine.

Robert drove me almost everywhere, so I rarely had to walk or ride the bus anymore. We danced every Friday and spent as much time together as possible. That's why I was so surprised when he broke up with me. He explained that he wanted me to be certain I was ready for more than just dating, and that he hoped I would take time to meet others so I could be sure of what I wanted. At first, I was so hurt, I knew what I wanted! But soon the Spirit comforted me, and I realized this was only a necessary and temporary step in our story.

The day after he broke up with me, I walked up to Robert at church, shook his hand, and told him I agreed, he was right we needed to do this for perspective. He looked at me with surprise before shaking my hand back. Just like that, we were friends again.

Our friendship carried on for a couple months. During that time, I found little ways to show him I cared, dropping off his favorite candy bar, bringing him a houseplant, or stopping by to check in. It was easy since one of my other good friends lived in the same apartment complex. I did as he suggested and dated others, but in truth, my thoughts never strayed far from Robert. The other guys were kind enough, but none of them compared. Robert was the only man I ever pursued.

Eventually, Robert had enough of our time apart. After seeking and receiving his own spiritual confirmation that it was right for us to be together, he asked me to get back with him. Of course, I said yes! It felt so natural, so joyful, to be Robert's girlfriend again.

True to his romantic nature, a month later he planned something unforgettable. He drove me up a mountain and laid out a picnic he had prepared himself. As we sat together, gazing out over the sprawl of Southern California with the sky wide above us, he turned to me and asked softly, "What are you doing for the rest of your life? Would you like to spend it with me?"

I had a feeling Robert would propose soon, but when the moment finally came, I sat stunned. Every part of me wanted to shout "yes!" Instead, tears filled my eyes as I wrapped my arms around him. "Yes," I whispered into his ear.

By then, the sun had slipped behind the horizon, and the mountain air had grown cold. Yet as we lay back on the blanket and looked up, the stars stretched endlessly above us. It felt as though heaven itself had opened, a quiet witness to the promise we had just made. The night was cold, but we were wrapped in a warmth that came not from the blanket, but from the hope of eternity together.

The next six months brimmed with joy and anticipation, days full of laughter, dreaming, and planning for our future, all while I did my best to navigate life in my mother's lair. As Robert came to know my family and saw their ways for himself, he only tightened his hold on me. Again and again, he reassured me that he loved me, and together we would create a beautiful life, one brighter than the stars above us.

The day of our wedding finally arrived. I had barely slept the night before, my last night in my childhood home. Most of my belongings were already in the little apartment Robert and I had prepared, waiting for me to join him after the honeymoon. That morning, all I needed was what would make me a bride.

Robert picked me up before sunrise. Together, we slipped quietly from the house to his car, the cool morning air wrapping around us. As the sun climbed the horizon, the warmth came with it, golden light bursting across our path as we drove toward Los Angeles. Fingers entwined, we talked with excitement, the sunlight pouring over us like a blessing.

Soon the square concrete lines of the Los Angeles skyline rose before us, sharp against the glowing sky. We passed through the city's noise and chaos until, at last, we reached the quiet of our wedding venue. Parking beneath the shade of a tree, we were greeted by smiling workers who guided us gently to where we needed to go.

The first time Robert saw me in my wedding dress was when I stepped out of the bride's room and walked down the hall toward him. He stood waiting in his white tuxedo, looking so handsome, broad shoulders filling his jacket, his strong hands ready to reach for mine. When his eyes met me, they sparkled with joy, and his wide smile, always enough to melt me, spread across his face. In that instant, I truly felt like a princess.

"You're stunning," Robert said, taking my hand as we walked together through the beautiful sanctuary. Just before we entered the place we would leave calling each other husband and wife, he stopped, turned to me, and looked deeply into my eyes. With a tender kiss, he whispered, "Let's go get married, my beautiful bride." Tears welled in both our eyes as we lingered in the bliss of that moment, thrilled to know we would never have to part again.

After the ceremony, as we strolled the scenic grounds toward the photographer, Robert squeezed my hand and said softly, "I'm never letting go."

Dear Lisa,

Waking up with joy and feeling focused every day was a new and beautiful experience for you. Your sobriety brought surprise and gratitude that you prayed over often, grounding you in the peaceful rhythm of your busy, meaningful days. Though your childhood limitations like not having a license was hard, your new community and friends supported you lovingly, helping you feel safe.

Dating Robert was a gentle unfolding of trust, respect, and shared faith. You allowed yourself to be vulnerable, sharing your past openly, and were met with love and acceptance, something you deserved deeply. His kindness and your shared devotion to God built a foundation that gave you confidence to embrace your union thoughtfully, and at a pace in alignment with your values.

When Robert paused the relationship to give you space, your spirit knew this was part of a bigger plan. You remained patient and hopeful, trusting the Spirit's comfort, which guided you back to him stronger and more sure of your love.

The day of your wedding was a joyful culmination of growth, courage, and choosing love amidst challenges. You stepped into your new life with hope and warmth, supported by the promises you found in faith.

Remember, dear one, your story shows how faith, honesty, and patience can build a loving partnership and a fulfilling life. Keep leaning on God and yourself, your journey of healing and love is sacred and worth every step.

CHAPTER 32

As we drove toward our honeymoon destination in Newport Beach, a "Just Married" sign fluttered on the back of the car. Passing drivers honked and cheered, flashing smiles and thumbs-up that made us laugh and squeeze each other's hands tighter.

When we arrived and checked in, we didn't head straight to our room. Instead, we slipped down to the shore for a moonlit walk. The cool waves rushed around our ankles, each crash against the sand invigorating us, while the silver light of the moon shimmered across the water.

The days that followed unfolded in a blissful rhythm, hours spent between the beach and our hotel, with little adventures exploring the city woven in. It was the sweetest beginning, a perfect time carved out just for us, ushering us gently into the life we were starting together.

After a week of bliss, real life began. I felt completely at ease stepping into the role of Robert Plumb's wife. We delighted in building our little nest together, planning meals, filling our days with fun activities, and settling into the rhythm of married life. Of course, we had to adjust to each other's quirks, but even that felt like part of the adventure.

I had simple dreams, to be a wife, a mother, and a martial artist. And here I was, living them. I had married a true gentleman, and together we were having the time of our lives.

At first, we had agreed to wait a year or so before starting a family. But within just a couple of months, the longing in my heart grew too strong to ignore. My baby craving couldn't be denied, and so, hand in hand, we decided it was time to begin our family.

We were blessed to conceive right away. Carrying a new life while working wasn't easy, especially in a daycare, fighting nausea, and tending to children all day, but I pressed on until the final months, when I could finally rest and prepare our little home for the baby. Gratitude filled me.

During my pregnancy, I was given glimpses of our child in dreams, sacred moments that felt like God letting me peek through a veil. Those dreams gave me a sense of knowing, as though I had already met this little soul. Ultrasounds weren't yet routine, so we would wait until birth to learn if our baby was a boy or girl. But in my heart, I already knew.

One year and six days after our marriage, our son Daniel entered the world. Labor was far more grueling than I had expected, leaving me trembling and weak when he was finally placed in my arms. Yet, the moment I held him, time seemed to stop. Awe washed over me, this perfect, wrinkled, cone-headed boy was mine. He was strong, hungry, and brimming with energy.

Within twenty-four hours, we were home. I cradled Daniel in my arms, humbled by the sacred covenant of motherhood, knowing that God had placed eternity in my keeping through this tiny, holy gift of a child.

Becoming a mother was the fulfillment of my deepest dream. Yet with that dream came a trial I hadn't anticipated. As soon as my motherly instincts stirred, so did my fears and anxieties. The weight of my past abuse and my sense of inadequacy sharpened my awareness of everything that could possibly go wrong.

Though my baby nursed well and I loved him more than life itself, a shadow crept in, stretching across both day and night. Sleep deprivation, anemia, and emotional overwhelm magnified my worries until they pressed in on every side. Motherhood was everything I had hoped for, but it also carried a heaviness I hadn't known to expect.

I was deeply grateful to be home with him, free from working outside the house. Yet, inside our small apartment, the walls seemed to close in. A gnawing thought haunted me. I would never be normal again.

When others wanted to hold my baby, I felt suspicion rise. Could I trust their intentions? Did they know how fragile he was? He was mine to protect, and I clung to that role with everything I had.

Then the past came crashing over me like a tsunami. Memories of my abuse slammed into me with the force of a punch to the gut. I hadn't been safe, so how could my baby be safe? Fear ruled my thoughts. I obsessed over every possible danger, every imagined loss.

I told myself I wouldn't survive if anything ever happened to him. And yet the darkest fear whispered: *What if I was the danger? What if I was the bad thing that happened to him?* His cries pierced me, and with every wail, doubt clawed deeper. *Maybe I'm a bad mom. Shouldn't I know how to stop this crying?*

I had no experience with babies and no real help except for Robert. When my mom finally visited, I was desperate enough to beg. "Mom, could you please help me with the dishes? I'm so tired."

She scoffed. "When I had you, no one helped me. And I had two other children to look after, too."

"Mom, please," I whispered through tears as I settled in to nurse. "I just need help."

Somehow, maybe out of a fleeting moment of compassion, she walked into the kitchen and began doing the dishes. But even then, her words cut deep. "You need a better routine. You can't be lazy. Holding him all the time isn't helping. And I expect gratitude for this. I didn't come over here to work."

I never asked her for help again. The days and nights blurred into one another as I counted the minutes until Robert returned home. His presence was more than just help; he was an anchor. As a father, he was extraordinary, never once complaining, his love for us shining in everything he did.

When he was near, the heaviness lifted and my pain eased. Each morning, when he left for work, my heart ached at his absence. Yet even in the loneliness, gratitude overflowed. I loved him beyond measure and marveled at the gift of his steady, unwavering care.

Yet the darkness crept closer. The flood of emotions and flashbacks only grew stronger. I couldn't believe what I had done. I brought this perfect, beautiful human into the world. I had no regrets about his existence, only about my own ability to be what he needed. I loved him fiercely, but I was convinced I wasn't the best for him.

Still, I couldn't leave him. I couldn't even bear to be apart for an hour even when he was with Robert. The weight of my emotions pulled me under, and my thoughts spiraled. Maybe it would be better for Robert and Daniel if I weren't around. Surely it would. My misery and negativity felt contagious.

Even as those destructive thoughts whispered, I knew something about them wasn't right. Yet, the idea of disappearing still carried a twisted sense of relief. But then another truth rose up, no one else in the world would protect Daniel like I would. And I did love him, with everything in me. That love anchored me, even in the storm.

When Daniel was only a few months old, the torment in my mind still hadn't let up. It rattled inside me constantly, and no one knew. One morning, he had cried without pause, and I knew it would be hours before Robert came home. My nerves were frayed; I couldn't take any more. Afraid I might snap, I set Daniel in his crib, and walked out of the room.

I collapsed in tears, my own sobs filling the silence. In that moment, I remembered, I could pray. Prayer had become a habit for me, but it was harder to keep up with. But this prayer would be different, I had to be specific. I had to tell God that I wanted to die. And for a brief moment, I considered that I would have to take my baby with me. I couldn't leave him alone. God wanted honesty, didn't He? Then I would give it. I told Him I must have been wrong to have a baby, because clearly I was too broken to be a good mother. Rage, sorrow, regret, and confusion tore through my heart, leaving me exhausted and hollow. I couldn't help but wonder, where were all the good feelings I had felt since my conversion? Why had they vanished when I needed them most?

I collapsed onto my bed and screamed into my pillow. *Why? Help me!* I prayed desperately, listening for any trace of an answer.

In the dampness of my tears and sweat, a memory rose, my baptism, slipping into my mind like a healing balm. I remembered how Christ had been baptized though He had no need, and how I had once arrogantly thought I was the same. I was the victim, not the perpetrator, so what could I possibly have to repent of?

But now, I was an adult. A mother. And I needed repentance as much as anyone. I recalled a definition I had read: *repentance is a change of heart and mind that brings us closer to God.* Repentance wasn't just for crimes or sins; it was for course correction, for noticing where my thoughts and choices were pulling me away from Him and turning back.

The realization stung. I wasn't guilty of the abuse that had been done to me, but I was weighed down by its effects, by anger, despair, and fear. I needed help. I needed to repent, to adjust my heart daily, to reach for healing and support. I didn't want to believe I was a terrible mother. I wanted to believe there was a way forward, a way to be whole.

As I poured my heart out to God, a familiar answer returned to me, one I had received the year before. *The rain falls on the just and the unjust, but I am with you even in the storms.*

Love and encouragement wrapped around me like a blanket still warm from the dryer. I was reminded that life would not always be easy, that storms would come, but it would be worth the struggle. This path, with God beside me, was far better than the alternative.

I thought of the prayers I had written down, reminders that my future did not have to be defined by abuse or addiction. A different life was possible. And in that moment, a scripture pulsed through my mind, steady and insistent:

This too shall pass. This too shall pass. This too shall pass.

I believed it. I couldn't deny how far I had come or all the comfort the Spirit had already given me. In that moment, I understood more deeply the scriptures describing Christ lamenting on the cross.

He hurt.

As I clutched my pillow, I felt a little less alone. Even He had cried out in anguish, pleading for the cup to be taken from Him. Even He had voiced the ache of suffering. That realization wrapped around me with unexpected comfort. My lamenting did not mean I lacked faith, it meant I was human.

I am not alone.

Even in that moment of despair, my Savior's comfort and love reached me. In my mind's eye, I saw Him, first agonizing on the cross, and then clothed in a brilliant white robe, smiling at me. He took my hand, pulled me into a tender embrace, and met my gaze with the kindest, most loving eyes. His voice was gentle yet sure: *"I understand. I will never leave you or forsake you. You are mine. Mansions on high are waiting for you."*

I realized then that I was not alone in my agony. My soul was soothed, my pain eased. Even when I felt abandoned, He was with me. All I had to do was return to this moment, hold it close, and let it steady me.

I lingered there for several minutes, hands crossed over my heart, eyes closed, resting in the warmth of His promise, before slowly returning to the world around me.

The peaceful feelings I had known so consistently for more than a year now felt distant much of the time. Still, the insights and quiet comfort of the Spirit kept me from harming myself or my baby. I found strength in remembering that even the Savior had faced agony. I was in good company. His promise was that my burdens would be made light, and I clung to that hope.

As the days wore on, I discovered a way forward, through the sorrow and into moments of joy. The Atonement of Jesus Christ took on new depth for me as I pleaded for Him to succor me, just as He had promised. In answer, comfort and hope came in waves, never all at once, but always enough to carry me through.

I clung to the assurance that this trial would pass, and that, in time, I would grow lighter, stronger, and more whole. The Savior's love steadied me, and in that love, my prayers naturally turned to my baby. I prayed for his safety, his happiness, his future, that he would always feel cherished, protected, and guided by God.

The love I felt for him was fierce, beyond words. It ached in my chest and brought tears to my eyes, a love so deep it demanded I keep going, no matter how heavy the days felt. I prayed that I might never lose sight of the

Savior's love, that I would always recognize it, feel it, and pour it into the life of my little boy.

Lisa,

Your honeymoon by the beach was a joyful beginning, filled with peace, connection, and hope for the future. Becoming Robert's wife felt natural and beautiful as you built a life together, learning each other's quirks and sharing dreams. When you became a mother, your joy deepened, but so did unexpected fears and anxieties. The overwhelming love for your baby also stirred memories and trauma, turning your days into a storm of exhaustion, doubt, and worry. Postpartum depression is common for abuse survivors, and what you faced was not weakness but the weight of old wounds pressing on the present.

You longed for help, and you needed it. But your mother's visit brought more pain than comfort. Yet Robert's steady love became a lifeline, reminding you that you were not alone. When despair pushed you to the edge, your prayers grew honest and raw. You remembered that even Christ cried out in suffering, yet He never left you, offering a love so deep and unwavering.

Though peace often felt far away, the Spirit's quiet presence held you steady through the darkest moments. Through it all, your fierce love for your baby blazed, you prayed he would always know how deeply he was loved, not only by you but by God. You prayed he would feel the Spirit guiding and comforting him always.

Lisa, your courage to keep going, praying, and loving was powerful. Step by step, you grew stronger, carried by hope and love. I'm so glad you survived.

CHAPTER 33

Studying the Savior's life was more important now than ever. I learned that *everything good comes from God,* a truth that gave me courage to seek wisdom not only in scripture but also in other good books that could guide me. Some of what I read confirmed what I already sensed, I needed therapy.

Even in the midst of precious moments with my little family, I found myself caught between waves of fatigue, deep sadness, and cravings for old addictions. I suspected my pain was rooted in my chaotic childhood, but I had no idea how to face it. Pride had no place here; I was willing to do whatever it took to feel whole and become better.

Still, I worried. What if a therapist dismissed or criticized my faith, the very thing that was holding me together? To protect that part of me, I resolved to meet only with a Christian therapist, someone who could honor both my healing and my belief.

"I don't even feel like brushing my hair," I mumbled to my therapist, a doctor of psychology. It was only our second session, and I wasn't sure what to expect, but I knew I had to let some of my pain spill out.

"But you did," he replied, calm and flat. The words hung in the air, offering little. I waited for more insight, but nothing came.

With each session, the ache to tell my story grew stronger. I longed for someone to really hear me, to help me make sense of the chaos I had lived through. I shared small pieces of my past, testing the waters, but he never seemed very interested.

Finally, he blurted out with confidence, "You can move forward from today. Make choices to do that, and you will."

But I was haunted by images of past sexual abuse, weighed down by a shame that ran deep. Move forward, how? "How am I supposed to do that?" I asked. "I want to, I really do... but what does moving forward even mean?"

"Don't let yourself get stuck in the past. Just focus on what you can do today," he told me.

I left feeling confused and misunderstood. Deep down, I knew my struggles were tied to my childhood. My whole body ached to release what I had suppressed for so long. I believed I needed to speak it aloud; to drag the shame into the light so it could lose its hold on me. But he never encouraged me to share.

On the few occasions I did open up with painful, vulnerable memories, his responses were flat, lacking clarity or compassion. Instead of relief, I felt heavier. My emotional pain deepened, and with it, my cravings to smoke and drink grew stronger.

Still, I needed help. And so, weary and uncertain, I kept dragging myself back to his office.

"I'm in so much pain," I confessed. "I'm ready to relapse."

"I'm sorry to hear that, Lisa," he replied. "But I will no longer be taking your insurance."

Panic rose in my chest. "I won't be able to afford therapy without insurance."

"I can't adjust my fee, and I don't know how to help you with this," he said flatly. "So, this will be our last session."

My voice cracked. "What do I do? I don't know how I'm going to go on and deal with this pain. I feel like an open wound. I'm not ready to be done yet."

"You can call me if it's an emergency," he muttered, his tone strained and obligatory. "But we won't be able to meet unless you can pay."

My head was swirling, and I didn't feel right. The tightness in my throat and chest intensified as I stood up and walked out of his office. I couldn't figure out what to do. I went home and, as calmly as I could, explained what had happened to my husband.

"I don't want to do this, but I'm in a lot of pain, and if I don't feel better, I am going to go get beer and cigarettes." I couldn't believe the words coming out of my mouth, but they were true. My confession was only to explain my level of pain. Expressing my renewed cravings took some of the edge off, bought me some time, and I avoided relapse that day.

My emotions were storm waves crashing in on me, with moments where the water was calm, but not for long. My sister and I were talking one day when she said that I should visit her therapist and that I probably had some funding due to me because I was a victim of a crime.

I had never heard about such funding. "Are you sure?"

"My therapist knows about you. I told him that you went to court as a victim of crimes, and he said he would help you access those funds."

So, I started therapy with Mel. Mel was much warmer and more compassionate than my first therapist, but he wasn't Christian, and I told him that concerned me. He reassured me that he totally respected my religious autonomy. He went on to explain that we would be working on healing from the abuse and that he was happy that I had something to give me hope. His words injected new life into me. *Maybe he can help me!*

Part of therapy with Mel was group therapy. The other women in the group were comforting most of the time, and it was helpful to know I wasn't alone. I never fully trusted anyone, but even so, I gained a lot from their support. One thing I kept hearing over and over was to write in a journal when I was upset. What to do when I was upset was my number one question. *What am I supposed to do with all these painful feelings?*

"Write in a journal, Lisa. Don't censor yourself; just write," Mel repeated to me multiple times.

"But that feels like torture, Mel! I don't want to."

"Lisa, just try it," he would say, and group members seconded.

One day, I finally couldn't take the wave of painful emotions flooding me, and out of desperation, I wrote. I had been trying not to swear and felt guilty at all the swear words that poured out of me, but they matched my thoughts and my emotions. My first journal entry was a long string of vulgarities. I screamed onto the page. After violently scratching across the page, I paused and noticed breath entered my lungs just a little easier. *This just might work!* The more I channeled all my energy, emotions, thoughts, cuss words, cravings, and pain onto the paper, the better I felt. Of course, the pain came back, but I had a way to deal with it now. The more I journaled, the happier and more functional I became. Energy came back to me so I could care for my son, do housework, and go to martial arts. I just knew I would heal, that I *was* healing, and I was so hopeful.

In fact, I was determined to heal. It became my passion, my motivation not to let evil win. Evil had attacked me my whole life, and I had seen it in its ugly face up close. I absolutely did not want it to win. I was on the right team, and I had been promised that not only would all of this be worth it, but life would be good, and I could have more and more joy. I clung to that hope with every fiber of my soul.

Dear Lisa,

Discovering the joy of studying the Savior's life gave you courage to seek healing beyond scripture, including therapy. Though you faced dark waves of fatigue, sadness, and cravings, your humble willingness to do "whatever it takes" was a powerful step forward. Your first therapy experience, however, left you feeling unheard and misunderstood, intensifying your pain and cravings instead of easing them. When your therapist abruptly ended your insurance coverage, fear and despair overwhelmed you, yet you bravely shared your struggles with Robert, buying yourself time and avoiding relapse.

Hope appeared when your sister recommended a new therapist who respected your faith and warmly welcomed your story. Group therapy helped you realize you weren't alone, and journaling, though so hard at first, became a vital tool to release your anger, pain, and cravings. Writing raw truths on the page helped your breath deepen and your spirit lighten, fueling your growing strength to care for your son and continue your healing journey.

You clung fiercely to the truth that evil would not win, that healing and joy were promised to you. Your passion to heal grew stronger, supported by faith, persistence, and the wisdom you sought in books and community.

Remember, healing is a process full of ups and downs. Trust your resilience, keep speaking your truth, and lean into faith and supportive connections. You are on the right path, and your hope will carry you forward.

CHAPTER 34

"This is the Dr. Laura Show. What's your question?"

I got through! My heart raced as I scrambled to form a question, my voice trembling. The screener on the other end was kind and patient, but as I waited on hold, my nervousness only grew.

My mind drifted back over the last year and a half of motherhood. What carried me through was the steady faith that someday I would be well. There had been many moments of joy with my son and husband, but also a deep undercurrent of pain inside me that I couldn't ignore. Training in martial arts became more than just an activity, it was an outlet, a lifeline, another piece of my healing.

However, I was obsessed with the idea of abuse, and in defining it. *Was I even abused?* Maybe I was overreacting and dramatic, just like Mom said. Had I made it too big a deal like my dad advised against? Anger welled up just thinking of my parents. Guilt followed in right after the anger. The commandments said to honor your mother and father, and here I was, full of hate. *Are all these feelings sins?*

My hope was that I could count on this blunt, tough-talking radio show host to tell me the truth. Dr. Laura seemed to know what she was talking about and never sugar-coated her opinions. She seemed to have a lot of wisdom without worrying about her delivery. As a self-proclaimed expert on abuse, would Dr. Laura tell me to suck it up? Would she tell me to honor my parents as she did so many others? She often "corrected" people who reported they were abused growing up, and with exasperation, explained the difference between abuse and parenting. Sometimes, I agreed with her conclusions but often recoiled at her harsh approach. I was willing to take the risk. But I was so vulnerable.

As the minutes ticked by, I considered hanging up. I didn't want to be shamed, but I yearned for her insight into my situation. My thoughts turned to how much I had longed for and loved my mom so much as a little girl. I missed her deeply when she was gone. When I was home alone, I often went into her bathroom and smelled her makeup, inhaling the thought of her. I walked in her shoes, making the clunking noise she made as if it brought her closer to me.

Dr. Laura's familiar bark startled me out of my memory. "You said that you were abused as a child. How were you abused?"

I was taken back by the quick and firm question broadcast throughout California and muttered, "Uh, my mom and her boyfriend, uh would um, they were in bed and uh they ummm…"

"Did they have sex with you?" Dr. Laura interrupted.

Stunned by her question and unsure how to explain, I said, "Uh, yes?" Memories rushed through my head. *Did what happened with Mom and Larry qualify as sex with me?* Before I could speak again, she muted my line and said on air, "Then as far as I'm concerned, your parents cut up their parent card." And that was the end of the call.

I was still on the line and could hear the show proceed. She went to break immediately, and the next sound I heard was Pat Benatar serenading me about hell being for children. As her voice rang out about bruises and secrets and payment in flesh, I sat down hard on the floor. *Hell is for children. What did the call mean? Was my anger justified?* I felt oddly comforted and, at the same time, slapped down. I had hoped to talk more. But she was playing that song right after my call, and she told me that my parents had torn up their parent cards. *Maybe I was abused?*

They tore up their parenting card. The truth of the abuse settled over me, and I felt more comfortable with my anger. Thank you, Dr. Laura, for permission to move forward. I sat on the floor of my bedroom, rocking and hugging myself as I relived the call over and over in my mind. I came back to reality when I heard my son wake up from his nap. I wanted so much to make sure that his life wasn't hell, and I was extra determined to do what I needed to do so that didn't happen.

In a group session that week, the topic of confronting abusers came up. My therapist pointed out that some perpetrators could feel cornered and retaliate in dangerous ways, and he didn't want anyone to get re-victimized. With this information, the consensus was not to confront abusers. But I was in full rage mode now. I was finally empowered to express it. My seething anger was no longer directed at myself. It belonged to the ones who caused it, and confrontation would resolve it, put it where it belonged. The therapist said that the anger could be directed where it belongs without telling the person, but I wasn't going to just journal or cry about it in therapy. I wanted to see my abusers' reaction as I expressed my appropriate anger, in the flesh.

I will find them.

How would they handle me now? I might even be taller than some of them. I could look down on them as they did me. Would they know how to handle an adult? Would my martial arts training come in handy? I felt more confident because of it. I wasn't planning on hurting them physically, but just in case, I visualized a few scenarios. I would look them in the eyes, watch them squirm, and see how they liked it! I would take my power back.

Dear Lisa,

How courageous of you to call Dr. Laura! You were searching for truth in the midst of confusion. Was it abuse or just "normal" parenting? Were your anger and grief sins? That confusion was the old indoctrination still whispering inside you, twisting reality. Yet step by step, you were un-indoctrinating yourself by listening to the Spirit, leaning into truth, and letting light untangle the lies.

When Dr. Laura, a strong proponent of the ten commandments, bluntly said your parents had "torn up their parent cards," it sounded harsh, but it gave you something priceless; validation. Someone you trusted named what you had lived through, and that recognition freed you to own your anger and call the abuse what it was.

Your determination to protect your son from ever knowing such a "hell" only grew. It also sparked a fierce desire to reclaim your dignity and stand unafraid. Martial arts embodied that strength, you were preparing not only your body but your spirit to no longer cower. Each kick, each stance, each disciplined breath was part of peeling away what had been forced on you, replacing fear with confidence. You were learning how to stand grounded in your own truth.

Your longing for love and validation is natural. Let the Spirit keep guiding you as you shed the lies of the past and live into the life of safety, strength, and love you deserve.

CHAPTER 35

I slammed the phone book on the table, rage coursing through me like convulsions. *I'll start with my first abusers.* My first memories were when I was five. John and Larry! My fingers frantically flipped through the pages to L. Where was he? I couldn't find John Lippert! Ugh! In frustration, I accidentally ripped a page as I flipped on to F, Feldman, Larry Feldman. Oh wow, there were a few. I picked up the phone, dialed without hesitation, and waited. Ring, ring, ring… and no answer. The same happened with all the Larry Feldman's. NO ANSWER! Ugh! Who else… I started a list. My hands shook as I wrote each child molester's name on paper. The visual was nauseating. I screamed as my rage demanded. "How dare you! All of you! What have you done to me!" I sobbed, thankful to be home alone so I could let my rage pour out without worrying about little ears overhearing. "I'm ruined. I'm demolished. I want revenge." *Revenge is mine, saith the Lord. But he isn't saying that there won't be revenge! I'll take note of that.* I grabbed another book.

The Bible was full of verses that told of God's great justice being served. Frantically flipping through for comfort, I mulled over the New Testament scripture: *But whoso shall offend one these little ones…, it were better for him that a millstone were hanged about his neck, and that he were drowned in the depths of the sea.*

Better that a millstone… I imagined God and I standing at the Ocean's edge. And he was mad. He was so upset at what happened to me that he grabbed up the molesters, hung millstones around their necks, and looked at me as he held them. One by one, he just let them go, dropping them into the sea. They sank, each of them, like a stone, no hesitation, no bobbing up, just straight to the bottom.

Plop.

I lingered at the visual for a while, my eyes smashed closed. And as the emotions lurched out of my body, I felt calm. My Heavenly Father cared about what happened to me! He really cared. He would turn everything that happened to me for my good. I felt that. I knew he didn't mean that abuse would ever be called good. No way. My mind explored how God could use these situations for my good. He could teach me compassion, allow me to feel comfort from the Savior, and give me wisdom and strength to survive with His help. And even though my earthly parents were not at all like my heavenly parents, I had a glimpse of what it would be like to have a loving and protective parent.

God was mindful of me! He showed me the righteous act of justice! I felt what it could be like to have a dad standing up for me. A dad who would express seething anger if he walked in on the abuse and saw what was happening to me. And then I saw how he would comfort me. At that moment, he was with me in my rageful sorrow, understood it, and joined in it. That gave me more comfort than I could have imagined.

I sat stunned. I felt grateful that I survived my childhood as many memories flashed through my mind. Then, remembering my struggle to be a good mom now, my thoughts turned from hope to darkness. Why hadn't they just killed me? *I wish they had killed me. I'm no good now. I'm ruined. I'm in deep and unending pain.* My anger flared up again, and I added my parents' names to the list. My mother sure earned her place with these abusers. My siblings were on it too. My father, well, where was he when all of this was happening? It was his job to care for and protect me, not tell me not to make a big deal about being molested by John Lippert. He was so wrong. He should have comforted me and enacted justice for me. Instead, he didn't even ask what John Lippert did to me, or how I felt, or offer any comfort at all. In fact, he had never asked about me or my life. When he picked us up on Sundays we were just supposed to be quiet and show gratitude for what he did for us. I felt disgusted at the perverted stuff we found in his apartment when he left us there alone. I wondered if leaving your children alone with access to pornography was molestation too? I realized I was glaring at my list and noticed that it was almost time for group class at Martial arts.

Thank goodness I had class to go to. The punching and kicking and shouted kiai's were the controlled violence that I needed so badly. It was appropriate to scream and release anger, disguised as practice.

After class, as I was catching my breath and wiping the sweat off my forehead, I decided to confront Bob. That ostrich-looking sleazebag was always in the background of my life, dropping off birthday cards and Christmas cards for me at Mother's house. *Why does he do that?* He seemed to think we were on good terms, that it was okay for him to be in my life. I would correct that thought. When I called him, Bob picked up on the first ring.

"Hi, Bob. Yeah, it's Lisa. I was wondering if you would meet me. I'd like to talk with you."

"Sure, I'd love that, Lisa." Bob sounded excited.

"Ok, great, I appreciate that. How about in the parking lot at church." I was careful not to sound upset because I didn't want to scare him away. I wanted to see the look in my abuser's eyes when confronted by their victim. I was waiting next to my car when he pulled up with a big smile on his face. "Hi Lisa, it's good to see you," he called out as he walked to me.

"It is huh. Well, I want to tell you to stop bringing cards around and stop visiting my mother's house." I clenched my keys in my hand as potential weapons, ready to strike and cut him if needed. "I don't want you around. You were an abuser to me, and I'm in therapy, and I'm struggling badly. I want you to know that I know what you did was wrong, abusive, a repeated violation, and honestly, you should have gone to jail for all you did to me."

His happy expression melted to surprise, "I thought you liked it, that you wanted to!"

"Really? You did, huh, even though I told you I didn't want to participate in all those perversions you imposed on me. You never listened to me and you threatened to leave me if I didn't do what you wanted, and you knew I was so sad when you said that. I told you many times that I didn't have anyone else, and I just wanted to be loved. I was only able to stop being with you when I found strength and comfort and hope in myself through God!"

His eyes tightened, and I felt a familiar wave of fear. I shook it off, reminding myself that I was not his anymore. I was safe and loved now. I caught my breath and stood up taller. With a firm tone, I reminded him, "I was fifteen when we first had sex, and you were twenty-five! That is illegal. Are you saying that you don't know the law? Do you have anything to say for yourself?"

He cocked his head and smirked at me.

"That is illegal, and you know it."

"Lisa, babe." He flashed his classic grin, the same one that used to manipulate me. Now it only stirred trepidation. "Does age really matter? I'll always find you attractive, no matter how old you are." His eyes swept over me, head to toe. "In fact, I was thinking maybe you invited me here today to... you know, remember old times." He raised his eyebrows suggestively.

"What? NO. Listen closely, Bob. Don't. Ever. Talk. To. Me. Again."

Unbelievable! His arrogance knew no limits. But it wasn't surprising. I had no more words for him. No reason to waste another breath. I turned, got into my car, and drove away. My therapist voice popped in my head, confronting abusers was rarely worth it, dangerous even, since they would deny everything anyway. But for me, this moment was so worth it. I had taken back my power and spoken the truth to the scumbag.

Next on the horizon was my father. My eyes were opening, my thoughts sharpening. Every day, I prayed to see clearly, and clarity came. I no longer doubted that my father should have been there for me. And now, he was going to hear it.

A few days later, I paced the narrow stretch of my living room while my father sat back on the couch, his usual glare locked on me, cold and unyielding. I had finally asked him the question that now burned in me, after telling him about so much of my abuse. Why hadn't he been there? Why hadn't he protected me?

His answer landed like a stone:

"Lisa, wow, you've had quite an extensive sex life."

His words sliced through me, leaving me stunned. I stood there, only a few feet from the man who should have been my protector, my guide, my father. Instead of love or sorrow, he offered dismissal. To him, molestation was sex, not abuse. He named the evil I endured as if it were normal, as if my childhood pain could be rewritten as choice.

I was a child. A lost, broken child. And he dared to call that a "sex life?"

Before I could even gather the pieces of my shock, he went on, his voice steady,

"And children under the age of three don't remember anything."

My head snapped back. My eyes flew wide. What had I just heard? Why would he say that? What did he know that I didn't? The nightmares that had haunted me for so long, were they memories after all?

Before I could respond, Daniel wandered into the room crying. My father rose, his never-ending glare still fixed on me, and muttered that he had to go. Without softening, without a trace of tenderness, he walked out the door, leaving me with his words echoing like poison.

"Children under the age of three don't remember anything?" The phrase seared itself into my mind as I bent down to gather my own three-year-old. I brushed Daniel's tears away, pulled him against my chest, and let myself breathe in his innocence. His eyes were wide with trust; his little body relaxed into mine. In that moment, I knew the difference between the father who withheld love and the mother I chose to be. I savored Daniel's sweetness and silently vowed he would always feel my love, even now, at this tender age.

The following week, I confronted my brother. I had barely begun to form the words, trying to explain how he used to hit me, chase me down... when he interrupted.

"Lisa, I'm sorry for what I did to you."

I stopped mid-breath, words slipping away. His words landed heavy, carrying a weight I hadn't expected. Part of me wished he had let me finish, allowed me to speak the truth aloud, but I understood. Maybe he couldn't bear to rake through the gory details.

Still, gratitude washed over me. After all these years, I didn't have to argue, justify, or beg for acknowledgment. It came in three simple, powerful words:

I am sorry.

No one else could bring themselves to say those three simple words, not even to appease me. But my brother did. The moment he spoke them, a calm settled over me. I didn't feel the need to press further; we both let it rest there.

"Thank you for saying that," I told him quietly. "You're the only one who has apologized."

The words I had longed to hear came from my brother. He had lived through the same chaos and carried his own wounds, but he had also harmed me in ways that left deep scars. His apology couldn't erase the damage, yet when he said he was sorry, something in me gave way.

Relief and sorrow welled up together, relief that someone had finally spoken the truth, sorrow for the pain we both carried. I grieved not only for what he had done to me, but also for what had been done to him. In that moment, I saw both our suffering. Out of everyone, only he offered even a flicker of accountability, the simple words I had ached to hear, *I am sorry.*

Lisa,

Your rage is right and shouted the truth; This was wrong. I deserved better. Screaming, pounding, writing names, you carved space for your pain instead of letting it stay hidden.

In scripture you found justice, a Father who would rise in anger on your behalf, who would stand at your side and heal you. That vision reminded you; justice will be served.

When you confronted Bob, your voice cut straight through his denial. He no longer held power over you. And when you confronted your father, he did not offer care, he revealed more of how he had hurt you.

His words carried a cold cruelty that pierced deeper than silence. That revelation was haunting, but it gave you clarity.

Your brother's apology, messy and complicated as it was, broke the silence at last with the words: I am sorry. They stirred something deep inside you, a small but undeniable shift. They would never have been spoken if you hadn't found the courage to confront him.

Martial arts were part of your healing. Every punch a release, every kick a declaration: I am strong. I am here. I can defend myself now. The balance, the breath, the shouted kiai, they were not just movements. They were your spirit reclaiming its ground.

Lisa, you are not ruined. What happened was devastating, but it does not define you. You are capable, you are growing, and you know what source to draw your strength from, it is always within your reach.

CHAPTER 36

A couple of years later, as I got ready for church one morning, I noticed how much had changed in me. Joshua had joined our family, that pregnancy and his birth so much easier on my body and spirit than before. I could feel how far I had come, stronger, steadier, more present. Daniel beamed with pride at being an older brother. He hovered near the baby, eager to help, though at three and a half, his patience sometimes ran short. One day, he sighed, "When is he going to be a kid so I can play with him?" I laughed gently, pulling him close. He longed for a playmate, and for him the wait felt endless.

Outside our home, nothing had softened with my parents and siblings. Their drama still swirled, but Robert and I had grown wiser at shielding ourselves from it. We kept our distance, choosing instead to build something different. Within our walls, I felt the healing take shape, peace where chaos had been, warmth where fear once lived. Our little family was my safe place, and here, our children were protected.

The last few years I had been focused on healing, and I could feel the difference in myself. That shift alone felt like a quiet miracle. I leaned on my tools almost every day, journaling to release my thoughts, therapy to untangle my past, and martial arts to channel my anger into strength. Prayer was the thread woven through it all, steady and constant. My relationship with my Savior was a source of strength that continued to comfort me.

Motherhood was my greatest joy. With two beautiful boys, I often caught myself marveling at the love that poured out of me. Before my second pregnancy, I had worried, *would I be able to love another child as much as I loved my first?* But when I became pregnant again, those fears melted away. My love didn't have limits; it expanded, growing stronger, wider, deeper than I ever imagined.

Robert and I were committed to doing the right thing, and our love, our faith, and our boys kept us moving forward. My therapist suggested he was a trauma survivor too, as we began to see the echoes of my own childhood in his. Carrying similar wounds, we worked to grow and support one another. Our commitment held us together and gave us the strength to keep building the life we longed for.

My depression and anxiety, though less intense than before, still surfaced at times. During the harder days, Robert carried more of the load, and together we worked through life the best we knew how. I was healing, slowly but surely, but one of the greatest obstacles was the constant drama with my family. Though we avoided them much of the time, my parents pushed themselves into our lives. They acted entitled, offering "help", often financial, but their help was always a setup. They denied ever doing anything wrong, yet treated me exactly the same as they always had.

I hadn't learned how to cut them off yet. I still believed healthy communication could heal us, if only they were willing to try. But they never did, rejecting every suggestion I offered. Even as I tried to protect my own growing strength, they found ways to undermine it. I grew frustrated with myself for continuing to try, clinging to the hope that things might change. I didn't yet understand that what was truly needed was to block them out of my life.

Still, I kept reaching. I wanted parents. I wanted things to be different. But each attempt collapsed the same way, their words and actions snatching hope out from under me, leaving me confused and ashamed for not knowing when to stop. Even so, protecting my boys was nonnegotiable, and in that choice, I felt my strength growing. They were never alone with them.

But we did have many good days. On one such occasion, the day started out pleasantly. I slipped on a new dress while Robert helped the boys into their little shirts and shoes. I packed a picnic basket with simple food, sandwiches, fruit, a treat or two, feeling grateful for the ease of the moment. After church, we planned to head to the park, spread out a blanket, and spend the afternoon together. I imagined the boys' laughter rising into the air, the sunlight filtering through the trees, and the cool grass beneath us as we rested side by side. These were the moments that filled me, reminders of how far we had come. This was what it was all about, love, safety, and being together.

At the park, Robert took the boys to the swings, and I had a quiet moment to myself. Lying on my back, I looked up through the branches at the wide blue sky and let my thoughts drift. It struck me that I had just recovered emotionally from another outburst from my mother. For the first time, I hadn't thought about it for a few days, an improvement from the way her words used to consume me, circling in my mind without end. I felt grateful for those days of forgetting.

Just the week before, she had dropped off my baby book, baby shoes, and old report cards. They came with a letter where she disowned me once again. She pointed to my absences from school as proof that I had been a "bad seed" from the start, and wrote that she was relieved to finally be free of me and my ungrateful attitude. I wouldn't return the items this time.

I plucked a blade of grass and held it between my fingers. *This time,* I thought, *I won't try to fix it. I'll let go.* My efforts to repair anything with her had never gone anywhere, and I was finally beginning to see that.

On the way back from our picnic, Robert stopped to check the mail we'd forgotten the day before. Inside was an unusual-looking envelope from Orange County, addressed to me. I tore it open and froze. It was an official letter from the court.

Court? For what? My heart pounded as if I had just sprinted. The name *Don Gordon* leapt from the page, and my knees buckled. I stumbled to the couch before I collapsed. The word *subpoena* sent a wave of fear and confusion through me. I was twenty-four years old, a mother of two. It had been at least a decade since I had heard anything about Donald Gordon. And now they wanted me to appear in court. Why?

I handed the letter to Robert and whispered for him to take care of the kids. Then I slipped into the bedroom, sat between the bed and the wall, and felt sick. My head throbbed as I rocked myself, memories rushing in, being left alone with him in that apartment, the fear I thought I'd buried. *What should I do? What does this mean?*

Panic pressed hard, but I fought to steady myself. Flashbacks flooded me until time blurred. At last, I pushed them aside and stood. I wanted to spend the evening with my little family. The rest could wait. *Tomorrow, I will call the court.*

I tried to push the memories back down, to pretend the letter hadn't stirred them up, but the irritation came fast. *Not again,* I thought. I had been feeling so good earlier, and now it was slipping away. I tried to stuff the fear and confusion, but it was like pressing a bandage against a wound that had been ripped open.

When I was out of earshot of the kids, I turned to Robert. "I don't understand," I said quietly. "What do they want? What does this mean?"

"Don't worry, Lisa," Robert said gently. "We'll figure it out. I'm sorry you have to wait to know more."

The next morning, right at eight o'clock, I dialed the number on the subpoena. My hands shook as I introduced myself. "Hello, this is Victim Baer. I received a subpoena to appear in court for Donald Gordon, but… I don't understand."

A calm voice answered, "Yes, Lisa. This is District Attorney Smith. You are listed as a previous victim of Don Gordon. We're asking if you would be willing to testify on behalf of his newest victim. She is the only one this time and quite young, it would be better to have another victim of his speak up too."

"Ummmmmm… Of course, I want to help in any way I can. Okay, yes, what should I do? What do you need?"

The DA went on to explain that I should appear on the listed date and be prepared to testify. *Just show up?*

"He was sentenced to ten years, and this is about the time it would have been up," I said. "How long has he been out?"

The DA then pointed out, "Actually, he only served five of the ten. You didn't know?" *Only five?* "I had no idea. How would I know?"

"Oh, sometimes victims are notified. I guess you weren't." *I guess!*

My chest tightened, heat rising in my face. Five years? I would have been eighteen when he got out. He only served five years for what he did to me, and the other girls.

"So he's been molesting for the past five years?" I asked, my voice shaking between anger and disbelief.

What if he had come looking for revenge, showing up at my childhood home while I was still living there when he was released? Did anybody care that he might have come looking for me? The fear that he might want to do so never really left me, it had only slipped into the back seat of my mind, waiting.

Panic surged through me. I hated that it did, snapping at myself; *Stop it!* But the panic was mine alone. The DA seemed completely unconcerned, as if there was nothing at all to fear. And was it really so far-fetched that he might want revenge? After all, I had exposed his photographer friend and cooperated with the district attorney to put him in prison.

Yet beneath it all, one truth remained, he still scared me.

"Will I see him?" The words spilled out between choked sobs. "Will Jody be there?"

I tried to picture his face, but it was gone. From the time I left the shelter home until now, his image had vanished from my memory. And yet the fear of him seeing *me* again gripped me harder than anything. I hated the thought of his eyes finding me. I remembered too many times how he looked at me, and I couldn't bear the idea of that violation again.

I didn't want him to see me as an adult. The idea of his eyes landing on me, sizing me up, sent panic through my chest. The thought of being exposed to his gaze made me want to disappear, to protect myself at all costs.

"See who? Oh, Donald Gordon. Yes, he will be in court."

"Do I have to see him? Is there any way that I can do this without having him see me?"

"No, that's not possible. He has the right to see everyone present in court for his case." He didn't even notice my fear.

But the victim needed someone. The lone victim. I wondered how old she was, whether she had good parents, how alone she must have felt. And what had he done to her?

My throat closed as my own memories of him crashed back. My whole body tightened, my mouth went dry, words sticking to my tongue. I felt so small, weakness spreading hot through my veins.

I forced the words out anyway. "Um… yes. Okay. So, I go in four weeks?" The subpoena showed a date the next month.

"Yes," he said. "I'll call you in a few weeks with final details."

I hung up the phone, trying to reassure myself. *I have to do what's right.*

The weeks that followed felt like slogging through three feet of mud with earmuffs on, dragging myself forward while everything around me was muted and far away. I tried to hide it, but the irritability and sadness crept back in, I worked hard to not allow them to be my full-time companions.

Three weeks later, the DA called to say the court date had been pushed back another three weeks. "I thought I'd give you a quick call before I run into court. The date has moved, but it's not finalized yet."

"Well…" I searched for words, but none came.

"Okay?" His voice carried a hurried tension, already halfway gone.

"Three more weeks?" I finally managed.

"Well, actually, it could be more than that, but for now, yes, that's the date."

"Ummm…

"I see that this is an inconvenience," he said rapidly, "but that's just the way these things go. I'll call you in a couple of weeks to finalize details, okay?"

"Uh, yeah, I guess."

"Okay, great, I'll talk to you then. Bye."

Another three weeks! Oh no. I was clinging to the thought of this being over. I can't... but I have to. I had just confided in a friend, finally telling her what was going on. She comforted me, even shared some of her own history of abuse. For a moment, I felt less alone. She reassured me it would be over soon and promised to help however she could. She even offered to babysit when the time came. But now the dates had changed. What if she can't babysit then? Who else could I trust with the kids? Tears shoved past my best effort to hold them back. *Suck it up, Lisa.*

Mom called with bright curiosity after my sister told her I'd have to testify again. "So, what did they say, Lisa?"

I tried to explain, but the words felt heavy, dragging out of me. I did my best, and she replied, "You know, Lisa, that detective is an awful person. I'd take you, but I don't want to run into him again."

"What detective, Mom?"

"That Detective Mendez. He didn't, uh, like me, and he's an absolute idiot!" she snapped.

My Detective Mendez, the one who made sure I felt heard, who arranged for me to keep playing softball while I was in the shelter home. The one who told me my mother was the worst kind of abuser. He had been kind to me. He had tried to help.

"Mom, I'm not asking you to take me. My husband is taking me."

I spent weeks psyching myself up. *You can do it, Lisa. You'll feel better again,* I told myself again and again. The day before I was scheduled to testify, the DA called. "Lisa, it turns out he decided to take a plea, so we won't need you to testify."

"What?" My thoughts spun out.

"Yup, so that'll be it then."

"That's it?"

"Yes. Thank you for being on standby. Take care."

All the energy, all the buildup of psyching myself up, came crashing down on me. I didn't know whether to celebrate or collapse. I had prepared to testify, telling myself it was okay that he would see me, steeling myself to be strong enough.

And now? If I didn't have to testify, then he wouldn't see me. Relief flickered, but so did disbelief. After all these weeks, *that's it?*

I couldn't process it fast enough. "Um… okay. Wait, can I still go if I want?"

"Why would you?"

Why would I? Because I'm an idiot, I guess. The thought stabbed at me. Shame churned hot through my body, twisting my thoughts. I had spent two months talking myself into this, believing it would be good, trying to keep being a good mom, a good wife, a martial artist holding it together despite the mess. And now they didn't want me to go, and somehow I felt guilty. Confused. Always confused. *Why am I always confused?*

"I don't know," I said slowly. "I just… I was expecting to go. My husband took the day off."

"I guess you can go if you want, but we won't be meeting you. If you go, you'll just be like the public in the courtroom."

"Um, okay. You won't be meeting with me then? Um, okay. We'll see. Thank you."

"Uh-huh, bye-bye."

Why did he sound annoyed? *What is my problem? I don't have to go, so why am I considering going anyway? What's wrong with me? I still don't want him to see me.*

Later that night, my husband comforted me. "Honey, let me take you. We were already planning on it. You can show me where their apartment was, and afterward I'll take you to dinner."

We decided it would be best to go. We needed some kind of closure to this whole process. This would be the last time I'd ever see him, and now, I wanted to know what he looked like. He wouldn't know I was coming so he wouldn't see me. What if I ran into him again someday and didn't remember his face? And besides, we'd been bracing for this for weeks.

"Let's just go and decide what to do when we get there," my husband offered.

"They don't want anything else?"

"No, that's it. They're done with me. He said I won't be hearing from them again."

"Okay, well, let's go, and we can always decide once we arrive."

I so appreciated my husband's encouragement and support, but I couldn't make sense of myself. There must be something wrong with me for even wanting to go. I felt consumed by it, obsessed, and I hated myself for that, for the curiosity I couldn't explain.

The morning of his hearing, we sat alone in the back of the courtroom. When the judge asked if there were victims present, the DA answered no. Then, for a breath-stopping second, Don, in jail clothes, turned and his eyes landed on where we were seated. I recoiled, ducking behind my husband on the bench and burying my face against his back.

My husband squeezed my hand as we hurried to the car. "He didn't see you," he said. Thank you, I thought, but I couldn't form the words, so I simply hugged him when we climbed in. He held me for a few minutes, then we tried to stitch the day back together, a slow drive through Santa Ana past their apartment, past the photographer's studio, then a quick stop at the beach. We ate at a restaurant and sat mostly in silence, each of us trying to reclaim ordinary moments.

The boys were asleep when we returned. My friend who babysat asked a few gentle, respectful questions and then left us to our quiet house. It was over, and I still felt tangled and unsure about what I'd just experienced. Back in the rhythms of life, I wondered if I'd ever be able to feel normal again. I longed to rewind to that day in the park before the letter, but there was no undoing it.

Lisa,

I'm so proud of how far you've come. You've built a family filled with love, even while carrying the heavy weight of your past. It's okay that your healing journey isn't perfect, depression and anxiety ebb and flow like the moon, and you're learning to ride those waves with faith and strength. Your husband's support is a blessing, and together you're creating safety and love for your boys.

Your family drama still stings, but setting boundaries, even imperfect ones, is growth. You're learning to protect your children from harm while navigating difficult relationships.

Getting that subpoena was terrifying. It brought back scary memories and made you feel vulnerable all over again. Emotions are time travelers. Your fears about seeing Donald Gordon show how trauma leaves deep marks, even when we try to move forward. It's natural to feel confused and conflicted, wanting closure and to help, but fearing the pain.

Remember, your fear is valid, and your feelings matter. The legal process is often cold and unkind, but your courage in facing it is a sign of how much healing you've already done.

You're not alone. Connecting with fellow survivors reminds you that empathy and shared experience can be a powerful source of comfort.

Though you struggle with confusion and exhaustion, trust that your journey toward peace continues. You are worthy of safety, love, and healing every day.

CHAPTER 37

Life went on. I focused on what I wanted to do and be better at; a better mom, a better martial artist, a better person, and I always fell short of my potential. But giving up wasn't an option, so I pushed away lingering thoughts about Don, and Orange County, and soldiered on.

"Ms. Plumb, push harder. Picture your opponent in front of you. Come on, you can do it!" my instructor urged. Then, softer but sharp, "You seem off lately. You need to be consistent if you want to progress." I mouthed an apology and kept moving through the kata.

He didn't let it go. "I know you can do it, but you should be farther along than you are, and you would be if you were consistent."

His words landed like a weight in my chest. I wanted nothing more than to be consistent, to flourish in my training, but each time I reached for that steadiness it felt just out of reach. My heart ached with the gap between who I wanted to be and where I was.

I put my instructors on a pedestal, especially the head instructor. Martial arts consumed me, I wanted, more than anything, to become an instructor myself, though I never dared say it out loud. Just walking up to the dojo door twisted my stomach and sent my heart racing.

I craved progress, the black belt shining at the end of the road. My instructor said I could do it, but one minute I was doing well; the next, I wasn't. He told me I had the talent, and yet I couldn't even be consistent in my progress, even though I showed up every day.

His words echoed as I left the building, *If I were just consistent...* and I vowed, again, to do better.

Martial arts made me feel alive, something I did for myself. It let me stay athletic while being a mom. It was my new dream. The old hopes of high school or college athletics were gently grieved and let go as martial arts took their place.

Being a mother was my top job, nothing was more important, and martial arts was the oil that kept that engine running. I loved being a stay-at-home mom and a martial artist, supplementing our income with side jobs when needed. When I scrubbed floors, delivered pizzas, or tossed newspapers, Ray's voice would steady me: *Lisa, there is no shame in any job. Whatever job you have, do it well.*

Even though I poured myself into the house and the dojo, I never quite felt good enough. The DA's letters and calls from Orange County shattered the calm I had gained, dredging up feelings I struggled to handle. It was like being yanked back into towering waves, clawing for shore, but I kept fighting.

I worked hard to be a healthy mom. Helping in the church nursery taught me how to be tender and present for little ones, the small rituals, the quiet rhythms. I learned simple songs to sing and practical parenting tools that actually helped. Watching those gentle women care for the children, I tried to mirror them. Sometimes, I would close my eyes and imagine I was singing to Little Lisa, holding her safe, and in those small acts something inside me began to heal.

I reflected in gratitude with how far I had come. I knew that if I hadn't found Christ and got sober, I never could have stayed clean through pregnancy. I thanked God every day that I didn't harm my babies with substances. I felt a deep compassion for women who weren't so fortunate. I was still amazed I was living my best sober life, and the church community gave me the belonging and support I needed as a mom.

Even on hard days, I loved my life. I knew I had work to do, and I was doing it: therapy, journaling, reading everything I could about healing. I'd been rescued. My husband and I were trying to be good parents and partners.

As a child, I'd wanted to be a marine biologist and a mom. Now I was a martial artist and a mom. I still loved the ocean. Then, quietly, a new tug began at my heart; maybe I should be a therapist. I laughed. Me? A therapist? I'd barely finished high school. I didn't have a fancy education. I could barely find my voice in martial arts.

I prayed that the thought would go away. Instead, I received a steady impression; it would be a long road, but the years would pass anyway, take it one step at a time. I was stunned. *Heavenly Father, you have the wrong person,* I told him. *I'm too much of a mess.*

But God had already performed miracles in my life, could He do another?

I knelt on my bedroom floor. "Is this true, Heavenly Father? Am I meant to be a therapist?" I waited, aching for an answer.

My heart knew before my head could argue. A quiet, clear impression settled over me; *Yes.* I didn't need to keep asking. I was to trust what I had received as an answer to prayer. I could continue to pray for strength and guidance, but the direction had already been given, and I could carry it in my heart as I walked the road ahead. I felt I must write it down, the answer, the experience, so I could reflect on it when doubts arose again.

The impressions kept coming: *One step at a time, line upon line. It will happen, but perhaps not on the timetable you hope for.* I wanted it to happen fast. But how fast could a master's degree be? Still, I'd learned from scripture and good books to *doubt not, but be believing,* to hold the picture of success in my mind and to chase out doubts the moment they crept in. So, I replaced fear with the memory of the answer to my prayer and pictured myself holding my diploma, taking it one baby step at a time.

I knew I had to get started with school. With my husband's support, I enrolled in my first college class. The first day, I felt overwhelmed. I forced that picture of success into my head to quiet the racing thoughts; that's what got me to class each day. It was just a typing class; I'd never learned to type. But as the weeks went by and my anxiety didn't ease, I decided to drop it. I hated that choice. *It's just one class. Just typing!* I scolded myself: "Gheesh, Lisa, how are you going to become a therapist this way?" I'd only dipped my toes in the water, and for now, that was all I could manage.

In addition to school, we were also working on our little family. When our third son, Matthew, was born, perfect just like his brothers, we were overjoyed. The older boys lit up; they were proud, gentle, and instantly protective.

My husband and I made parenting a deliberate project; we stepped in early to prevent fights, taught peaceful ways to solve problems, and refused to allow hitting. It was everything we hadn't had growing up, and we were determined to do it better.

When our youngest was finally old enough, I tried college again. My husband had started school before me, and we even enrolled in the same class so he could support me. The idea of studying together felt hopeful, but the old anxiety rode with me into the lecture hall. I felt like I was in Junior High again. I tried to listen, to follow along, to make myself concentrate, but I couldn't force it. I never officially withdrew, and my first college grade was an F.

I was discouraged, but I didn't let the failure erase what I'd already felt in prayer. I kept that picture of success in my mind and held on to the tiny, stubborn belief that I could do better in the next class.

About a year passed before I was able to try again. A new hybrid class was offered on a subject that interested me: Sociology. I would be able to watch some of it on TV and go in once a week. I not only passed this class, but I enjoyed it! Relief washed over me, and I even got a B. This gave me just enough confidence to sign up for another class. I passed it with an A. I built my tolerance for schooling, studying, and climbing my way toward the required schooling one class at a time.

If I took one class a semester till I got my degree, I was ok with that. I was more and more comfortable with the slow pace. My confidence in myself and my brain was slowly but surely building.

Lisa,

I see your fierce determination to be better, a better mom, better martial artist, better person, even when it feels like you fall short. That inner fire pushing you forward is your strength, even in your hardest moments. It's okay to struggle with consistency and self-doubt; those are part of healing and growth.

Martial arts became your sanctuary, a place to feel alive and connected to yourself beyond motherhood. You worked hard to balance your dreams with your realities, and that's courage. Remember, progress doesn't have to be fast; small, steady steps are enough.

You are healing old wounds through tender moments with your children, learning new ways to love and care, something Little Lisa never got to experience. Your faith and sobriety gave you a foundation to build a new life, even if anxiety and past trauma still show up.

The idea of becoming a therapist surprised you, but deep down, it's a calling that matches your heart and your journey. You don't need to have it all figured out now, just trust the process and take one step at a time.

You are doing an incredible job balancing family, school, and healing. Celebrate every small victory. Keep holding onto that vision of success and be gentle with yourself when the path feels slow or uncertain.

You are creating the good you envision! Way to go!

CHAPTER 38

It was the day before Halloween, and I was on cloud nine as I pulled into the grocery store closest to our new home in Apple Valley. At thirty-three, we finally owned a house, on a hill, no less, a place that was truly ours, with land and a view that felt like a promise. We had only moved in the day before, and boxes still crowded every room. Leaving Riverside had been the right choice. That city carried too many shadows; too many corners etched with pain.

The crisp autumn air carried a hint of change, pumpkins grinning from porches as I drove through the neighborhood. Everything about this place felt like a fresh start, as if even the season itself was celebrating our new beginning.

We left Riverside when Matthew was still a baby. Then we lived for a few years in Adelanto, near our friends, and now, at last, planted ourselves in Apple Valley. The high desert stretched for miles, wide and unbroken, and we found our own little high desert paradise on a hill. Our home was modest compared to the larger ones nearby, but to us, it was the best space we'd ever known. And the land, our whole acre, felt like freedom. We could grow a garden, keep animals, and give our three boys room to run and play. Victorville Community College was only fifteen minutes away, close enough to keep me moving forward with school while we built this new life.

I had just dropped the older boys at school, my youngest still strapped in the back seat, sleeping softly. We only needed a quick shopping trip before heading home to unpack boxes and settle into our new house for fall. But the instant I parked, the world shifted.

My stomach dropped hard. My chest seized. My hands, still on the steering wheel, turned clammy as my body locked in place. My eyes bulged, my mouth hung open. *No... it can't be.* For a split second I questioned reality, but my body knew before my mind caught up. Recognition ripped through me, cold and merciless.

Her shape, her gait, unmistakable. Burned into my memory, impossible to ever forget. Like the blurry outline in that infamous Sasquatch video, her silhouette had haunted me for years. And now, there she was, walking casually into the very store I was about to enter with my toddler.

My pulse thundered in my ears. Breath shallow, heart racing, I could barely swallow. Shock, disbelief, terror, every nerve ending screamed the same name.

Jody

How... why is Jody here?

I sat frozen in the car, disbelief pressing down on me until my son's babbling broke the silence. Shaking my head, I forced myself to breathe. "It's okay, honey. We're just going to sit here for a minute, alright?" My voice sounded steadier than I felt.

What to do? What to do? My hands trembled as I shifted the car to another spot, angling for a better view, her car, the store, everything in sight but from a safe enough distance. I couldn't let her see me. I told myself I would wait, watch, and when she came out, I would follow. I needed to know where she lived, where she came from. Was she my neighbor now? I could always check Megan's Law for her zip code, but that wasn't enough. I needed answers *now*.

Fifteen long minutes crawled by before she emerged. She didn't glance in my direction, moving quickly, her posture hunched yet unmistakable. She slipped into her car and sped off. I started the engine and tailed her, gripping the wheel tight. But the streets were still unfamiliar, and within minutes I lost her.

Obsessed, I circled block after block, searching for her car, for her unmistakable slouched figure. Nothing. She had vanished.

Defeated, I finally headed home and called my friend Sharon. My voice trembled as I recounted what happened, and I told her what I already knew I had to do, go straight to the Sheriff's office.

That afternoon, I met up with Sharon, and together we drove to the sheriff's office. On the way, I filled her in with more details about Jody's past.

"Lisa," she said firmly, her voice steady, "I'm here for you. Let's go figure this out."

I clung to her words. I already knew Jody's name would be on the sex offender's registry. Years earlier, the judge had made it clear; she was required to register every time she moved. Now, Megan's Law, made it possible to search for sex offenders by zip code at the sheriff's department.

We pulled into the small parking lot, my heart pounding. Inside, the lobby felt stark and cold. I walked up to the glass window, feeling like a deer caught in headlights.

"Hi, uh, I need to look up a registered sex offender. I want to make sure she isn't my neighbor." My voice shook despite my best effort to stay calm.

The receptionist glanced up from her desk. "She?"

"Yes… she." My throat tightened. "She was a perpetrator of mine when I was a child, from eleven to thirteen. I just saw her at my local grocery store, and the abuse happened almost a hundred miles away from here."

The woman behind the glass leaned forward, her tone more attentive now. "Okay, ma'am. What is her name?"

"Jody Jones, or um, they got married in jail, so Jody Gordon."

After waiting for a few more minutes, the receptionist explained they couldn't find her on Megan's law. "I don't understand. She is supposed to register, but you don't see her anywhere in California?"

"I'm sorry, no."

I explained to the receptionist that Jody and Don Gordon perpetrated against me when I was a child, and were both supposed to be registered sex offenders. She acknowledged what I said and went away for a few minutes before returning and asking for his full name.

"Donald Lee Gordon."

"Ok, the full name makes a difference. Let me check again."

After a few minutes, she opened the door and quietly motioned for Sharon and me to follow her into the back. Her expression was grave, her tone deliberate. She confirmed the city I had just moved from, then looked me straight in the eye.

"We found him," she said carefully. "He was paroled to Adelanto this past year."

"When?" My voice caught as my eyes widened so far I thought they might pop from my head. *My town. The very place I had just lived for the past few years!*

"He's been there about eight months," she answered.

Speechless, I tried to process it. Eight months... A memory stirred. Around that time, I had heard a radio report, two high-risk sex offenders had been paroled in Santa Ana, one of them named Donald Gordon. The neighborhood had raised the alarm, a Megan's Law notification went out, and it made the news.

I remembered the panic in my chest as I called the radio station immediately, desperate to confirm. I poured out a message on their machine; I was a victim, I thought I had just heard his name, please... please... call me back so I could know for sure. No one ever returned my call. The silence stung and I was frustrated by their insensitivity, but what else could I do?

I forced myself to let it go. It was a trigger, yes, but a small one I could shake off. I knew he'd get out eventually. I was determined to live my life without being dragged backward by the abuse and the court cases. And I managed to, until now.

"He's been in town for eight months? *My* town... the one I just moved from."

She lowered herself into the chair across from me, her eyes narrowing slightly, mouth pulled down at the corners. Her tone softened, almost soothing. "I'll call his parole officer and have him reach out to you."

"Okay… but what about Jody? My son is still playing soccer in that town. It's not a big place. Do the neighbors even know he's a high-risk sex offender?"

"Ma'am, I can't say for certain. What I can tell you is that you have the right to notify the neighborhood. In fact, anyone does. If a high-risk offender is living there, the community has a right to know."

My pulse quickened. "Well, where exactly is he living?"

"We're not allowed to give out exact addresses," she said firmly. "Only zip codes. But I'll make sure his parole officer contacts you right away."

A chill swept over me as questions spiraled in my head. *Does he know I lived there? Did he see me? Did he see my kids?*

"Okay, thank you. I appreciate your help."

She walked us out, holding the door open as we stepped into the sunlight. My words tumbled out in a rush. "Sharon, you still live there! I'm sure Jody is with him. And all of our friends are still in that town, they *need* to know!"

Sharon nodded firmly. We agreed then and there; we would notify the neighborhood as soon as possible.

Later, I stepped into my own living room, still cluttered with unpacked boxes and dominated by the giant pumpkin I'd picked up on discount for Halloween. From outside, I could hear Robert's laughter mingling with the boys' voices. The moment they noticed I was home, they bounded in, faces bright with energy.

I forced myself to shake off the stunned, hollow feeling, pulling a smile across my face. "Who's hungry? Who wants dinner?"

The boys were finally tucked in, their soft breathing drifting from their rooms as Robert and I settled onto the porch swing. The epic sweep of city lights stretched out before us, glittering against the night sky. I had once thought a view like this could chase away any sadness, that it was impossible to be depressed with such beauty laid out before me. Yet tonight, even the lights felt distant, unreachable.

We rocked gently in silence, the chains of the swing creaking softly as the cool evening air wrapped around us. I tried to swallow the despair pressing against my chest, willing myself to reach back toward the joy I had felt that morning. My voice cracked when I finally spoke. "Robert, I'm sorry. I know it can't be easy, being married to me, with my history, and all of this surfacing again. I'm just... so sorry."

He turned toward me, his arm pulling me close in a quiet, steady embrace. The rhythm of his heartbeat grounded me against the weight inside. His words came low and certain, carrying more strength than the night around us. "Lisa, I love you. I'm grateful every single day that I married you. No matter what, we'll get through this together. I have no regrets. I love you, and I love our little family. Forever."

For a moment, the ache inside me softened, and I let the city lights blur into the night, their shimmer mingling with the safety of his arms.

Lisa,

Sometimes, life throws us unexpected moments that bring old pain rushing back, like seeing someone who hurt you years ago or finding out they're living nearby. The sudden shock can trigger intense physical and emotional reactions, leaving you anxious and unsettled. It's completely natural to feel this way. When trauma shows up like this, it can catch us off guard and shake the safety we've worked so hard to build.

It's especially painful when the system, meant to protect us, doesn't seem to have our back. Learning that someone who harmed you has been living close by, without warning, feels like a betrayal, reopening wounds you thought were healing. It makes sense you feel scared, and angry about that. Your feelings aren't weakness, they show you're human and that your safety matters.

You were brave, you sought help, protected your family, and kept moving forward, one step at a time.

Healing isn't about pretending the past didn't happen or that the fear isn't real. It's about learning how to keep moving forward, protecting yourself and your loved ones, and finding moments of peace and joy again. You are doing exactly what you need to do to stay safe and strong, even though it's hard. Your courage and resilience are your greatest allies, and you deserve all the safety, love, and happiness in the world.

CHAPTER 39

The phone rang, and when I answered, a steady voice introduced itself.

"Ms. Plumb? This is Officer Ash, Don Gordon's parole officer. I understand you're a previous victim of his and that you live in the high desert. Could we meet? If you're comfortable, I can come to your home, or we could meet somewhere else."

"It's okay, you can come here," I agreed. We set a time for a couple of days later.

Those days crawled by with me on high alert. At least Don and Jody were in another town now, but that town was full of children. The cheaper housing had drawn in young families, parents eager to start fresh, never imagining the danger living among them. I could hardly rest, my mind circling over and over until the meeting came.

I had so many questions. I needed to explain that Jody should be a registered sex offender, so why wasn't she? I needed help with neighborhood notification. And most of all, I had to know: did Don Gordon know I was living here?

The day of the appointment finally arrived.

Knock. Knock. Knock.

I moved slowly toward the door, my pulse quickening. "Hello?"

"Hi, I'm Officer Ash."

"Hi… uh, come on in."

He stepped inside, clearing his throat as his eyes flicked away from mine. "Okay, where would you like me to sit?" The strain on his face was unmistakable, tension written in every line.

I gestured toward the empty couch. "Please, have a seat." I sank onto the other couch across from him. "We just moved in, so… excuse the boxes."

"Yeah. Hi," he said, shifting awkwardly. "I'm sorry this has happened. He isn't supposed to be within twenty-five miles of you. Why didn't you tell us where you were living?"

I stared at him, stunned. "What? I didn't know that. No one ever told me he couldn't live near me. I was never told anything."

He narrowed his eyes, shaking his head slowly before leaning back. "Really? That's hard to believe."

"Hard to believe? What do you mean? How was I supposed to know this?"

My eyes fixed on him, sharp and searching. "No one ever told me I should be notified about his parole, or that I was supposed to report where I lived." My voice quavered. "I didn't even know he wasn't allowed to live near me."

"Yeah, well, we'll have to move him now," he said, exasperation creeping into his tone.

He studied me for a long moment before continuing. "Umm… what can I do for you?"

"I don't know for sure," I admitted, "but I want a neighborhood notification. And I need to understand why Jody isn't a registered sex offender."

A chill ran through me. *Does he know I lived there? Does he know what my kids look like?*

I went on, laying out the relationship between Don and Jody, how she was fully complicit and why I knew she should be registered too. I then told him plainly why I was terrified of them being so close to neighborhoods with children.

My voice wavered, thin and shaky, as I fought back tears. My throat ached, my chest tight, but the words forced their way out. "Can you check him?

See if he has pictures of me... or my kids... or anything that shows that he might have known that I was living there?"

The room tilted for a moment under the weight of what I'd just said. *Do I sound paranoid? Crazy?* Heat prickled across my skin, shame crawling up my neck. My mind spun in jagged loops, *does he think I'm overreacting; what if I really am?* I clenched my hands together, desperate to hold myself steady.

"I know he probably doesn't know," I blurted, the words rushing out before I could stop them. "But it feels like too much of a coincidence." My voice cracked, trembling with the weight of it. "Even if it's only a one percent chance, or less, please, I need you to check him. Check his things. Please."

He cleared his throat and rolled his eyes, then softened his tone. "Uh, yeah. I can do that. I have access to him and he has to comply with my requests or for any searches. And for the neighborhood notification you go to the police station there to get that initiated"

"Okay, thank you, I really appreciate it. I know it's not likely, but I just need to be sure." The words spilled out in a rush, and inside I groaned. *Oh my gosh, I sound crazy. But I have to know.*

Something in his expression shifted, his eyes softening. "Okay. No problem."

"I really appreciate it, thank you. When will I hear back, about you checking on him? And about the move?"

"I'll be in touch," he said simply.

And then he left. I sat still for a moment, staring out the window at the bright sweep of my new view, fighting the pull to sink into oblivion. The sunlight poured across half-unpacked boxes, and I forced myself to move. I busied my hands with unpacking, trying to keep the darkness at bay, each folded shirt and stacked dish a small defiance against oblivion. *No,* I told myself. *I will not let this steal the joy of my new home and family.*

I kept moving. Determined not to sink, fixed on what I could do; searching for the address of the police station, making a plan with Sharon to go with me, anything to keep momentum alive. I called Sharon and set a time to meet later that day, relief mixing with dread as the plan took shape.

Keep moving, Lisa. Don't fold. Don't let this crush you.

Later that afternoon, we walked into the Adelanto police station and explained my situation. The officer at the counter cut me off sharply, raising his hand in a stop sign. "Hold on, just hold on. Let me get my supervisor."

His tone hit me like a slap. I had expected help, not resistance. Moments later, a sergeant approached the window, his voice edged with irritation. "Okay, what's going on?"

I took a step back, my stomach tightening. *Why are they so angry with me?*

"Umm, I'd like to do a neighborhood notification for a high-risk sex offender," I said.

I went through everything again, gave him the parole officer's number, Don's name, and explained that I knew I had the right to notify.

The officer frowned. "Okay, lady, just a minute. We'll have to get back to you. We don't know about this. Call back in a couple of days and we'll let you know if you can do that."

My chest burned hot. "Oh, I *know* I can! I have the right, and the people in this town have the right to know a high-risk sex offender is living in their neighborhood!" I was seething, unwilling to back down.

"Look," he said flatly, "we have to call the parole officer and confirm it's okay. Just come back or call in a couple of days." His hand flicked in dismissal, cutting me off.

And then he walked away. My eyes clenched, my fists balled up. Fury propelled me out of the police station and into my car. I drove up and down the streets, scanning every corner, every house, desperate for a glimpse of him, of Jody, of anything that would prove where they lived. I was on the hunt now. *Where were Don and Jody?*

Nothing. Street after street, there was nothing. The afternoon turned late, the light thinning into shadows that crawled across the streets, and with unease tightening my chest, I finally turned toward home. But I wasn't finished. I would be back. I would do a notification. This fury needed a place to land, it belonged in action, not buried inside me.

In the days that followed, I called the police station again and again, no new information. But I did my own digging, looked up my rights, to arm myself with information. They had to know by now that I had the right to make the notification.

As I went to search the neighborhood again, I tried to pull together a group to help. I reached out to people I knew, from church, who were still in Adelanto. I was sure they'd want to know and want to help. Instead, after I explained the situation, one friend's husband mocked me with, "What does molested mean anyway, did you scream and resist or did you like it?" My friend just sat there and did nothing about her husband's vulgarity. Shocked, I walked out in silence and never spoke to them again. Later, another woman sneered, "You just think your problems are harder than everyone else's?" Shocked again, I couldn't believe the cruelty I was experiencing from people meant to bear my burdens with me. I was so confused by her response. I gave up on my plan to raise up the neighborhood and instead I turned my focus to the support I did have, tucking those betrayals away for later, much later. I couldn't deal with them at that point.

Officer Ash called the next Monday. His tone was clipped. "Ms. Plumb, because you didn't inform us of your address, Don was moved to Adelanto. Now we have to relocate him again, and finding another placement is not easy. If you start a notification before that, it will only create additional complications for us."

"Officer Ash, the people have a right to know. I have a right to notify them."

"You may do as you see fit," he said flatly. Then, almost as an afterthought: "And Jody doesn't live with him. They aren't allowed contact as part of his parole conditions."

My jaw dropped, how can they be so naive? "Jody is in the high desert." The words shot out of me. Of course they were in contact, why else would she be here? I didn't believe for a moment they weren't in contact with each other.

The anger broke through before I could stop it. "You tell me I can do it, but every time I try the police prevent me from doing it. Which is it? Do I have the right, or don't I? Because you guys keep blocking me from acting, making it impossible."

His voice clipped and icy. "I told you; it's your choice. But if you go through with it now, you'll only make things harder."

His persistent dismissal cut deep; it physically hurt. I forced myself to push past it, to ask the one question still gnawing at me, the most important one. My intensity sharpened, laced with fear. *I had to know.* My jaw clenched as I pressed harder, my voice dropping low, trembling with fury I could barely contain. "Have you checked him yet?"

His voice snapped, curt. "Checked him?"

"Yes," I shot back, my voice tight. "You said you would search his home and person for any information about me or my family."

A short, clipped exhale. "I did not."

The words slammed into me, his cold dismissal hitting like a wall. My stomach dropped, air catching in my throat. My hands trembled around the phone as panic and fury twisted together. *If he had anything on him about me, he's had time to hide it, or destroy it.*

Tears broke through before I could stop them. I sobbed into the phone, my voice raw. "Officer Ash, you said you would search him. It's been a couple of weeks now. I just wanted to know, I just wanted to make sure."

"Well, I didn't."

My breath hitched. "Will you please? And will you let me know, please?" Shame surged through me, but I couldn't stop myself from begging.

His answer came cold, final. "I don't think I'm going to be able to do that."

My throat tightened, my chin quivering. My voice strained through the constriction, barely holding together. "Give me your supervisor's name and phone number."

"Fine, here it is."

I slammed the phone down, my body shaking. *Is this what a nervous breakdown feels like?* I'd heard of them before but never really understood. I couldn't pull myself together. I was drained, wrung out, and at the same time burning with rage. Rage and shame tangled inside me, demanding release. It couldn't go back inward, not again. I couldn't sink into that abyss.

Why didn't he just search him like he said he would? He could've even lied about it and told me he had. At least then I'd have something to hold on to.

I gulped air, grabbed the phone, and called Officer Ash's supervisor.

"Hello, this is Officer Pent."

"Hi... um... I just got off the phone with Officer Ash." I couldn't stop the sobs now; they came like a tide. I rammed the words out, "He said he'd search, he didn't, he probably wouldn't, maybe it's only a one-percent chance he even knew I was there, but what if, what if he had pictures of my sons? I needed to know. I'm scared. I'm furious, he was unkind."

A beat of silence. Then, clipped and annoyed: "Excuse me, Ms. Plumb. You know, you really should go to therapy."

The words hit like a fist, punch, punch, punch. In my head I saw my hand smashing into his smug face. I wanted to strike more than anything. Instead, his words did the smashing.

Keep it together.

Therapy. Oh wow. Brilliant. What a revelation. He must be the messiah of mental health. Thank you so much, Officer Pent, hadn't thought of that. Did he want a medal for diagnosing me over the phone? Maybe next he'll tell me not to cry, to calm down, to smile more. Maybe he'll tell me the sun rises in the east and my whole life is my fault.

Rage and shame tangled until I could hardly breathe. One voice inside sneered, *He's right. You're a mess. Pathetic. Sobbing. Begging.* But another voice burned hotter, *No, they're the ones who should be ashamed.*

I sat on the phone shaking, humiliated, furious, tears streaming while fire roared underneath, ashamed that I was still crying, angry that I had to beg for a simple human act, check him, protect my kids. Was that really too much to ask? My chest so tight I could barely breathe, the phone suddenly heavy in my hand, snot running down my face as I choked out, "I want your supervisor's number," only to hear, "What? I couldn't understand you." I stammered, "You, you, give me, you don't care, I need," before he cut me off with, "Look, get some help and we'll be in touch," and the line went dead. I screamed, throwing the phone, collapsing to the floor, punching a pillow until I couldn't scream anymore, sobbing until I felt something crack in my brain.

Lisa,

You were left in the dark by people who should have protected you. They kept you uninformed about the things you had every right to know, then had the audacity to turn the blame back on you. And when the parole officer and police brushed you off, dismissed your concerns, and even lied to you, it was devastating. You wanted answers, safety, and support, but instead you were met with cold shoulders and silence. That kind of treatment cuts deep, making you question yourself and your reality.

And then, facing people who mocked or disbelieved your pain, it carved the wound even deeper. It's like being dragged back into that same lonely, frightened place you fought so hard to leave. Their dismissal wasn't just cruel; it added fresh layers of judgment on top of the old hurt. It's disorienting, even crazy-making.

But listen closely: every feeling that rose up in you, fear, anger, frustration, grief. is real and valid. You are doing the hardest work there is; standing up, demanding safety for yourself and your family, even when it feels like the world refuses to listen. Keep reaching for the ones who truly see you. Keep holding onto your strength, even when it feels buried beneath everything.

I'm here beside you now, holding space for your pain.

CHAPTER 40

"Hello?" The voice on the line carried a note of hope. "Is this Lisa Plumb?"

"Who's calling?"

"This is Officer Smith with the San Bernardino Sheriff's Office. I have some information I believe will be helpful to you. Your maiden name is Baer, correct?"

I hesitated, my voice cautious. "Yes, it is."

"And you're a victim of Jody Gordon and Don Gordon, is that right?"

"Uh… yes."

"Well," he continued, "I wanted to provide you with Jody's current address."

"For real? You do? Okay… thank you."

"Yes," he replied. "Are you ready?"

As he began to give me the details, I thought, *See, Lisa, there are good people in this world.*

"Okay, Officer Smith, thank you so much."

"I just felt you had a right to know," he said. "Technically, I'm not supposed to give out a sex offender's address, but I wanted you to have it anyway. Take care of yourself."

A redeeming call! For a moment I wondered, *Who was this officer, and how did he even know about me?* But the thought was quickly drowned out by joy.

When the line went quiet, I leapt up. "Heck yeah!" I shouted. "Oh my gosh, I know where she lives!" The call ended, leaving me with a sliver of relief and an address on a scrap of paper.

Wait. I studied what I wrote on the paper. She lives in Victorville? *That's not Adelanto. She doesn't live with Don? But I know they are together, meeting up. Why else would she be in the high desert?* Victorville, Adelanto, and Apple Valley were small communities clustered together in the high desert 100 miles east of Los Angeles. She may not have been in his same town, but she was close to him. I called the local police department in her town of Victorville and gave them her address. I explained that she should be registered as a sex offender, and she wasn't. They took the information and said they would get back to me.

Then I took a drive. As I neared her house, my stomach dropped, she lived less than half a mile from the college I attended. *Of course she does.* I recognized the car that I had followed that day from the store. Same license plate. I knew where she lived now, and that brought a rush of relief, yet it tangled with a current of angst that I couldn't shake.

The Victorville police eventually called me back about Jody. They confirmed she was in their jurisdiction. But their response stunned me; they claimed she "didn't know" she had to register. They gave her a warning, and she promised she would register.

"But I told you she wasn't innocent, that she'd reoffend even without Don. I was there in court when I was thirteen, I heard the judge tell her she had to register. I told you that."

No one listens to me.

"I told you she molested me too, she wasn't just baking cookies in the kitchen while Don molested me, she was fully involved." My mind flashed back to my twenties, when I was contacted to testify again. I knew Jody had been involved in that girl's abuse as well. They told me she was Don's wife still, yet still she wasn't charged. She should have carried more strikes, but somehow she walked away with only one.

Whatever she does from here is not on me. I tried. I told the police the truth.

A few weeks later, I got another call, this time from Don's new parole officer from wherever they sent him, of course I didn't know where that was. He told me Don had been belligerent and obnoxious, and that he intended to put him under *civil commitment*. He explained that civil commitment is an involuntary hospitalization for offenders considered a danger to society and likely to reoffend.

Even though Don had technically "done his time," the parole officer said he had the authority to act in order to prevent further crimes. He made it clear he didn't believe Don was sorry for anything. In fact, the evidence told the opposite story, pictures, porn, and movies discovered in Don's residence that showed he was still steeped in the same behavior.

He found pictures!

When I asked about the pictures, he said he couldn't disclose who or what was in them, only that he wanted me to understand why this next step was being taken. Then he did something unexpected. He apologized. He acknowledged the ordeal I had been put through and thanked me for following up with the neighborhood notification, even though the Adelanto police had stalled the process and kept it from moving forward. He reassured me that I *should* have been allowed to do it.

Before we ended the call, he urged me to contact the Orange County District Attorney and request to be notified when Don was released, so this situation wouldn't repeat itself.

I thanked him over and over. Hanging up, I felt a surge of gratitude, finally, a professional who treated me with respect. In fact, it was the second one within days. And Don was going back behind bars!

Lisa,

I can see how your heart lifted when Officer Smith read that address to you. After shouting into the wind, here was someone who didn't just hear you, they acted for you. You mattered enough for him to take a risk. That call gave you more than an address; it gave you proof that there are people in the world who will go above and beyond to help someone who's been hurt.

I also see the sting that came soon after, the Victorville police brushing you off, talking to Jody like she'd just forgotten a form instead of reminding her she had harmed a child. That's the cruel whiplash of interacting with flawed systems; one moment you're honored and believed, the next you're erased.

It makes sense you felt both relief and rage, Lisa. Having her address brought a measure of relief, finally, something concrete, but that relief was tangled with anxiety, knowing she lived so close to your school. Your drive-bys, your phone calls, your persistence, those were acts of reclaiming control in a situation designed to take it from you.

Please remember; the failure of a system is not your failure. There were people, even within broken structures, who chose courage and compassion over indifference. Hold on to those moments. And congratulations that Don's new parole officer put him away again. Your voice matters!

CHAPTER 41

Fall slipped into winter, then spring, and still my involvement with "the system" wasn't over. One day, an assistant Orange County District Attorney called and asked if I would testify in Don's upcoming civil commitment trial. They explained that men like him, those diagnosed with a severe mental disorder and deemed unsafe to return to public life, were placed in secure psychiatric hospitals where treatment was offered but not required. Many refused it, knowing that agreeing to therapy might look like an admission of guilt or a sign they weren't truly rehabilitated. Instead, they gambled on a trial, hoping a jury might give them their freedom. This was Don's plan.

Perpetrators like Don also knew the law itself was under constant challenge. The ACLU was pressing courts to view civil commitment as unconstitutional, arguing that since these men had already served their prison sentences, continued confinement was unlawful. Offenders clung to the hope that one day the law would shift in their favor.

That made my testimony essential. Only by speaking could I help the jury see through Don's polished lies and manipulations. The truth was plain; he wasn't safe. His record, his repeated choices, his refusal to change, everything showed he remained a danger. Without the voices of survivors, it was too easy for him to dress himself up as rehabilitated; to pretend he deserved freedom. If the jury could hear us, the façade cracked. With our words, the jury had the evidence they needed to keep him where he belonged, civilly committed, unable to harm another child.

How could I say no? Just hearing the word *testify* hit me like a wave, pulling me under, dragging me back into memories I wanted to leave behind. Saying yes felt like the only right thing to do, but the moment I agreed, dread sank deep into me.

They couldn't say when the trial would be, when I would be needed. The idea of waiting. The not-knowing. It pressed on me like a weight I couldn't lift.

Inside, the arguments battled;

Why did I agree?

I don't want him to see me.

But if I don't, he could walk free.

He could hurt another child.

An idea came to me, something that might give me back a sliver of control. "I need you to understand," I explained. "I can't handle another surprise call. Please give regular updates. I'm sorry, I have to have this."

The contact at the Orange County District Attorney's office agreed; they would update me monthly on the status of Don's civil commitment trial, as long as I was the one to initiate the call. So, at the start of each month, I checked in. Each time, the answer was the same, no trial date yet, no way of knowing when it would happen. Month after month, the same conversation, the same uncertainty hanging over me.

I did my best to only think about it on that one day a month when I called the DA. The rest of the time, I turned my focus to my family, my schooling, and our new town. Apple Valley was beautiful, mountains rising in the distance, rugged desert stretching around us. Our cute little home, the view, the garden, the pets, all of it rooted me.

But then Jody began to appear. At Walmart. In the doctor's office. Not once, multiple times, as if she were haunting the edges of my new life. Each sighting struck like a blow, my chest locking up, my mind racing, *Why?* It felt less like coincidence and more like a warning. No matter where I went, the past could still find me. Each time I saw her I slipped out of view, unwilling to meet her eyes or hear her voice again. I never knew if she noticed me. Once, trapped in a doctor's office, I watched her helping an elderly patient and assumed she was working as a caretaker. The irony hit hard, a registered sex offender in California wasn't supposed to hold that kind of job. Yet there she was.

Of all the people I could have crossed paths with, it was her, I saw her more often than my own neighbors. The unfairness of it pressed in. I wanted to escape. But where could I go? We had worked too hard to create this life, the kids were finally settled, and moving again was beyond our reach. And deep down, I now knew no place came with a guarantee of safety from the past.

So, I chose to keep living. Shaking it off the best I could each time I saw Jody. I continued with school and tried to be a good mom and wife. But sometimes I was sure I was losing my mind. The sightings gnawed at me. I found myself doing things I never would have before, trying to carve out some small measure of control; driving by Jody's house became part of my routine, a way to check that she was where I thought she was, to see with my own eyes that nothing had changed. Sometimes, I spotted her in a window. Other times, I only saw her car, or nothing at all. Then I'd confirm on Megan's Law that she was still local. Once, I even found her standing outside. Knowing where she was gave me a shaky sense of control, enough to quiet the panic for a while. I told myself I didn't want it to affect me, didn't want her shadow dictating our days. Still, the fear lingered beneath the surface, and my anger grew sharper; at times it even teased me with thoughts of revenge I didn't want to admit.

The pressure built until it felt like something inside me would snap. When it did, the crack sent me down into a very dark place, I started to believe my family might be better off without me. I couldn't stop imagining Jody walking free and hurting someone else. If the police and the legal system wouldn't stop her, a raw, furious part of me whispered that maybe *I* should. I wanted all that raging energy to go straight at the source, the one person who kept turning up in my life.

Even as those thoughts roared, another part of me heard how dangerous they were, and how far I could fall if I followed them. I didn't act on those impulses, but the pull of them frightened me.

Sometimes, when my emotions felt overwhelming, I'd get in the car and circle her house, usually after a chance sighting during some errand earlier that week. I called Robert once, my voice unsteady.

"I, uh, I think that uh, ummm, I should just kill Jody, and then she wouldn't hurt anyone else, and I'd be in prison, and then you and the boys could move on without me being a burden."

My mind supplied scenes so vivid they felt real; me forcing my way into her house and ending her, quick and final. Other times, the images were darker, patient, and cold, waiting for the right moment. The fantasies were terrifying in their clarity.

"Lisa, no. We want you. We don't want someone else. It wouldn't be worth it," he pleaded, fighting back tears. I felt so worthless, so pitiful, for putting him through this.

Waves of pain swelled up, I felt like a ticking time bomb.

Tick. Tick. Tick.

She is going to harm more children.

Tick.

She shouldn't be free.

Tick.

I'm never going to be ok again.

Tick.

I should do something about it.

Tick. Tick. Tick.

One day my worst fear was confirmed. I checked Megan's Law and saw new charges against Jody, recent charges. Even though Don was locked away in civil commitment, there she was, convicted of having sex with a young teenager. A cold certainty settled in my bones: I had known, deep down, that she would hurt more children.

No. One. Listens.

It felt like watching a car wreck unfolding in slow motion, the same horrible scene I'd seen in my nightmares, playing out exactly as my premonition had warned. I felt like Kassandra from the ancient Greek myth who was fated by Apollo to utter true prophecies, but never to be believed. Prophecies of impending doom. I covered my ears and rocked, shaking my head in disbelief. You should have done something. *Lisa, you failed that child!*

I called the police station, asking for the officer I'd spoken to about Jody before. No answer. I left a voicemail, my voice breaking with anger and grief: *"This is Lisa Plumb. I told you Jody would re-offend. I told you she wasn't innocent. I. Told. You. Now what?"*

This should have been her third strike, first with me, second with the victim I was called to testify for in my twenties, and then for not registering. Now she was caught with a teenager. Had law enforcement acted when they should have, she wouldn't have been free to hurt another child. I never heard from that officer again. A part of me pitied him. I'm sure at first he thought I was crazy. But now he knew better. How did he carry the guilt? He had believed her when she claimed she didn't realize she was supposed to register. He should have arrested her then. Instead, it was too late for him to redeem himself, and for her most recent victim.

All I had were scraps of information from Megan's Law. No professional ever kept me informed. And within months, Jody's name was gone from the website, erased as if she had never existed.

Off.

Where did she go? How did this happen?

I knew Jody was originally from Illinois, so I checked their sex offender registry. And there she was, listed in Illinois, but with a lesser charge than she'd carried in California. How could that be? Did leaving the state mean her crimes were softened? She wasn't flagged as high risk there, even though in California she had been.

I called the Illinois police to report it. The woman I spoke with was kind, thanked me, and said she would do what she could to update the record. But nothing ever changed. She stayed listed as a low-level offender. Sorry, Illinois, I tried. Again.

A few months later, Megan's Law shifted from providing only zip codes to listing full addresses. Finally, thank you, Megan's Law. Now I could see exactly where Don was, and where Jody and Glenn lived. None of the other offenders I'd known appeared, but at least these addresses gave me a sliver of control. However small, it was something. I could steer clear of those streets, avoid those neighborhoods. The relief, though fragile, was real.

I carried on with life as best I could. The Orange County District Attorney's office never could give me a timeline for Don's civil commitment trial, and after almost a year of waiting, I stopped calling. I wanted to live a peaceful life, one that didn't involve the DA or anything connected to Don and Jody. I still carried emotions that sometimes threatened to overwhelm me, but they lessened. I did my best not to think about it anymore. And I didn't aside from the occasional glimpse at Megan's law, just to make sure.

Don was locked away in a state mental hospital. Jody had returned to Illinois. Glenn lived down the hill in Perris. Megan's Law gave me an occasional reassurance of where some of my childhood abusers were living.

And then, without warning, the rollercoaster lurched again, Glenn and Jody vanished from Megan's Law. Gone, as if they had never existed.

How?

I called the DA and learned the truth; both Jody and Glenn had used a loophole in the law to reduce their charges, making them disappear from Megan's Law.

My face flushed, my hands shook, fists clenched. They were high-risk sex offenders, and now they were no longer searchable. The one thing that had given me a shred of power, knowing where they lived, was gone. I felt stripped bare, helpless. *Shake it off, Lisa. You can't change this. Let go, let God.*

I had a life. I wanted *my* life. I never asked for any of this, never wanted it to invade me. I didn't want to be damaged, not by my childhood, not by this. But then the voice inside whispered; *You are damaged, Lisa.*

Still, I wanted more. I wanted meaning and purpose. I wanted to do better, and to be happy. So, I forced myself to let it go, again and again, as many times as it took. My life was mine to claim, and no loophole, no abuser, no system's failure would take that from me.

One day, while training at the dojo, the pain welled up again. Outrage surged through me, but I knew I had to redirect it. *I can't live like this.* I tried to laugh instead, pounding the bag harder as I remembered the parole officer who once told me to get therapy, to let it go, to move on. I wondered what he would do in my shoes. If he thought he could do better, I'd love to see how. *Don't think about it, Lisa. Focus on the good in your life.*

For a moment I wanted to punch his face, but I caught myself and redirected again. *Lisa, you can train your thoughts like you train your muscles.* I replaced revenge with compassion, drawing on scripture and the spiritual experiences that had once filled me with peace. *If you don't focus on the good, you'll explode. You'll lose everything, even your peace.* I reminded myself of eternal justice, of a God who sees and who holds everyone accountable. One day, they would know how they hurt me, and I would also understand how I had harmed others.

But training my mind was hard work. Rage often crept back in. Tick. Tick. Tick.

At my core, I knew what I wanted; to be understood. More than that, I longed for everyone to know peace, for people to care for and support one another. I focused on what I could do for myself, my family, and my future career. I let it go again. Sometimes, when the anger flared, I'd taunt the officers who had dismissed me, shouting into the air with sarcasm, *"Let it go!"* Then I would pray, pray to forgive them, forgive everyone. *Help me. Help my family.*

Slowly, the fire cooled. The rage and pain came to me less and less. Eventually, weeks passed without them rising up at all.

Then one day, the phone rang. My sister's voice was solemn on the other end of the line.

"Lisa, Mom died."

Lisa,

You were carrying a heavy weight, the knowledge that danger was still walking free, and the agony of being right when no one listened. You lived with the constant hum of "tick... tick... tick" in your chest, and every sighting of Jody, every loophole in the law, every contact with the DA was like another hand tightening the clock's spring. I know how exhausting it was to keep trying to "let it go" when the world kept dropping it back into your lap.

You learned something hard but powerful; forgiveness is not a gift you give to the person who hurt you, it's a gift you give to yourself. It's not excusing them, and it's not forgetting. It's reclaiming your peace so their choices no longer dictate your emotional state. Forgiveness is about loosening their grip on your spirit, so you can keep your hands free for the life you want to build.

That doesn't happen by pretending the pain isn't there. First, you have to face it, feel it, and understand exactly what you're forgiving. Sometimes healing means using therapies like EMDR to reduce the emotional intensity of memories, or somatic work to release what the body has held onto for years.

Letting go isn't a single moment; it's a practice, a muscle you train like you trained at the dojo. You won't always get it perfect, but every time you choose peace over revenge, you are winning your life back. I'm so proud of you!

CHAPTER 42

Her voice was respectful, as it had been for the past few weeks, a welcome reprieve from the usual chaos that flowed from my sister.

"I'm coming down. I'll see you soon," I told her.

I grabbed my keys and called my husband as I drove. "Mother's dead. She passed away early this morning. I'm going down to see her."

"Go take care of what you need to," he said gently. "We'll be fine. I'll make sure the kids are picked up from school and get where they need to go."

This day, this day had finally come. I told Robert I was going because it seemed like the right next step. In many ways, I had already grieved both her and Father while they were still alive. I had gone no contact with them out of necessity, to protect myself and my family. My mind drifted back over the last few years with Mother. I had swung between wishing her peace and wishing her suffering. But ultimately, what I wanted most was for her to have peace.

When the time came, I visited her on her deathbed. She couldn't speak, and I could have used that silence to be cruel. Instead, I chose kindness. I sang gentle songs and read her beautiful poems, the very things I would want if I were the one lying there.

Even though no earthly consequences ever came to her, other than being briefly investigated by the police after Don and Jody were busted, I knew she still awaited eternal consequences. I knew God is both just and merciful, and that in the next life Mother would face the truth, find healing, and be sorry for what she had done.

The real issue pressing on me was how things would go with my sister once I got to Riverside to see Mother's body. That relationship had always been awful. She had a way of finding the cruelest words at the hardest times. I told myself, *For now, I can be kind. Just get through this.*

I pulled up to the mortuary, my stomach tight. My sister was waiting out front. Together we followed the funeral director as he led us back to the room where Mother's body lay.

"Here she is." He opened the door and gestured for us to step closer before quietly stepping back.

We approached, and there she was. Oddly, she looked just the same as she had the last time I visited her. What had I been expecting? I reached for her hand, but as soon as I touched it, I recoiled, the stiff coldness of death had replaced life.

The funeral director said, "It's okay, you can touch her." I nodded but pulled back, I couldn't bear to feel that coldness again. As I stood there, a strange sensation crept in. I could almost hear her breathing. Wait, I *could* hear it. My heart kicked into double time. *But she's dead. She's dead.* My mind felt twisted, my thoughts bizarre. The sound was there, loud enough to notice, faint enough to doubt, audible only because the room was otherwise so silent.

I forced myself to clear my head and trace the sound back to its source. The funeral director. His heavy, rhythmic breathing filled the room. Why was he doing that? Minutes dragged by, each breath unnerving. Finally, I turned to my sister. "It sounds like Mom is breathing."

She agreed instantly, as if she'd been holding it in. The funeral director flushed, muttered an apology, and shifted his breathing, the spell breaking. We'd had enough and stepped out to the parking lot, sharing a rare moment of laughter at the funeral director's expense.

For a few minutes, my hopes lifted. I let myself lean into the ease of it, a sister-to-sister moment I had longed for and missed. Maybe, with Mom gone, things could finally be different between us. We had shared good times before, though they were scarce. For now, I chose to accept this small piece of good.

Just as we were wrapping up, saying our goodbyes, we agreed to share the cremation costs. My sister suddenly pivoted. Her eyes narrowed. "You know the scar on Mom's nose? You know how she got it, right?"

Of course I did. That salacious story had circulated my whole life; Mother as a teenager performing a sexual act for her boyfriend while he drove, the crash that shattered her nose and leg.

Why bring this up now?

I stayed silent, furrowing my brows, instinctively stepping back to create distance.

Then she struck, her voice like a blade; "You're just like her, aren't you, Lisa?"

There she was, the sister I knew. Disappointing, yes. But not surprising. Still, it left me aching. The rage she sparked in me simmered, but I refused to give her the satisfaction of seeing it. I walked away in silence, climbed into my car, and sped out of Riverside. Only when the city was far behind me did the sobs break free, spilling out in waves. I wasn't sure if I was crying for Mother, for my sister, or for myself, maybe for all of it, all at once.

My sobs eventually gave way to numbness. I fixed my eyes on the long drive up the Cajon Pass, grateful at least that I had a safe place waiting, with people who loved me. Forcing myself to breathe, I turned to prayer. *Please bless and guide my mother in the way You know is best, and my sister too, and everyone...*

It's in God's hands now. *You don't have to be around your sister Lisa, that's why you set boundaries in the first place.* And she set them too, reminding me years ago, "Lisa, I don't love you, and I never loved you."

I took a deep breath, tightened my grip on the steering wheel, and tried to comfort myself. *It's okay, Lisa. You are safe. You are loved. God understands, and He can make good out of what isn't good, through our growth, our leaning on Him, through His rescue.*

Drive. Just drive.

As the car curved through the canyon, a memory blindsided me. Dry yellow grass. Stale air. The sting of disappointment over a missed ice cream cone. Scrunched, glaring eyes. A rough grip pinching my arm.

Why now? Why was John Lippert, my abuser at just five years old, suddenly haunting me here? *What the heck? Why am I thinking about him?*

I shook it off and forced my gaze back to the present; jagged tan rocks rising beside me, the road climbing higher toward the clean air of the desert. *Here I come, clear blue skies.*

Mom would have loved this drive. She always liked drives. Now, she was in His hands.

Images crashed through my mind again, flashes of me in the car with John, driving into the field. *Okay, brain, I know that happened. But why now?*

Then new images began to surface, splicing themselves into the ones I already knew were real. My stomach dropped. I swallowed hard, sweat breaking across my forehead. *What? Are these real?*

The visions tangled together, old and new, while heat surged through my body, my hands trembling. Pain prickled, sharp and confusing. *What the heck, why now? My mother just died!*

I shook my head violently, desperate to push it back. "No!" I shouted into the empty car. As I neared the top of the pass, the desert stretched wide before me, Joshua trees standing like silent sentinels, welcoming me home. I drew in a deep breath, grateful at least that Mother was no longer in pain.

I didn't even know how she died. My sister wouldn't tell me, and the nurses said I wasn't on the list to be informed. Once again, I was left in the dark. *Let it go. Stop paying the price for caring.*

She's gone, that's all I know. And I know this; God is good. He will sort it all.

The cool drop in the high desert air felt refreshing, and I cracked the window to let the chill brush against my face. *That's what Mother feels now, cold air. Except she doesn't feel anything anymore, Lisa.*

Again, flashes of John broke through, images of being grabbed, the sweat, the shoving, forcing their way into my mind. *Lisa, why now? Stop. Don't go there. Just focus on getting home.* I reached for the radio and turned it on.

At last, I pulled into my driveway. The rugged beauty of the desert and the endless blue sky looked muted somehow, though I still noticed their quiet pull. A strange mix pressed on me, heavy and light at once. No more worries about Mom. I'd never had a parent die before. *It's okay, Lisa. You haven't needed her in a very long time. You are independent now.*

Then a wave of sadness crashed over me. *I don't even miss her. I won't miss her. She made it that way, Lisa, not you. You already grieved her long ago. So why was this sadness here? Where did it come from?*

When I stepped into the house, dinner was waiting, and everyone greeted me with sweetness. Warm hugs, a gentle evening.

But the next morning, I woke up gripped by terror. I tried to steady myself; Mother is okay. You are okay. There is nothing to fear.

Images forced their way to the front of my mind, John Lippert's mouth moving, words spilling out. They felt urgent, like my life depended on them, yet they came through muffled and jumbled. I could hardly make sense of it.

No. I'm not going there. Why is he invading my mind now?

I got busy with my day and then settled into the couch. Cleaning was too much right now. I stared out the window, the wind blowing up dirt and pushing clouds closer. Then the phone rang.

My sister sounded breezy, like we'd parted on good terms. "Lisa, do you have enough money for Mom's cremation? I don't, I don't know what to do."

"But you were taking care of her. You have legal authority, you got everything."

"I don't have the money, Lisa. What do you want?"

"Don't worry about it. I'll handle it."

I hung up. Not interested in fixing, explaining, scolding, or pleading. It's under four hundred dollars. I can do that to cremate our mom. The irony stung; her last job was selling pre-paid funerals and plots. Even more; she sneered once, "I'm not preparing for my funeral because you kids don't deserve that. I hope you feel burdened when I die."

No burden, Mom. A quick cremation and it's over. Letting it go.

In the days that followed, John kept breaking through, his glare, his half-formed threats, haunting me. My body wasn't settling either. Yes, my mother had just died, but I'd grieved her long ago. I should be okay. So why this heaviness? Why the fear, the depression, the constant anxiety?

I prayed for guidance, for help in facing these feelings and the intrusions that wouldn't stop. *Do inner child work, Lisa.* I realized, *what if this isn't just grief, what if it's a flashback?*

What if? The thought froze me; I couldn't push through. Despondency washed over me, utter, sinking. How do I feel better? *Listen to Little Lisa.* The thought came like a nudge, pulling me toward the closet where I could be alone with her. In the dark of the closet, his face returned.

Grabbing. Blood. The field. My body flung, like a ragdoll. Shoving.

Why have I never had this memory before? Did I forget? Did I bury it? I can't believe this.

Were these images just Little Lisa's worst fears acting out in my head? Or did it really happen? I'd always remembered John in the living room, the ice cream, the trip to a field, but these felt new and strangely familiar at the same time. *Am I inventing it? Why won't this leave me alone?*

You don't believe me, Little Lisa's sad voice whispered.

My gut wrenched at her suffering, and I blinked into the darkness. John's face appeared again, and I noticed he was speaking. I calmed myself down to listen.

But it's not real.

Shhh, just listen.

John's stern voice burst from his sweaty face, 'Do you love your mom?'

His grip around my shoulders tightened. *It hurts.*

Answer me!

Yes. I nodded frantically.

Then if you don't want her to die, don't ever speak about what happened here. Don't tell, then she won't die, okay?

I didn't answer fast enough. He yanked me hard.

"OKAY!" His red face pressed inches from mine. His breath, hot and sour sprayed across my face.

All I could do was nod, yes. That's what he wanted. My small, worn-out body ached with pain and confusion.

"Shhh, Lisa. Don't speak. Let Little Lisa show you."

If that happened, then these feelings must belong to that time. Lisa?

You're making this up, I told myself. Each time I said it I felt worse.

"I need you to believe me," came a little hurt voice, barely audible. "Believe me."

"Lisa, just go with it," another voice urged. "It doesn't matter if it's real, no one has to know. Just treat her like it happened."

So, I listened. I started to answer Little Lisa: "I believe you. I believe you. I believe you," while hugging her.

With each repetition, the pain softened. I wrapped my arms around myself, rocking gently. "I'm so sorry, Lisa. I love you. It's okay. I believe you." My body began to loosen, the tears slowed, and the noise in my head quieted. Warmth spread.

A sudden realization swept over me. This is surfacing now because it's finally safe. Little Lisa can speak at last, because Mother is gone. He can't hurt her anymore. No more burying. No more hiding. No more need to keep it locked away.

Oh, Lisa! I pulled my arms tighter around myself. It makes sense now.

"Oh, sweet girl, it's okay. Yes, she's with God now. You're safe now to share this. Thank you for trusting me. I'm so sorry you had to hold this alone for so long. You're safe now. I love you."

I rocked Little Lisa in the darkness, back and forth, back and forth, cradling her with love.

Lisa,

Saying goodbye to a parent who caused deep harm is one of the most complicated experiences to face. It's normal to feel many emotions at once, numbness, sadness, anger, and even relief. Our hearts try to make sense of what feels impossible.

Offering kindness at the end of a parent's life can be healing, even when that parent could not, or would not, offer kindness back. That compassion is a gift you give yourself. That's true strength. You may not be able to control siblings or repair fractured relationships, but you can protect yourself and honor your own healing.

When unexpected memories or emotions rise, it means some part of you finally feels safe enough to speak. Those flashes of pain are younger parts of you asking to be seen and believed. Though frightening, they are also invitations to listen, hold yourself gently, and remind those tender parts inside that they are loved. When you do you heal, you feel better, you put the feelings where they belong.

Grief is not only about losing someone; it's also about mourning what you longed for but never had. Giving yourself permission to feel it all, without rushing, is part of the healing journey. You are safe now. You are not alone. Healing unfolds one compassionate breath at a time.

CHAPTER 43

As weeks became months, and months became years, I kept training my mind toward forgiveness, hope, and faith. Five years after my last contact with Orange County, I sat in my brand-new office, reflecting on the long road behind me and the place where I had finally arrived.

I've come so far. A smile of deep relief spread across my face as I held my Master's degree in my hands. At forty-one, my education was complete. From failing grades in junior high and high school to earning a Master's degree. Gratitude filled me. I had set my heart and mind on this path, and I did not allow anything to stop me.

Today, I am a Marriage and Family Therapist!

My internships during school were working with trauma survivors and those struggling with addiction. When my schooling was complete, I stepped into full-time work doing the same. A few years later, I stepped into private practice. I could hardly believe it, I was thriving, holding down a fulltime workweek as a Marriage and Family Therapist.

I remembered the days when even part-time work felt impossible. Back then, sometimes my heart ached so deeply it was hard to function. Now my heart swelled with gratitude. The picture I carried in my mind throughout school, me a thriving and a capable professional, had become reality.

I felt profoundly thankful to walk alongside others on their healing journeys. Client breakthroughs and affirmations from supervisors seemed to arrive just when I needed them most. I had two teenage boys still at home and one away at college, soon to be married. I marveled at the life I was living; the success God had helped me build, the warmth of family and meaningful work all around me.

I did my best to live fully in the present. The trauma of my past felt far away, more like history than a wound. Even Orange County area codes flashing on my phone no longer rattled me, just spam now, nothing more. I couldn't have been prouder of Little Lisa and the woman she had become. She had not only survived, she had grown, thrived, and achieved her dreams.

We had imagined living out the rest of our lives with that beautiful Apple Valley view. Our little orchard, the pumpkin patch, the quiet neighborhood, it all felt like home. And while we built some wonderful memories there, life shifted. The area was no longer what we wanted for our boys, and then the economy took a sharp downturn. Determined to give our teens the best future we could, we let go of Apple Valley and started fresh in Arizona.

Robert had grown up there, and his roots and family ties gave us a sense of familiarity. We already knew the area well from years of visits, and with Arizona's economy thriving compared to the California high desert, moving wasn't just a leap of faith, it was the logical next step.

Arizona was beautiful, and on the very day we moved into our new home, we were welcomed by a haboob, a towering sandstorm born of the summer monsoons. At first, the wildness of the haboobs and the drama of the storms made the transition feel almost magical. But the adjustment proved harder than hoped, especially for our youngest, still navigating high school. His struggles made us question our decision more than once. Still, we believed the move was for the best, and we committed to making it work.

I trusted that we had been led to Arizona for everyone's best interest, and I prayed fervently that it would all be worth it, that my youngest would adjust. One morning, as I knelt in prayer, a wave of peace washed over me. Then came a flood of joy. Surprised but deeply grateful, I rose to continue my day, and the feeling only grew stronger.

By evening, the love and clarity I felt in the very core of my being were so profound it was as if an umbilical cord stretched from my belly button straight to God. For three full days, I was wrapped in this peace, my own little miracle. The message I felt again and again was clear: *You are so loved, Lisa. You always have been, and you always will be. Everything will be okay.*

In those few days I felt only deep peace and love. I knew, with unshakable certainty, that God was mindful of me, of us. I recorded the experience in my journal, wanting to hold onto every detail. I knew this umbilical connection was temporary, but it left me with a soul-deep awareness, a glimpse of what awaited in the afterlife. I sensed that I would need to return to this memory one day for comfort. And over the months that followed, I did. Again and again, I reflected on this beautiful gift, this fleeting yet eternal taste of peace.

One challenge of our move was discovering that I couldn't transfer my marriage and family therapist license from California to Arizona. Without it, my dream of opening a private practice was put on hold, and I had to work in agencies until Arizona eventually changed its licensing laws. What first felt like a setback turned out to be a blessing in disguise. Each agency role gave me invaluable experience, introducing me to trauma-healing tools and terminology I hadn't yet learned.

One of my positions was at a suicide prevention agency, where I worked as a clinician assessing children newly placed in child protective custody. The agency was solid, my boss supportive, and my coworkers incredible. Still, the work was heavy. Traveling from case to case, sitting with traumatized children, I often found myself wondering; how would I have answered those same questions if the state of California had assessed me when I was removed from my home? That thought stayed with me, sharpening both my empathy and my determination to do this work well.

On the morning of February 11, 2016, I pulled into my favorite local gas station before heading out to assess children. I had a busy day ahead and was in a hurry. As I reached for the gas station door to pay, my phone rang, startling me. I glanced down and laughed softly, an Orange County, California area code. Probably just a solicitor, I thought. I still had my California number, after all.

After paying, I plopped down on the front seat and opened my voicemail before pumping. A firm voice came through; *"This is Investigator Davis from the Orange County District Attorney's Office. We're wondering if you would be willing to testify for the civil commitment trial of Donald Gordon..."*

What? Did I hear that right? I froze, stunned, unable to move. It felt as if I were glued to my seat, eyes locked on the phone. A wave of disbelief swept over me, my mind racing, calculating. *Over ten years... it's been over ten years since the last contact.* In an instant, that entire decade vanished, collapsing into this single moment.

I sucked in a shaky breath and shook my head, as though trying to wake from a heavy dream. Rubbing my forehead, I struggled to wrap my mind around the flood of feeling that hit me. I replayed the message to be sure. Yes, I had heard correctly.

Another long minute dragged by before a flicker of my fighting spirit stirred: *Maybe… maybe I should.* But the weight of it crushed me. After all these years, *why me, again?* How did they even find me? My body felt like lead, as if I weighed a thousand pounds. The thought of calling back felt impossible.

Still, one truth pressed through the fog, Don was still dangerous. My hands trembled as I whispered to myself, *You can't ignore this. Not forever.* I didn't know how or when, but I knew eventually I'd have to call him back. And I couldn't put it off any longer.

With a deep breath, I dialed Investigator Davis. The line clicked and quicker than I was prepared for a male voice answered, "This is Investigator Davis, Orange County District Attorney's Office."

"This is Lisa Plumb; you just called me and left a voicemail." There was a pause, then he said, "Yes, thank you for calling back so soon. And I also noticed from your voicemail that you're a marriage and family therapist?"

Before I could say more, he carefully verified my identity. "You are Lisa Plumb? Formerly known as Lisa Baer? Lisa Marie Baer, born May 16th, 1968? You grew up in Riverside, California? You're a victim of sexual abuse from Donald Lee Gordon?"

"Yes… all of that is correct," I was sure he could hear the shakiness in my voice.

His tone softened slightly. "That's really good, what you've done with your life." Then he added, "We would love to have a witness like you, someone who is successful, someone who can speak well and understands the language, but who can still show that it still does affect you. Will you help us keep this sexual predator away from the public?"

It was obvious what he meant. He wanted me to appear simultaneously professional and capable, yet wounded and vulnerable. His reasoning upset me and made sense because victim-witnesses are often browbeaten in court. He was hoping that I would be able to handle that because of my title.

And yet.

At his request to perform, something in me felt like it broke. Beneath his polished words, I heard the manipulation, how useful I would be, how important my testimony could sound, yet not a word about what this sudden call might cost me. No acknowledgment of how jarring, how disruptive it was to be pulled back into this without warning. Just the expectation that I would step up and deliver. Afterall, I was a marriage family therapist!

Tick, tick, tick.

The dynamic rang all too familiar, being asked, not seen. Fear curled in my stomach, tangled with duty. I wanted to say no, and I wanted to say yes. Both lived in me at once. In the end, how could I refuse?

"I will help if that is the right thing to do. If it will keep him off the streets and protect potential victims, I will help." The words left my mouth, almost without my permission. And in the back of my mind another question pulsed;

"How did you even find me after all this time?" I asked, the sharp edge in my voice fading into defeat.

There was a short pause before he replied, steady and plain, "Uh… well, we have our ways."

He was excited that I said yes, and I wanted to be excited too. Instead, I was paralyzed, too stunned to feel anything else. After our brief call, with his promise to get back to me soon, I cranked up my favorite fight music and pulled out of the station.

Halfway down the street my stomach lurched. I hadn't even pumped my gas. My heart kicked harder as I whipped the car around and sped back. Relief flooded me when I saw the pump still open. Shame washed over me as I slid out of the car and finally filled the tank. *What just happened?*

Don't slow down. Push through.

I threw myself into work the rest of the day, assessing children while my mind swirled. I tried to keep the thoughts at bay, but beneath the surface I felt trapped, shoved back into absurdity, the weight of it all waiting for the smallest spark to ignite.

Lisa,

Look how far you've come! You once believed school was impossible, yet you pressed forward and earned your Master's degree. Today you are a Marriage and Family Therapist. That is extraordinary, and it happened because of your courage, your determination, and your faith.

And then the phone rang. After more than ten years of silence, Orange County found you again. No warning, no care for the disruption to your life, just the expectation that you would step in. Your heart raced, fear and confusion swirled. Why me, again? Can I do this? Even in your hesitation, you found the strength to say yes, because you wanted to protect others. That is who you are. Brave and always wanting the best for everyone.

It makes sense that you felt paralyzed, that your body carried the weight of dread. The past still touches you, sometimes invades you without notice, but you will survive, you are a warrior!.

When fear or flashbacks come, it's okay. It doesn't mean you're weak. Your fight, flight, freeze, and fawn feelings are your body's way of keeping you safe. You can learn to listen without letting them overwhelm you. It takes practice, but you can do it now even if you didn't know how to then.

Keep holding on. Your story isn't over yet, or your joy.

CHAPTER 44

I waited until I knew Robert was free before calling. After I told him what happened, he said, "Who called? They didn't tell us they would contact you again, after this long. How on earth did they even find you? More importantly, how are you?"

"I don't know," I admitted. "I asked Investigator Davis how he found me, and he wouldn't say. I just feel so heavy, Robert. I don't know what to think, but I know I have to keep moving."

"Then let's walk when we get home," he said gently. "We'll sort through it together. I love you, Lisa."

"I love you too. Thank you for being here for me. This is all so crazy... I'm so sorry."

"Lisa, you don't need to apologize. I'm always here for you and I always will be."

It was almost dark when I pulled into the driveway. The fight energy that had carried me all day was nearly gone. I'd planned to walk with Robert the minute I got home; I knew if I sat down I might not get back up. I had to walk. I felt unbearably heavy.

But I ignored the part of me that was screaming at me, *don't lay down*. Almost in slow motion, I fell onto the bed. And there I was. Stuck. I couldn't move. I tried to will myself up. *Lisa. If you don't walk now you might not get up again. You can take this fighting or lying down.* But I couldn't move. My body chose for me. I stared at the ceiling, my eyes burning.

I felt disoriented, as if I'd slipped into another time zone, and a heavy wave of self-doubt settled over me. Part of me wanted to call Orange County back and explain; *Wait, I'm not really successful, not in the way you think. Please don't assume that just because I'm a therapist, it means I have it all together.* But shouldn't it mean that? The thought lingered, but I didn't pick up the phone. Instead, I let it sit and decided to wait for him to call me back.

When Robert came home, he found me still lying on the bed. He leaned down and wrapped me in his arms. "We'll get through this, Lisa. I'm here for you," he whispered. I held on tightly, grateful for his steady presence. I didn't rise again that night.

I tried to stick to the plan and go to work the next day. But from the moment I woke, everything felt off. I was irritable, exhausted, wishing only to stay in bed. *When did he say he would call me back?* The thought circled endlessly as I sat on the edge of the mattress, moving slowly, as if wading through five feet of mud. *Just get ready,* I told myself.

Snapping out of a daze, I dressed and then forced myself into the car and down the street. But at the corner, I turned around. I couldn't do it. Not today. My schedule was already full of appointments, but I couldn't face them. I called my boss, apologizing. "I'm sick today, I'm so sorry," I said, leaving out the truth. *Would she even understand?*

Back home, I crawled under the covers, curled tightly into a ball. I pressed a pillow over my head, shutting out the light, the world, everything. I was forty-seven years old, a therapist, yet one phone call had me unraveling instantly. Still in disbelief, I replayed it in my mind, word for word. Sitting motionless, my thoughts raced through every possible option.

I tried to put myself in the DA's shoes. Of course, I wanted justice. Of course, I wanted to help protect others. But alongside that was my own need for support and understanding. Was that even possible? What I didn't want was another bad experience, to be mishandled by the system all over again.

This time I knew myself well enough to realize that I was triggered. Even so, I didn't really understand why I was having such a hard time. Maybe this time would be different working with the professionals in the justice system? I was still shocked they contacted me, yet again. It had been thirty-five years since Don's conviction.

I shoved the covers over my head and clung to the dark. Could I show up the way they wanted? The thought gnawed at me. People already saw the damage when they looked at me, or so it always felt, and I knew juries judge the witness as much as the testimony. I'd read the studies; victims' presentation can sway outcomes. They wanted me to appear competent and composed. I was falling apart.

A scream lodged in my throat. I'd fought for healing my whole life, built a life around it, and yet here I was, unspooling, shocked by how raw the pain still felt. I had believed I was past this.

Investigator Davis finally called back the next day, though the wait stretched for what felt like weeks. His voice was businesslike. "We'd like you to send us any photos of yourself from the age when Don assaulted you. Do you have any?"

"Yes… I think I do," I answered, my voice small and hollow.

"Okay, great. Just email them to me once you've found them."

"Alright. They're buried in old boxes from my childhood, so it may take me a little time." My throat tightened at the thought of digging through those remnants.

"That's fine. Just try to get them to me within a few days."

"And after that… what happens next?"

"Well, we're preparing the case. The Assistant District Attorney and I will schedule a phone interview with you. After that, it should only be a few weeks before you're due to testify."

My eyelids felt like bricks, heavy and unwilling to stay open. My body seemed pressed down by invisible cement. I was sure he could hear the panic vibrating through my voice. "A few weeks? Will this really happen? I've been contacted before…" I explained about the calls in my twenties, then the ordeal in my thirties. "Now I'm forty-seven, and here it is again."

My throat cinched so tight that my words broke into a squeak. I tried to keep emotion from spilling over, but it leaked out anyway, impossible to contain.

"I see. Well, let's get this done. I'll follow up after you send the photos."

I swallowed hard. *What did you expect, Lisa?* I whispered to myself, managing only a faint "Okay" before he hung up.

I collapsed onto the bed, my body folding in on itself, and didn't move for the rest of the day. I lay there, drained and lifeless, as though every ounce of strength had leaked out of me.

The next morning, I forced myself to face the task. I opened the old boxes of photos and keepsakes, my hands trembling as I sifted through the dust and time. Each snapshot of my younger self cut into me. I hadn't looked at these pictures in years, not because I'd forgotten them, but because they hurt too much. Every image of little me stirred that old ache, lost, alone, and full of pain.

I managed to pull together about five photos of myself from ages eleven to thirteen, scanned them, and emailed them to Davis. The effort drained me completely. I hadn't eaten in over a day, and I didn't even care. After sending them, I crawled back into bed, staring at my inbox, waiting for confirmation that he'd received them. Nothing came.

The following day, I met with my therapist. She knew pieces of my history but not the whole picture, I had only started working with her a couple of months before this new contact from Orange County. As I filled in more of the blanks, I watched her face shift between compassion and something heavier, like sorrow mingled with disbelief. Finally, she said gently, "Lisa, this contact and the way Orange County is treating you; it mirrors the same dynamic as the sexual abuse you endured."

The validation hit me like a bright, unexpected light. Suddenly there were words for what I'd been living. I hadn't thought to call it the same dynamic before; hearing it named gave me just enough lift to finish the day with a fragile thread of hope.

Morning arrived and shattered that thread. Why hadn't he emailed back? Didn't he understand how hard it had been to dig those photos up and send them? The questions swarmed, louder than reason. I forced myself to get ready and drove to my first appointment, but after the assessment the car became a dangerous place for my thoughts. *What if I just crashed and didn't have to go to the next appointment?* The idea was a cold, sharp whisper. I pulled over, breathed, tried to talk myself down. *I can't do this,* I thought. *I can't work.* Everything felt weighted, like walking through mud.

Dejected, I called my boss. Her voice came over the line and I couldn't hold it in. the sobs spilled out before I could stop them.

"I'm so, so sorry. I'm going through such a hard time right now, I just can't finish my day."

She listened quietly, her voice warm and steady as I explained what was happening in my personal life. With genuine compassion, she encouraged me to take the rest of the day off and come back tomorrow with a clearer head. Her understanding surprised me, and I felt deeply grateful. I did exactly as she suggested.

Back at home, I collapsed into bed. I tried to think the best of Davis, to give him the benefit of the doubt. Maybe he just didn't realize how much this had cost me, or maybe he'd never been trained in how to talk to survivors, or why quick, kind responses matter. I had recently completed training on working with trauma survivors in stress states; fight, flight, freeze, or fawn, and I even had tools I could share with him. I imagined the vicarious trauma he must carry from his job.

If I explained my needs with kindness and compassion, surely it would make sense to him. With that renewed hope, I picked up the phone and called Davis.

Voicemail.

"Hi, Investigator Davis. I… um… sent you the pictures you asked for, but I haven't heard back yet. I was just wondering if you received them. And, I'm sorry, I know I sound emotional. I'm just really overwhelmed right now. I probably just need some validation. I know it might seem small or silly, but reassurance means a lot, even though what happened was thirty-five years ago. I'm not doing well… not at all. I really do appreciate your concern and caring. I also have some tools as a therapist that might help you understand trauma responses, and maybe even ease some of the stress in your work. I'll email you some links and handouts. Please let me know if you have questions about them. Thank you."

Days passed in silence. Finally, an email arrived from him asking for a time to meet with him and the DA. No mention of my voicemail. No mention of my email. I wrote back, asking, "Did you get the pictures I sent? And the information on working with people who are traumatized?"

At last, he replied. One word; *Received*.

Received.

I could have screamed. My thoughts spun, *did he even listen to my voicemail?* I shot off a quick email; *Did you get my voicemail?* If he had, surely he would've answered with something kinder than one word.

I swallowed hard and forced myself into the car. Before I even reached my first appointment the tears started and wouldn't stop. *What is wrong with me?* I thought, panic hot and hollow in my chest. I held my head in my hands and sobbed, then screamed once, the sound tearing out of me. I didn't want to bail, but I couldn't work. I couldn't do it.

I called my boss and tried to explain through the shaking. I apologized again and again. She said softly, "Lisa, I'm sorry you're having such a hard time, but you can't keep doing this."

Her words landed like a verdict. I whispered back the truth I already felt; I can't keep doing this.

All I could manage was a string of profanities at her before I slammed the phone down. The instant the call ended, my anger evaporated and a new voice started screaming at me, loud, furious, unforgiving.

Oh no, Lisa! What did you do? That's it, it's all over. You just threw away your career. Your life is finished. Great job. You cursed out your boss, totally unprofessional. You're ruined. You're ruined.

Lisa,

That phone call wasn't just information; it pulled you back into old betrayals. Once, someone who should have kept you safe shattered that trust. Now, a system meant to protect you moves forward without tenderness for your heart. That's betrayal trauma. It leaves you doubting yourself, feeling isolated, and so so sad.

I see you lying there, staring at the ceiling, frozen no matter how hard you try to move. You keep telling yourself you should be fine, stronger, further along. But trauma doesn't follow "shoulds." You were being retraumatized. This is your body remembering. Emotions are time travelers, carrying you back to moments when trust was broken and you were left unprotected. It's not one wound but layers of hurt, each new betrayal pressing into the old ones.

When you lashed out at your boss, shame rushed in, you felt unprofessional, ruined, small. But this wasn't a reflection of your worth. It was your nervous system, raw and overloaded, firing from survival. The words came from pain, not your true self.

Your emotional load had reached beyond its capacity. Curling up, crying, unable to work, these are trauma responses. Healing begins with naming it; I'm triggered. From there, gentle steps can follow, grounding, resting, seeking support, offering yourself the compassion you were once denied. I'm sorry you had to face this without someone guiding you, helping you understand. You deserved that care all along.

You are not ruined. Look at us now! You are still worth protecting.

CHAPTER 45

I sat in the car, stunned. We needed my income, and in one moment I'd shattered the life I'd built: my career, our family's security, all the schooling I'd worked for. *I am ruined,* I thought, and the word felt like a hand around my throat. I screamed until my voice gave out. My head throbbed, my face burned, hot tears carving tracks down my cheeks. I didn't even wipe the snot running from my nose. Who cared? I wanted to mash the accelerator and see what would happen. Then a smaller, steadier voice cut through the chaos: *No, Lisa, not here. Don't hurt innocent people.*

After what felt like an hour, I tore out of my space, safely. I needed to get out of that pain. My thoughts raced faster than the car, but it was my emotions that slammed me down; loser, ruined, nothing, dumb.

I ended up near Tempe Town Lake and pulled into a lot, not sure where to go. It seemed fitting to be near the lake while it emptied its contents. It was being drained, like me. The loss of the water revealed many rocks and fish that were not visible before. It now was so easy for the herons to take their pick of the almost stranded fish. They stabbed their chosen fish with their beaks, flung their heads back, and shook violently till the fish was dead. Then they slammed it down, unimpaling it, and flung it up into their mouths. Such a violent scene. The cycle of life had gotten a lot easier for the birds but much harder for the fish.

I had been told by a friend, "Lisa, you don't have to testify, you know." I felt gut-punched when she said that to me. I coiled back from her comment. It was if she was saying to me that I had a choice not to feel so miserable and destroyed. As if all I had to do was say no to testifying and I would be just fine. Yes, technically, I could have refused. They probably wouldn't have subpoenaed me like they had in my twenties. But the truth is, the damage had already been done. The phone call alone had triggered me, ripping open old wounds. Even if I walked away, I'd still be left with the aftermath. *How do you say no to helping keep a sexual predator behind bars?*

My head spun from the intensity of it all, the shock at how raw I still was; the inconsiderateness of the investigator that magnified the pain. Most of all, the bitter truth that after all these years, I wasn't healed. I had believed I was. I thought God and I had a deal. I couldn't believe it. I couldn't find relief. *My God, why am I forsaken?*

Like the fish in shallow water, I was floundering and not able to protect myself. I just couldn't do better. I was lost. I had so much empathy for the fish and was glad that their suffering, though intense, was temporary.

Having my fill of the spectacle before me, I started my car and headed home. I considered driving in a completely different direction and contemplated what it would be like to drive for hours to an unknown area and disappear. But I thought about my kids and drove back home. *I love them so much.*

Dread pooled in my stomach at the thought of confession to my husband that I had just ruined our lives. I pulled into the driveway and walked straight to my room. *There is no good way to tell him.* I had failed at the one thing I swore I would do right. I had vowed to be a good mom and provide a better life, a much better life, for my children.

I heard him come in the front door and greeted him, "Robert, can I talk with you?" I said as I tried to appear pleasant, so as not to worry our children.

He came into the room after me, and I sat down and dropped my head in my hands. "I'm... I'm sorry. I messed up bad. I... I... I told my boss to leave me alone with the worst profanities. I'm so sorry, Robert. I think I've ruined my career and I can't even work anyway. I'm so messed up. I'm so, so, so sorry." *I'm not sure what is wrong with me.*

I knew Robert wouldn't rage, but a small part of me still braced for it, maybe because I felt I deserved it. I wondered how I would respond if the roles were reversed, if he were the one unraveling.

Before he even spoke, his gentleness disarmed me. "Lisa, honey, don't worry. I'll support you. I'll take care of us. We'll figure this out." His calm stunned me. How does he do that?

"Robert, I'm so sorry," I whispered, turning away as I lay back on the bed, my eyes fixed on the wall.

He rested a steady hand on my side. "It will be okay, Lisa. We'll get through this. We'll be okay." Then he slipped quietly out of the room, closing the door softly to give me space. I had no idea how he would make it all work, but I felt so deeply grateful for him.

After my outburst at my boss, she emailed asking me to respond right away. It took me until the next morning to find the strength to reply. To my astonishment, she wasn't angry. In fact, she offered compassion: *"You can go on medical leave. Take the time you need to finish the process with Orange County. Testify, and then we can revisit when you're ready to return."*

I was dumbfounded, she wasn't punishing me, she was holding my job. Her kindness brought tears to my eyes. Yet shame rose up just as quickly. I couldn't imagine ever facing her again, knowing the things I had said in that fit of raw, out-of-control emotion. I feared others at work might know, too, and I couldn't bear the thought of their judgment. I didn't think I would ever have the ability to work again, but I didn't have to figure that out at that moment. I thanked her sincerely, apologized, and let the relief sink in.

When I shared the good news with Robert, I reminded myself that while my paycheck was gone for now, I didn't have to force myself back to work just yet. For the first time, I started to believe him when he said we would make it somehow.

The day finally came for the official interview with me, via phone, since I was out of state. Investigator Davis and the Deputy District Attorney Peter explained the legalities of my talking with the deputy district attorney. It must be done only in an official manner, always with someone else present, as he was the attorney trying the case. Davis would be my main contact. "Do you understand?"

"I think so. Why can't we speak without someone else like Davis present?"

"It prevents the appearance of impropriety."

"Okay."

The deputy district attorney began with general questions, where the abuse with Donald Gordon had taken place, what had happened. After a few minutes, he remarked how good it was that I was a therapist, a professional.

I cut in quietly, "I'm actually not doing so well emotionally. I'm on medical leave right now."

Silence. Neither of them responded. After a brief pause, the questions simply resumed.

By the end of the interview, they told me Orange County would fly me out when it was time to testify.

"Alone?" I asked.

"Oh, yeah," came the quick reply.

"Well, I'd like my husband to come with me so we can just drive," I said.

"Oh, you feel you need that? We don't want you to drive," came the response.

"I do. I really do feel I need that."

"Alright then, we should be able to get another ticket approved. We'll let you know."

And with that, the interview was over. The deputy district attorney had what he needed, and my part was to wait for further instructions. Just wait.

Most mornings I spent at Tempe Lakes, watching herons spear fish and pacing the paths. There was something strangely comforting about watching the lake slowly drain, about being close to the river. I usually never walked outside alone, but at that point, I felt I had nothing to lose. As long as I kept moving, I could hold myself together. Once I was home, though, I sank back into bed, unable to rise above the weight pressing me down.

I could no longer afford therapy, and even if I could, I wasn't sure it would help. My therapist had offered validation in the beginning, but after that, she seemed lost. The worried look in her eyes, the heavy silences between her words, it was clear she didn't know what else to do with me. She didn't offer any suggestions for how to survive this nightmare. I felt like too much for her, too broken, and sitting across from her became another reminder that no one really knew how to help.

One Saturday morning, Rob said gently, "Lisa, let's go to Lynx Lake. Just you and me. Let's get out into nature."

It wasn't much different from the days before, except this time my husband was home, trying to breathe life into both of us. I could see the strain on his face, though he denied it whenever I asked. I agreed to go. At least I'd be out of the house, and maybe it would keep my heaviness from spilling over onto our teens, who were working, studying, and didn't deserve to carry the shadow of all this.

During the hike, I started rambling about how scared I was to be on the stand. Shame flowed up in me when I thought about it. It seemed so surreal. I hadn't spoken much recently, but now my worries flowed freely. He did the best he could to comfort me, but as we walked in the forest we both became silent and just breathed in the fresh air. We realized there was nothing to ease the pain either of us felt, and we just had to push forward.

The drive home was taut with that unspoken tension. I knew some of what I'd blurted sounded irrational, but I couldn't control it, I didn't even understand it myself. He didn't have the right words, so he apologized and sat with his worry. For the next few days, he hovered, careful and quiet, probably terrified of saying the wrong thing. Meanwhile, my mood frayed by the hour and everything felt heavier. Desperate, I begged him, "Robert, I need help. I need to feel better. I don't feel better, I don't know what's wrong with me. I feel so messed up." He stared at me, searching for something to say, but the words wouldn't come.

I thought about the toll this was taking on him, but I couldn't shake the darker thoughts that kept surfacing, that maybe I didn't deserve to be here, that I was ruining everything and causing so much pain. Some friends knew pieces of what was happening, but their check-ins were sporadic;

some didn't check at all. When they called they were kind, but I didn't know how to ask for more. How could I explain the rawness of what I was experiencing, or the strain on our whole family? My friend's offhand remark, that I didn't have to testify, kept looping in my mind like an accusation; *am I doing this to myself?* I felt deeply misunderstood and unsupported. The DA and Davis seemed oblivious to how fragile I was, and all I wanted was someone to truly see me and know how to help.

Once again I was doing everything wrong, my old story, replaying. Rob and I tried to hold each other up, but this was bigger than us. Neither of us had steady, healthy support; trauma had already hollowed us both out. It felt like nobody cared, like nobody could see the wreckage. The pain was everywhere, crushing us, and I was drowning under its weight. I wanted to do better, but living with the proof that I wasn't was slowly sinking me. I kept slipping into a dark abyss and, strangely, it felt like where I belonged. I began to imagine myself as already gone, and that thought brought a quiet, awful comfort. The God I'd leaned on, the one I'd felt close to just a month before, seemed to have vanished. Was he even there? The doubt shocked me; my whole life had been built on faith and on moments when I thought I heard him speak. Now, there was nothing. I heard nothing.

I pulled a bottle of pills from the cabinet, drove to the supermarket, and sat in the car with the engine off. I pictured a way to make it stop, the memory of whiskey after so many years made me gag, and that disgust felt somehow right, like punishment I deserved. I imagined a lonely stretch of desert where I wouldn't be found. My mind landed on the psychiatrist who'd trusted me with those pills, the thoughtful man who believed I could manage them. I pictured letting him down, and a small, shame-filled part of me hoped it would make him think twice before trusting someone else. Sorry, kind psychiatrist.

Relief felt dangerously close, a hush I'd chased before in other numbing ways. I pictured the moment when the noise would finally stop and a strange, aching peace would settle over me. For a flash, I felt steady, as if everything might simply end and the pain would be gone. *Lisa, what are you doing?* I admonished myself, trying to force my focus back. Still, that quiet determination pulsed through me, and with it a hollow calm; it'll be over soon, I told myself, and the weight will lift.

Lisa,

When helpers don't know how to guide us, it feels like abandonment. But their silence doesn't mean we're beyond help. It only reveals their limits. Real support exists; tools, compassion, and guidance to carry us through.

You're convinced you've ruined everything; your career, your family's stability, your very worth. You screamed until you couldn't, because no sound could match the pain inside. And when that pain felt unbearable, your mind began whispering an escape plan. That was your nervous system crying out for the pain to stop.

Flashbacks and triggers feel like time collapses, you're back in the betrayal, powerless again. The emotions come in tidal waves that feel like they'll never end. But they do pass, even when your body swears they won't. Remember that please.

Your friend's words "you don't have to testify" landed like blame, when you needed care. The DA and investigator's coldness deepened the wound. This is why victims need trauma-informed systems, so they are not re-injured by the very people meant to help them.

You are not "choosing" to be broken. You are responding to deep pain with the tools your body knows: fight, flight, freeze, fawn… and sometimes, the urge to disappear. Those thoughts don't mean you want life to end, they mean you want the pain to end.

In those moments, stay connected to a person, a helpline, any lifeline. Your life matters. Even in the heaviness.

You are not ruined, You are loved. You are worth saving. Always.

CHAPTER 46

I unlocked my car door in the grocery store parking lot, oddly proud of myself for following through with the plan. Inside, I would buy what I needed. I pictured Jack Daniels in one hand, pills in the other, and the promise of relief they would deliver together. The image brought a wave of calm over me, almost like hope, hope for release, hope for rest. For a brief moment, the sorrow quieted, replaced by the thought of escape and a break from the ache that never seemed to end.

But the calm quickly shifted into unease. I cracked the door open, ready to step out, then just as quickly shut it again. *Lisa, what if God is here? What if somehow you will be okay?* I didn't really believe that, not deep down. Still, a memory stirred, just days earlier, a friend from California had reached out unexpectedly. A strong Christian, they hadn't known what I was going through when they first contacted me. When they later learned the truth, they offered compassion and a willingness to stand with me, even from afar. In that moment, I felt a nudge, a quiet urging: *Message them.* Reaching out seemed safe, safer than facing the silence alone.

Me: Can you please bear your testimony to me of God?

Friend: Now?

Me: Yes please, I am in crisis. I need help. I'm not well. I want to die and I'm ready to do it.

Friend: Lisa, all our trials are but a moment. Someday soon you will see that. You'll see that all of Earth life was worth it.

Me: I don't feel God anymore.

Friend: Lisa, even when you don't feel him, he is there. Remember the times you did feel him.

I sat quietly in my pain for just a few moments, trying to recall. I remembered I had felt the Spirit many times, but I couldn't remember the feeling now.

> **Friend:** I can see why you are in so much pain, Lisa. You have been through so much, and now this, this just sucks bad. Life hasn't been fair for you. I can understand why you want freedom from the pain.

The validation from these few lines of text drew a sob from deep in my chest. And from the same place in my chest, a minuscule amount of hope grew, just enough.

I'm ok, I'm ok, I'm going to be ok. The validation from my friend spread through me, a rush of relief, a reprieve from the hopelessness. I had just enough faith in their words and compassion that I started to trust what they said was true. I remembered times when I had a lot of faith and comfort. I missed that feeling.

> **Friend:** You are not alone; you are in good company of suffering. Our Savior on the Cross understands and is there for you. You will be able to feel his succor again. This awful pain will pass. I promise.

In that moment, I knew I wouldn't follow through with my original plan. *They're right, Lisa, you can do this. Don't make a permanent decision from a temporary feeling.*

Talking with them gave me just enough comfort to hold on for another day. There was no judgment, just gentle encouragement. Their words felt like a steady hand reaching across the distance, holding mine, reminding me I wasn't completely alone.

I was steady enough to drive myself home and crawl back into bed. As I lay there, my friend's words lingered, circling in my mind. Softly, almost under my breath, I prayed: *"Heavenly Father, if You are listening, please bless my family and help me in whatever way You know is best."* I didn't feel radiant with faith, far from it, but I prayed anyway. I remembered the umbilical-to-God experience from earlier that year, faint but still tucked deep inside me, just enough to keep me from letting go. Maybe, I thought, someday I'll feel that light again.

I decided I might as well see this through, I had already come this far. So, I pressed on, doing my best to cooperate with the Orange County district attorney's office. Even the logistics, like arranging plane tickets, felt overwhelming. I explained to the assistant investigator helping with travel that we were broke. Thinking mostly of my husband, and with no appetite of my own, I admitted I was on medical leave and really didn't have the money to cover food while I was there.

"We're already covering the extra cost of your husband's ticket and the hotel room. We can't do a food voucher too!" His tone was clipped, almost annoyed, as if my asking for food was unreasonable. I was too worn down to argue, but the sting hit deep. *Why does he sound angry at me for needing help?*

I tried once more, softer now, nearly begging. "We don't have money to eat out so many times. Could you please double-check?" He never did.

When I turned to victim services, hoping for support, I was told to use my own PTO (paid time off) from work. Because the crime was thirty-five years ago, they insisted I shouldn't need anything now, no help with rent, no lost wages support, no real assistance. Their words didn't just deny me resources; they shamed me. I questioned myself, *Am I wrong to still need help? Shouldn't I be over this by now?* They mentioned they could cover therapy, but the paperwork and red tape were so overwhelming that my therapist couldn't navigate it.

Inside something stirred, a small, fierce refusal that would not be silenced. I knew they were wrong; I deserved help and I wasn't going to let this go. With no energy left, I folded myself into waiting, conserving whatever strength I could until the case was over. But when I was able, I would make them answer for what they'd done and by demanding the accountability and resources I deserved.

Lisa,

I see how heavy your chest was in that parking lot, how you were drowning in a longing for relief and how that ache drowned out every other voice. Thank you for reaching out; that small, scared "please help" text mattered, it kept you here. You held on, and that is huge.

When hopelessness rushes in, slow it down; breathe deeply, count in and out, and tell yourself, "Not today. I will wait and check in again later." Do the exact thing you did before, reach out to one person and ask for one concrete thing, like "stay on the phone" or "pray with me." Small requests are easier to receive. Remember a single moment you felt held, a faint tether to God, a kind text, a steady hand, and let that memory prove that comfort can return. If a plan to harm yourself comes back, call local emergency services or a crisis line right away; you deserve immediate help and protection. When systems shame you, conserve your energy instead of shrinking; save your strength and later use it to demand the accountability and care you deserve. Try a tiny habit; write three words from that exchange with your friend and keep them where you'll see them in the morning. You are not alone, and I am proud of the fierce, small refusal to give up that stayed with you.

CHAPTER 47

The day of testimony finally arrived, and for once it hadn't been postponed. They flew us out the day before so I could be in court at the start of the morning.

On the way to the airport, we stopped at the Circle K for a drink. By then, any trace of hope had drained away, only a suffocating sense of doom remained. The pressure inside spilled out in sharp edges. I was curt with the clerk and glared at the slow people in line. *Who was I becoming?* Shame stuck in my throat as I walked away, carrying not just my purchase but the heavy disappointment of myself.

I didn't carry my usual concern for safety as the plane lifted into the sky. Whatever happened, happened. Gazing out the window, the desert stretched beneath me, stripped and bare. We had often driven this route on our trips to California, but seeing it from above was different, miles and miles of emptiness unfolding. The cars below looked like toys, inching along so slowly. From the cold, sterile perspective of the airplane, it was hard to remember what it felt like to actually be down there, hours of driving with my husband, talking easily, music playing, and the warmth of the desert air during rest stops.

When we landed at John Wayne Airport, Davis, the investigator, was waiting for us at the terminal exit. Alongside him would be the victim advocate. I dreaded her presence, she had offered me nothing, no real support, no answers to my pleas. But no one asked what I wanted. Perhaps she was there more for him than for me, so he wouldn't stand alone.

As I stepped off the plane, the weight pressed down hard; it felt like I was walking toward my own trial, my own sentencing. A question gnawed at me: what if I had just said no? Would that have been easier, or even worse? Deep down I knew the answer. I couldn't say no. If there was even the smallest chance my testimony could help stop Donald Gordon from harming another child, I had to endure this. Refusing would have left me with a heavier burden than testifying ever could.

My husband knew he would have to be the steady one while we were in Orange County. I had always hated being there, and now I was in the thick of it again, barely holding myself together. Sensing this, he took my hand firmly and led the way.

At the designated meeting point, Davis approached us. "Lisa Plumb?" he asked, extending his hand. I assumed he recognized me from the childhood photos he'd received. I shook his hand out of obligation, careful to keep it brief, hoping he wouldn't mistake my politeness for warmth.

When I noticed the compassion in Davis's expression, my guard lowered just slightly. "Nice to meet you, Lisa, and you must be Robert," he said warmly. Then the victim advocate extended her hand, her smile overly bright, as if we were meeting up to go to a party. "So, how's the weather in Phoenix, really, really hot, right? Well, welcome to Orange County! It must feel so nice to be here!"

It must feel nice to be here? Is she kidding? Does she think this is a vacation? I gave a sharp shake of my head, trying to brush off her comment. "What?" I spoke sharply, fixing her with a hard stare. She looked away without a response and she and Davis just turned and started walking.

I leaned toward my husband and muttered, "I want to punch her in the face." He squeezed my hand firmly, and in his grip I felt his silent understanding as we followed them toward Davis's big black SUV. The whole scene struck me as absurd: Investigator Davis, armed and serious, leading the way; the victim advocate, flitting along in her too-short skirt, belittling my hometown with her chirpy small talk. We slid into the back seat, enduring her chatter as her hands fluttered with every word. At least it distracted me from watching her skirt inch higher and higher up her thighs. Her eyes kept darting toward Davis. *Is she actually flirting with him?*

I turned to my husband after enduring a few minutes of this. "Keep. Her. Away. From. Me." That's all I could say. And I meant it. I wondered what her degree was in and how she could even manage getting a degree. How on earth did she qualify for such a job?

We pulled up to the courthouse, and Davis and the victim advocate escorted us to a witness waiting room. Soon the deputy district attorney entered, and we met face-to-face for the first time. He was energetic and seemed entertained by this scenario. He said, "I'm going to bring you the police report, but don't look at the folded-over pages. Before I do, though, tell me what you remember." I started to think about his request and what he must've missed from our phone interview, and before I could respond, he continued, "I guess Don Gordon showed you about the same amount of attention as he did the other girls and didn't see you that often."

I pulled my head back, brow furrowed, confusion flashing across my face. Why would he even say that? I spoke slowly when I realized he wanted an answer, "That's not how I remember it, unfortunately. He spent a lot of time with just me and Jody, and later, a lot of time with just me. I remember other girls being there, but not often, when I was there, and mostly in the beginning. I don't know how much time he spent with them. But when I was there, most of the time, it was just us three. It wasn't occasional, it was at least weekly."

As the words left my mouth, it felt like I was racing toward the edge of a cliff, powerless to stop. How awful to have to spell out that Don abused me so often. The shame and weight of it pressed in until I shook my head, wishing I could make it unspoken.

Panic swelled through me as images of Don's leering, his hands, his lectures flooded my mind. I wrapped my arms around myself, bracing against the memories of the countless times I'd been abused. What the deputy district attorney said to me didn't make sense. A lump rose in my throat, along with that same crawling, sick feeling I used to have whenever I was trapped with Don. *Why is he making me review this? He knows that, right? I forced out more explanation.* "Remember Don made me watch Pretty Baby over and over."

I dropped my head into my hands, nausea rising until I thought I might vomit. His confusion left me reeling. Why didn't he already know this? Davis and the victim advocate just sat there, silent observers, as I stumbled through my answers.

"And Don and Jody took me on a trip through three different states, just the three of us," I said, my voice tight. *Didn't I already tell him all of this? I* paused, then forced myself to continue. "I wish it hadn't been that way, but it was, right up until they got busted after visiting the photographer."

The deputy district attorney piped in, "Wow. you have a really good memory! You shared everything you said when you were a child, and it's in the police report, plus some. I'll leave you and Robert, and you can glance over it. We'll be back in a little while." He seemed so happy. *He already knew, but made me tell him like he didn't know!*

They left the room together, the door closing behind them. I turned to my husband, exasperated. "Why did he act like he didn't know what happened to me?" For a moment we sat in silence, the weight of it hanging heavy. Then my eyes drifted to the police report on the table.

I had no intention of following his instructions to avoid the folded-back pages. Instead, I opened the report from the very beginning. *This is about me.* How surreal. Then my eyes fell on the first folded page, and one line leapt off it; Jody said, "Lisa was his favorite victim."

I squeezed my eyes shut. *What?* Did Jody really say that to the police? She called me a victim. Jody, I had loved her. I thought she cared for me too. Near the end she seemed to hate me... maybe I wasn't imagining it.

A chill shot through me, spreading across my skin, then flipped into a hot flush. I stood, trying to shake off the disgust crawling in my core, the deep sadness pressing into my chest. *This is too much.*

The assistant DA played me, tested me. He knew I wasn't just some occasional victim of Don and Jody's. Why would he force me to prove it? I turned to Robert, "Why would he even ask when he knew what Jody said in the police report?" Robert just shook his head, lost in his own shock.

I dropped the report onto the table without finishing it. *Why would Jody say that?* The question echoed as I sat there, stunned.

The minutes dragged on. Then all three returned to the room as if in formation. I kept my head lowered, unwilling to meet the deputy district attorney's eyes or be pulled in by his polished words, delivered with the slickness of a car salesman. Rage bubbled under my skin. I wanted to scream at him, shake him, make him feel even a fraction of what I carried. But what good would that do? He would walk away untouched, free to test and manipulate me without consequence. And me? The cost of losing control would fall on me, and I had no strength for anything beyond the one task ahead; to testify.

The truth was crushing; there was nothing I could do about any of it. Nothing but testify. Endure this, get through it, and maybe afterward I could figure out what came next.

The victim advocate sat across from me on the other couch. When the deputy district attorney finally stopped talking, words I hadn't even absorbed, she drew in a careful breath. "I just want to apologize," she said gently. "I realize now I should have reached out to you more. I'm not used to working with victims whose cases are from thirty-five years ago, and I didn't anticipate your needs correctly. I'm sorry. I should have built a relationship with you."

My eyes widened, and I clenched my jaw to keep it from dropping. Her words surprised me, unexpected in their honesty. "Wow... thank you. I appreciate that." I meant it, but at the same time her apology had come too late to change much.

Once the deputy district attorney and Davis finished their back-and-forth, it was time for us to head to the hotel. The deputy district attorney sent us off with his trademark cheer; "Enjoy your afternoon and evening. I'll see you in the morning. Then we'll do this! Bye." The ever-cheerful deputy district attorney. He really did seem to enjoy his job. I couldn't tell if it was the prestige that energized him, or a genuine sense of justice. Either way, he was in it to win it.

Davis explained that he would take us to the hotel, check us in, and then leave us on our own until the next day when I would testify. His expressions always carried a trace of compassion. He was the calm one next to the district attorney's intensity, and that steadiness made me feel a little better about the whole situation. Even the victim advocate had finally shown a humble response to my distress, and while it didn't erase the hurt, it was enough for me to at least tolerate her now.

Davis drove us to the hotel, checked us in, and then walked us to our room, like he was babysitting us. After inspecting the room and bathroom, he laid out the expectations for the morning. "Be completely ready at 7:30 a.m. and don't be late. Meet me in the lobby at that time. Make sure you eat before 7:30." His tone was firm, as if he suspected we might bolt and he wasn't about to risk it. In that moment, the gentle Davis gave way to the tough, thorough one, checking off every item on his list. He looked directly at me, holding my gaze until I responded.

"Okay, we'll be there," I told him, and with that he left us for the day.

We hadn't been given a rental car, and I couldn't bear the thought of staying shut inside the hotel. My husband had already asked his brother and wife to pick us up, and they kindly offered to take us out to dinner. After we settled in, they arrived, and at my urging we drove straight to the beach.

As we pulled into the parking lot and stepped out, the steady rhythm of waves welcomed me. The cool, salty air wrapped around my skin, loosening something tight inside me. I breathed in deeply, filling my lungs with the scent of seaweed and sand, letting it settle me in a way nothing else could. The cries of gulls overhead, the sparkle of sunlight on water, the endless horizon, it was all so steady, so much bigger than me, than my fears, than the weight I carried.

I slipped off my shoes and let my feet sink into the damp sand. The ocean breeze brushed against my face, soft and constant, like a hand smoothing down my tension. I hoped the Pacific might carry away some of the heaviness I bore, washing it out to sea. Maybe it couldn't take it all, but here, with the tide stretching in and out, I felt a rare stillness. For the first time that day, I could simply breathe.

In the beach parking lot, a tsunami evacuation sign caught my eye. I stopped and stared at it, thinking of all the people in Indonesia who hadn't known to run when the earth shook and were overtaken by the massive wave. I knew better. If the ground shook, I would know to run. I knew what to do if I felt the earth shake, but what would I do tomorrow on the stand?

Lisa,

I see you on that plane, carrying dread like a stone in your chest. Even the simple act of buying a drink felt heavy with shame, and stepping off in Orange County felt like stepping into your own sentencing. You wondered if saying no might have been easier, yet deep down you knew the heavier burden would have been turning away while others remained at risk. That strength, even when wrapped in fear, was your quiet courage.

I know how much it stung to be mishandled by those meant to protect you, how their careless words and polished tones felt like tests instead of support. That shame was not yours to carry. You were being asked to revisit horrors no one should have had to endure even once. When the prosecutor made you repeat what he already knew, it wasn't because you were unclear, it was because the system often forgets survivors are people, not evidence.

But you held on. You reached for truth when it was painful, you endured the weight of old betrayals, and you stayed present enough to see what was real: your husband's steady hand, Davis's quiet compassion, even the victim advocate's late but genuine apology. And then, the ocean. You let the waves remind you there is something larger than all of this pain, steady and eternal. That moment at the shore showed you your strength: when the world tried to reduce you to evidence, you found a way to breathe again.

CHAPTER 48

"It's time!" the assistant DA announced sharply, then turned to Davis. "You didn't get my message? We need to be down there now!"

I shot up from my seat, relief and urgency colliding inside me. After hours of restless waiting, my body was more than ready to move. My heart pounded, a light dizziness spinning through me as we descended the narrow metal stairs toward the courtroom. They were grimy, rusted, littered with scraps of trash. The assistant district attorney glanced back with a quick apology. "Sorry about the stairs, they don't get much upkeep. Other than that, the job's great. Just do what comes naturally, answer my questions, follow my lead." He picked up his pace, I struggled to keep up, breathless and unsteady, the weight of what lay ahead pressed on every step.

Two flights down, the assistant district attorney lowered his voice. "Okay, I'll go in first and bring you in as soon as they give me the go-ahead." I pulled in a deep breath, desperate to steady myself. I didn't want to walk in drenched with sweat. My hand brushed across my forehead, dry, thankfully, but my heart still hammered without mercy. I looked around, noticing the people lining the benches outside the courtroom, their eyes fixed on me. When I met their gaze, they quickly looked away. Why were there so many of them out here?

The doors swung open. "Witness Lisa B., are you ready?"

The assistant district attorney turned toward me with brisk energy. "Okay, here we go."

I'm going to see him. He's going to see me. It's okay, Lisa. It doesn't matter.

He led the way into the courtroom, stopping just a few feet inside. The short distance I walked behind him stretched out endlessly, every step heavy as though I were crossing miles.

Before proceeding further, I raised my hand as instructed. The clerk said, "Do you solemnly state that the evidence you're about to give in the case now pending before this court shall be the truth, the whole truth, and nothing but the truth, so help you God?"

After the swearing in I paused at the back of the courtroom. My eyes scanned the courtroom, the jury to my right, the judge straight ahead and to my left, in front of me, there he was. His straight brown hair hadn't changed much in thirty-five years, and just touched his broad thick shoulders. It was him.

Don.

He was in a wheelchair. An Indian woman sat next to him. Was she his attorney? A woman! *Of course,* I thought, shaking my head. He shifted, angling his head to catch me from the corner of his eye. A wave of red-hot anger flowed over me. It surprised me. *I could run up behind him and put him in a guillotine hold and choke him until his neck broke.* I felt kind of proud of my response. I wasn't scared.

I was *enraged.*

I would not get away with choking him before the bailiffs pulled me off of him. What a scene that would be! I could do it though.

The bailiff said to me as he pointed, "Have a seat right up there in the witness box in that black chair."

I had to walk in front of the jury. *Don can see my back now.* I hurried to the witness box and looked at as many of the jury as I could. They didn't look back at me. I sat down. Everything seemed in slow motion. I felt Don's stare before I saw him. The intrusion felt familiar. *It's ok Lisa, you are safe now.* To my surprise, I immediately looked right at Don, dead in the eyes, impressed by the courage that rose up in me. He didn't turn away.

What a jerk! I refused to be the one to look away first. I held my gaze, steady and unblinking, staring straight through him. He broke into a smile, rocking slightly in his chair, and for a sickening moment it looked as though he might reach toward me. He mouthed something like, *Hey, come on, good to see you Lisa*, like he was greeting an old friend. Did he really not grasp why I was here? *Idiot.*

The seconds stretched, thick and heavy, until finally his attorney nudged him. Only then did his eyes flick away, conceding the stare. I won! Victory charged through me like an electrical current. For the first time, I overpowered him. Yes!

His attorney leaned in, whispering, "Don't look at her." It only made the scene worse for him; I watched him squirm, enjoying watching him trying to avoid looking at me. *How does it feel to be the one squirming now?* I was steady, rooted. I felt strong. I imagined I had lasers coming out of my eyes, and they were disintegrating him.

A distant voice got increasingly louder. "Lisa.. Lisa… Lisa, are you ok?" I came to the present moment and looked at the assistant district attorney, who was positioned off to the side so as to neither interrupt my staring contest or block the jury's view. He repeated my name with an extra shocked and distressed tone. "Are you ok? Do you need to take a break?" Under the assistant district attorney's mask of distress was the gleam of triumph.

"Uh. No. I'm okay."

"Are you sure? We can take a break if you need to." And there was the attorney, in his element, on stage. It was fascinating to watch him work. A surge of energy rushed through me, sharpening the room into focus. The courtroom seemed brighter, crisper, and I felt myself sitting taller, lifted higher in my seat. I wasn't crying, at least not yet, remembering Peter's earlier suggestion, "However you respond is okay." I knew what he meant, hoping I showed something to help the case.

Peter-Q: Hi, Lisa.

Lisa-A: Hi.

Q: Do you know of a man by the name of Donald Gordon?

A: Yes.

Q: And how did you first come into contact with the man named Donald Gordon?

A: He showed up at my house one day. And my sister went on a trip to Indiana to visit our grandmother on a train and apparently Donald Gordon and his partner in crime befriended her, and they found out that they all went to nudist camps before. And apparently I was volunteered up, so they came to my house. I was 11 years old and I was told to go with them to a nudist camp whether I liked it or not.

Q: So let me step back for a second. Your birthday was May 16 of 1968, you were 11 years old, is this approximately 1979, 1980?

A: Yeah.

Q: Okay. And you were first introduced to Mr. Gordon through your sister? Do you see someone in the courtroom today that you recognize and identify as Mr. Gordon?

I studied Don, then lifted my eyes, trying to merge the man before me with the image I had carried from thirty-five years ago. I knew it was him, yet my mind stumbled over the contrast. Back in the shelter home, I had forgotten his face for a time, but now the memory returned. He looked so different, aged and diminished, though his hair was still the same. He was an old man now. I thought he was old even then. He was forty when I was eleven. Now he must be seventy-six? Why is it that some people live so long while others, good people, have their lives cut short?

A: Yes.

Q: Could you point to him and identify where he is in the courtroom?

A: Right there. (witness indicating.)

Q: And the respondent -- and who else was with him?

A: Jody Jones. Jody Gordon.

Q: So, your mother let you go with respondent and Jody to a nudist camp?

A: Yes.

Q: And where were you living at the time?

A: Riverside, California.

Q: So, after that first initial meeting where you went to the Glen Eden nudist camp, when you got to the nudist camp, if you recall, what, if anything, happened while you were there?

A: Well, just initially when I first got in the truck with Don and Jody, they immediately let me smoke cigarettes. Before that I wasn't able to smoke in front of adults. So. We started smoking and then we just went there and --

Q: So, when you got to the nudist camp, did everyone get nude?

A: Yeah. It's required if you go to Glen Eden.

Q: What was the frequency with which you saw the respondent after you first went to Glen Eden, that first time that you met him?

A: About every weekend.

Q: And how is it that you saw the respondent every weekend?

A: He drove up to riverside to pick me up.

Q: So, he personally would drive and pick you up?

A: Yes.

Q: And --

A: And any time that I wanted to -- my mother wasn't a very a good mother and Don Gordon knew that and would point that out. And whenever I had an argument he said to give him a call and he would come and pick me up.

The court reporter's eyes met mine as I paused. She leaned forward slightly and whispered, "Would you like some water?" In her gaze I felt more than an offer, it carried the message; *I'm here with you. You are not alone. We feel compassion for you. I'm sorry this happened.* My chest tightened with quiet gratitude. I thanked her, hoping she could feel how much I meant it. Then Peter carried on.

Q: And did you call him when you would get in arguments with your mother?

A: Sometimes.

Q: And he would come and pick you up?

A. He would drive from Santa Ana to riverside to pick me up.

Q: And then where would you go from there?

A: Back to his apartment in Santa Ana. Its own little nudist camp.

Q: You just said his apartment was its own little nudist camp? What do you mean by that?

A: As soon as you walk in the door, your clothes came off.

Q: And this is when you were 11 years old?

A: Uh-huh, yes.

Q: Were you the only child around that age that there taking your clothes off?

A: Sometimes no, sometimes yes.

Q: Over the course -- well, you said you went there almost every weekend. For how long did you go approximately every weekend to the respondent's house from Riverside to or his apartment in Santa Ana from when you first met him until it stopped?

A: Until I was 13 years old.

Q: So about a year and a half to two years?

A: Yes.

Q: How often -- you said that every time you went into the apartment, the clothes came off. How often were other children there with you when the clothes came off?

A: I would say 50 percent of the time, although near the end it seemed like it was just me.

Q: And what would happen after everyone took their clothes off?

A: Well, I was given free access to alcohol, and a lot of times marijuana, Atari. I played Atari. Don liked to watch *Pretty Baby* with me.

Q: What was the movie?

A: The movie was *Pretty Baby* with Brooke Shields.

Q: What did that involve?

A: That was about a 12-year-old girl who was raised in a brothel and -- well, she wasn't 12 yet, but when she was 12 her virginity was auctioned off to the highest bidder, and, in fact, they showed Brooke Shields' naked body and they show her having sex basically for the first time.

Q: And the respondent liked to watch this movie?

A: Yeah, a lot.

Q: You say a lot. How often did he watch it? If you remember?

A: I just -- sure we watched it at least, I don't know, 10 or 20 times.

Q: 10 or 20 times just with you?

A: Yeah, just with me.

Q: Did you ever see pornography?

A: Yes.

I gripped the edges of the witness stand, steadying myself as my eyes swept the room, the jury, the judge, and finally Don. *I will tell them everything you did, Donald Gordon.*

Lisa,

I see you walking into that courtroom, every step echoing with thirty-five years of memory. You knew he would be there, but nothing could prepare you for that first sight. However you would have reacted would have been fine. You found strength from deep inside and met his eyes. You didn't look away first. For the first time, he was the one squirming. You reclaimed your power.

Testifying can't be rehearsed into predictability. You never truly know how your body, voice, and heart will respond when the past is summoned into the present. That's why a survivor needs a strong support system, not only at home, but right there in the courtroom.

Sometimes that support comes in small moments, the bailiff's calm instructions, the court reporter's quiet offer of water, the compassion in her eyes. These gestures may seem minor, but they tell the nervous system; You are not alone. They provide validation in a place that can otherwise feel cold and clinical.

When court staff show empathy, they help a person heal. They create an environment where your voice can be steady because you feel seen and respected. This kind of compassion doesn't erase the pain, but it

291

can soften the edges and help a survivor leave the stand with their dignity intact.

You were more than a witness that day, Lisa. You were a woman standing in her own courage, telling the truth, fully, clearly, and without turning away. You are doing awesome!

CHAPTER 49

Pornographic images flashed through my mind, tangled with the memory of Don's insistent voice. My breath hitched as I was pulled back into the nightmare, trapped with no place to turn, no way to look away. Then, Peter's voice broke through:

Q: And who showed you the pornography?

A: The respondent.

Q: Okay. Now, you had said that your mother was not a good mother?

A: No, she wasn't.

Q: She allowed you to go every weekend to the respondent's apartment in Santa Ana?

A: She wanted me to go.

Q: Why do you say that?

A: She told me to go. And Don Gordon would point out to me how my mother was crazy and make great attempts indoctrinating me as to why what he was doing and wanting to do was good. And also pointing out that my father wasn't a real father. That if I had a real father, I'd would want to have sex with him. I remember asking Don, does that mean you want me to call you daddy?

Q: What did he say?

A: He snickered. He laughed. He thought it was funny.

Q: Is it fair to say you didn't have a good relationship with him [your father] either?

A: That's fair to say. As Don and Jody would point out how terrible my parents were, which was convenient for them.

Q: Why do you say that?

A: Well, because I was a desperate child and apparently that works out better for perpetrators.

Q: Ma'am, I'm going to show you a photograph. Do you recognize the person in the photograph?

A: Yes, I do.

Q: Who is it?

A: Me.

Q: Do you remember your approximate age in that picture?

A: 12.

Q: And is this in that same time period around November of 1980 that you were continuing to spend virtually every weekend with the respondent and his girlfriend or wife Jody?

A: Yes.

Q: Did photos ever get taken of you when you were nude?

A: Yes.

Q: How often?

A: It's hard for me to really remember that. I just know that we were always naked in the apartment and there just seems to be a camera around.

Q: So when you say we were always naked, are you referring to both yourself, the respondent and Jody?

A: Correct.

Q: At any time did physical contact start between you and the respondent?

A: Yes.

Q: And in what way?

A: How did it start?

Q: Yes. Do you remember the first time it happened?

A: Well, I remember one day I was in shopping with Don, and he told me that my sister said I wanted to have sex with him, and I said "What? No, I don't." No. I was petrified. I was terrified. And he like said, "It's okay." You know, and I was very freaked out, very upset and I asked him not to tell Jody because I thought she would be upset. And he, from what I remember he agreed not to, but as soon as Jody got in the car he said, "Lisa wants to have sex with me," and I was -- I don't really have the words, but I was very upset. And she said, "Well, that's okay. That's fine." but I didn't and I didn't say that. I didn't say that I wanted to have sex with him.

Q: Was there ever a point in time where the respondent put any part of his body on or near any part of your body in an inappropriate or sexual way?

A: Yes.

Q: Do you recall when that first happened, not the specific date but the first incident?

A: I believe I remember the first time.

Could I say it out loud? My heart dropped at the thought. It was too ugly, I felt grotesque. Every ear in the room was straining to hear. Peter nodded encouragingly. A man in the jury furrowed his brow. The judge stared forward, still as a statue. Don crossed his arms, a silent threat.

And then, something shifted. Suddenly, I could speak it. I could say any-thing if it meant keeping him locked away. My breath came uneven, shud-dering instead of steady, but I pushed through. The words spilled out, the truth laid bare, every twisted, perverse thing Don had done to a broken child.

Q: Did that happen on more than one occasion?

A: Yes, it did.

Q: After that, after that first sexual interaction with respondent and Jody, did he include -- well, separate from the other times that you engaged in that type of sexual interplay with the two of them, was there any other type of sexual conduct that the respondent had with you?

A: Well, yeah. He wanted me to willingly give up my virginity to him, so there was a lot of discussion how that could happen, why it would be a good thing and it would actually be, you know, sort of him doing me a favor.

I explained for all to hear how Don, on many occasions, attempted to con-vince me to have intercourse with him. He had been animated and vulgar, gesturing with his hands and arms, pulling me to him, mimicking the act with me. All the while claiming he would be performing a laborious act, doing me a favor, and that I should be happy he would be the first, you know someone who really cared about me. Be grateful for his stepping up. He'd even pretend to wipe sweat from his brow as if he just strained himself from a hard day's labor in the heat, mimicking what a chore it would be for him.

The room went dead still as I described the times he pulled me to the couch, put on the movie *Pretty Baby*, and groped me while making me watch the movie with him. Sometimes when he was frustrated that I didn't act grate-ful for his attention and give the go-ahead, he would call me a sissy. Then he'd grab Jody and show me how it was done. He always made sure I was watching, or I'd be in trouble.

Q: Is that something he did frequently?

A: Yeah.

Q: Did you ever go on any trips with the respondent and Jody?

A: Yeah.

Q: I am sorry to interrupt you. But separate from him driving and picking you up and bringing you to Santa Ana, separate from coming to Orange County or being brought back home to Riverside?

A: Don and Jody took me on a three state trip to Arizona, Nevada, and Utah, just the three of us.

Q: How old were you at the time?

A: I was probably past 12, as I had already, I believe, I had already started my period which I started at Don and Jody's apartment, of which Don was very vulgar about that.

Q: How do you mean?

As I described Don's comments and gestures about my first menstrual cycle, I glanced at the jury. They all looked shocked. An Asian man looked like he might get sick, the color drained from his face. A blonde woman widened her eyes in horror. An older man's face scrunched in disgust. *They won't look at me.* Any embarrassment was overpowered by my newfound strength to tell the truth about Don. So many times, I drowned in shame over this, now he would drown in the shame.

Q: And it was after that that you went on this trip?

A: Yes.

Q: How long was the trip going through the three states?

A: Seemed like forever, but I think it was about three weeks.

The Court: Mr. Peter, I think we need to take our break now for lunch.

Mr. Peter: Yes, your honor.

The Court: Please remember it's your duty not to converse among yourselves or with anyone else on any subject connected with the trial, form or express an opinion until the case is submitted to you. Report back, please, 1:30. See you then.

(whereupon the jurors exit the courtroom.)

I left the courtroom feeling proud of myself and surprisingly okay, but had no idea that while I was eating lunch with my husband and Davis, Don's attorney was already at the bench, plotting to dismantle my entire testimony.

Lisa,

Lisa, you did something extraordinary in that courtroom. You spoke aloud the very things that once silenced and shamed you. Don twisted reality and tried to convince you that his cruelty was somehow a gift. He relied on your desperation for love, your need for family, and the confusion of childhood to keep you quiet. But in front of strangers, a jury, and even him, arms crossed in threat, you found your voice.

Your breath shook when you spoke. Your voice carried not only the truth of what happened, but also the proof that he no longer had power over your silence. You turned shame inside out. Where once it drowned you, now it was his to carry.

It is important to remember that perpetrators thrive when children feel unseen, unsupported, and desperate for care. They deliberately exploit vulnerability. By telling the truth, you not only protected your younger self, but you stood as a shield for other children who might have been harmed.

You are not grotesque; you are brave. You reclaimed what was stolen, your voice, your strength, and your right to be believed.

Hold this close; courage does not erase trembling hands or shuddered breaths. Courage is speaking anyway. And you did!

CHAPTER 50

I met my husband's eyes, and he pulled me into a tight embrace. "Good job, Lisa. You're doing great." Davis stood beside us, steady and present, then gestured toward his vehicle as we stepped into the parking lot. "Let's go get some lunch." His voice was warm, his expression kind, but beneath it, I sensed his unspoken role; making sure I was cared for, and making sure I came back to finish what I had started.

"Okay, Davis, let's go." Energy surged through me, fierce and undeniable. The weight was gone. No chains, no mud pulling me under. I felt sharp, awake, reborn. I had emptied out pieces of the nightmare, and instead of fear, I was hungry to say more after lunch.

"You know what, Davis? This is alright after all. Did you see the judge? He looked at me with compassion. The jury, horrified. And the bailiff? He looked like he might either vomit or take Gordon out himself."

Giddiness surged through me, but it carried the heat of fire. For the first time, I saw them all standing with me, surrounding him, forcing the truth into the light. Don couldn't twist it, couldn't silence me, couldn't stop the record from capturing every word. I felt the power shift. I didn't want it to end.

As we pulled up to the restaurant, I wondered if Don had ever imagined this moment, sitting in a courtroom, forced to hear every vile detail of what he had done to me. Maybe that's why he always insisted the *courts* ruined his children, not him. He used to tell me they were fine until the system interfered, that the process itself was what damaged them. It was his way of brainwashing me, warning me never to testify.

But his plan failed.

I was no longer the silenced child he preyed upon. As an adult, I could finally expose him. Every word I spoke in that courtroom was for Little Lisa, the girl who had been forced to carry his secrets alone.

Inside Davis's favorite restaurant, I noticed something shift in his face, his compassion sharpened by a trace of sadness. I leaned toward him and asked softly, "Are you okay, Davis?"

"Are you okay?" he asked gently.

"I finally feel like all of this was worth it, that it's going to be okay. We're on the same team, and I feel really good about that."

But even as I spoke, my concern shifted to him. How did he carry this weight day after day? The endless stories of trauma, the survivors he had to protect, the darkness he had to face alongside us. I worried about what it cost him. I wanted to hand him tools, to tell him what I now knew about vicarious trauma and how it wears people down. Instead, I asked, "Davis, how do you cope with all this stress?"

"Oh, I drink," he admitted with a half-smile. "My wife drags me to church sometimes, but I just go for her." Then he went on, "It's actually a good job, what I'm doing now. I had some health problems, had to leave patrol. This is easier for me."

He asked about Arizona, sharing his own hopes of retiring there one day. A quiet closeness settled between us, the kind that comes only after walking together through something heavy. Part of me wanted to ease his burden, to be the friend who made it okay for him the way he was making it okay for me. But I knew the truth, after the verdict, our paths would almost certainly part. For now, though, I chose to relish the moment, grateful for this bond with my team, and for the rare safety of not being alone in the fight.

I ordered the cheapest item on the menu, knowing we were paying for ourselves. My appetite was still hollow, but I forced down a few bites. When the check arrived, Davis slid it toward himself. "This one's on me," he said.

Robert and I exchanged a glance, uncertain. Davis caught it and added with a grin, "Next time we eat together, you can cover it."

The simple kindness disarmed us. Our walls dropped another notch, and we accepted. As we stepped back into the sunlight and headed toward his

SUV, I felt a surge of unity. We weren't just three people leaving a restaurant, we were warriors, walking side by side, preparing for the final battle.

Lisa,

I see you leaving the courtroom lighter than you've felt in years. The weight that had pressed you down was replaced by the strength of having spoken your truth and been heard. You caught the compassion in the judge's eyes, the shock on the jury's faces, and the quiet solidarity in the bailiff's stance, clear signs that the wrong done to you was seen and understood. Don understood too, his squirming reflecting his powerlessness. It's ok that that felt good.

Davis walked beside you, not only as an investigator but as an ally. His steady presence and genuine care helped create safety in a place that could have been unbearable. When someone in that role listens and treats you with respect, it builds the trust needed to share your story fully.

That afternoon, the lunch you shared wasn't just a break, it was part of the healing. The gesture of covering the meal and speaking openly created a sense of partnership, a reminder that in this fight, you had people in your corner.

You returned to court not as the silenced child you once were, but as a woman with a team around her. And Little Lisa could feel, perhaps for the first time in such a setting, that she wasn't alone.

CHAPTER 51

While Davis, Robert, and I shared our quiet celebratory lunch, another battle was unfolding back at the courthouse. Don's attorney had pressed her way before the judge, insisting my testimony be thrown out. She argued it was inadmissible because I had described incidents not captured in the original police report.

Peter stood his ground. He reminded the court that I was the victim, that my memories and experiences carried weight even decades later. The judge agreed, ruling there was no legal precedent to support her attempt. She was out of line. My testimony stood, relevant, valid, and now officially part of the record.

Davis pulled into the employee lot, sliding us in among rows of police vehicles. He hopped out quickly and opened my door. "Are you ready?"

"I sure am. Thank you."

As we made our way back toward the courthouse, Robert's hand gripped mine, steady and strong. I squeezed back, fueled by his quiet strength. My pulse quickened, I was charged, ready to step back onto the stand. In my mind, I repeated the details I still needed to share, truths I had never been able to speak before. This was my chance, and I wasn't about to let a single word slip away.

As we stood outside the courtroom, Peter came over and warned, "Lisa, Don will be passing through here. Do you want to stay or move to where he won't come by?"

Before I could answer, Don rolled past, only six feet away. We instinctively stepped back. Robert broke the silence, his voice steady but edged with contempt. "I'm sure he doesn't need that wheelchair. It's all for show." Then, shaking his head, he added, "The way he squirms in his seat and reacts to your testimony, he looks like he can move just fine."

I leaned toward Robert and whispered, "You notice him squirming?"

"Oh, totally," he replied without hesitation. "He's so uncomfortable with what you're exposing."

A smile broke across my face. "You see that?"

"Yes, big time."

In that moment, I flashed back to Little Lisa, sitting frozen on Don's couch, confused and abandoned, her voice stolen. All those times I had squirmed, helpless against his harm. He had all the power then. But now, it was different. Now *he* was the one squirming, on display, powerless, exposed. I silently promised my younger self, *I've got you. He doesn't get to win anymore.*

I drew in a deep breath and pictured wrapping Little Lisa in the kind of hug she always deserved, safe, strong, and unbreakable.

Stepping back onto the stand felt like a relief. I could return to business, finish what I came to do. As I walked toward the black chair, the jury avoided my eyes, but I felt their presence with me, my silent warrior tribe, bearing witness, recording every horror. *Thank you, Jury.*

The judge turned, his gaze steady, his voice carrying a softness. "Are you okay? Are you able to resume?"

Compassion from the bench, the very face of justice, was asking if I was ready to keep going, ready to continue exposing evil. And I was.

"Yes, Your Honor. Thank you," I said aloud, steady and sure.

Inside, I turned toward Little Lisa with a smile. *I've got you, honey. You're safe now.*

> **The Court:** All right. The record will reflect the jury is back. The witness is on the witness stand, still under oath. Proceed.

> **Mr. Peter:** Thank you, your honor.

Direct examination (resumed)

By Mr. Peter:

Q: Lisa, when we broke off you had just started talking about a three-state trip from Arizona, Nevada and Utah, do you recall that's what we were talking about?

A: Uh-huh, yes.

My eyes fluttered as I drew in a steady breath. I pressed my feet firmly into the floor, anchoring myself to the moment. My gaze went right over Don's bowed head and landed on my husband, sitting just behind him to the left, a lifeline. For a moment it felt surreal, like I was slipping into a dream. *Am I really here? Am I truly staring down Don Gordon? Is he... afraid?*

He had been instructed by his own defense not to look at me. How many times had I wished for that, to have his eyes off me? Now, all my protectors stood in place, and he sat powerless. I could feel his urge to shut me down, to punish me, but that power was gone.

I was the one in the power seat now.

I am ready.

Q: Okay. Do you remember during the course of that trip if you stopped and stayed anywhere?

A: One of the places was a nudist camp in Nevada. Also, we went to the respondent's parents' house in southern Utah, Paragonah, Utah.

I had memorized that weird name, never forgetting it all these years.

Q: You went to -- I'm sorry. You went to the respondent's parents' house where?

I didn't know it at the time, but Gordon's plan was to "parole" to Paragonah Utah. He had told his team that he had never perpetrated abuse there.

304

And here I was exposing his lies, ruining his plans! I drew in another deep breath and pressed on, determined to keep pace with Peter.

A: Paragonah, Utah.

Ms. Lozin: At this point I am going to object. As to relevance, as to anything that happened in Utah.

I remembered that the out-of-state abuse hadn't been included in Don's original charges, California had no jurisdiction over what happened beyond its borders. Now, his defense attorney was trying to block me from speaking of it again.

Go ahead. Try.

The Court: Counsel, approach for a minute.

The Court: Overruled.

Yes! Good call Judge. Finally, a ridiculous loophole is being closed.

Q: So, the three of you stayed in the camper the entire time you were there?

A: Yes.

Q: And how long did you visit the parents in Paragonah, Utah? Approximately is fine.

A: Couple days.

Q: No one inquired who you were or why you were with them while you were staying there?

A: I do remember Don used to say that more than a mouthful is a waste when referring to my chest, and I said that once in the presence of his parents and I got in trouble for that.

Q: Trouble by who?

A: Don.

Q: What did he say?

A: And Jody. "shush. Don't -- why are you saying that?"

A: We also stayed in Flagstaff, and my main memory from Flagstaff was I found myself alone in the camper trailer in KOA campground very drunk. I don't know what happened before. I was just conscious all of sudden and Don and Jody weren't in the camper, so I stepped out into the campground and obviously I was -- apparently I was very drunk and making a scene, which I got in trouble by Don and Jody as well, that I would step out of the camper so drunk.

Q: You went to respondent's home weekend after weekend over the course of a year and half to two years was your earlier testimony, correct?

A: Correct, yes.

Q: Why did you keep going back?

Ms. Lozin: Objection, your honor, relevance.

The Court: sustained.

Mr. Peter: All right. May I have one moment, Your honor?

The Court: Sure.

Q: Is there any other sexual conduct that you engaged in or witnessed as it relates to the respondent that we haven't already discussed?

A: Yes.

I laid it bare for the entire courtroom, every horrified face taking it in, how Don invented twisted "games" that revolved around sex acts. On that trip, he didn't stop. He created new games that we hadn't played before.

Mr. Peter: Okay. Thank you, ma'am. No more questions.

The Court: Okay.

Ms. Lozin: Your honor, I have no questions of this witness. Thank you.

The Court: Thank you, miss. You can step down.

Mr. Peter: Thank you, your honor. The people call our next witness; may I step out to get her?

The Court: Sure.

Mr. Peter: Thank you.

That's it? I wasn't done. My list wasn't finished. I felt abruptly shut down, silenced when there was still so much left to tell. Begrudgingly, I stepped down and followed Davis, who rose as I moved toward him.

Out in the corridor, the words tumbled out of me. "Davis, I had more to say, why did he cut me off like that?"

"I don't know," he said, steady but gentle. "But you did good. You did real good. Hopefully, we all did enough to put that man away. We'll find out soon enough."

Lisa,

You walked back into that courtroom, empowered like never before, ready to give every detail Little Lisa never got to say. You were grounded, determined, and prepared to finish your list. Then, just like that, it was over. You hadn't finished. That's the part no one prepares you for: sometimes the legal system moves on before your heart is ready.

Defense attorneys often try to limit a victim's words, not because they doubt the truth, but because creating doubt is their job. They challenge memory, twist motives, and push to exclude anything that might strengthen the case against their client. These strategies can echo the silencing of abuse, leaving survivors feeling dismissed or unfinished.

But, Little Lisa, you were not silenced this time. You stood before him, the jury, and the judge and told the truth about what he did. You were believed. Every detail you shared became part of the record, part of dismantling his power.

It's normal to grieve what you couldn't say, but your courage isn't measured by getting every word out, it's measured by showing up, speaking your truth when it once had been stolen from you, and refusing to turn away.

Even when cut short, you walked out with more than you realize: your words heard, your presence felt, and your power reclaimed. You did so good.

CHAPTER 52

"Robert, Peter just stopped asking me questions, then dismissed me!" The words spilled out, sharp and fast, as tears welled. I swiped them away, my face burning with the fury of being cut off. "I wasn't ready! I had more to say."

Davis leaned closer, steady and calm. "Do you want to go back in and hear the other victim's testimony?"

"Yes! I can do that?" My trembling hands clasped together. "Let's go."

Davis, Robert, and I slipped back into the audience seats.

Now I had the chance to watch Don squirm while another victim testified against him. She was the very woman Orange County had once asked me to testify for, back when I was in my twenties. That was the start of their unexpected calls to me, and here she was now, on the stand, speaking after me. Our strange connection hung between us, though we had never met.

As I watched her testify, I silently dared Don to glance back at me. I wanted him to see my husband sitting beside me. I wanted him to know I wasn't alone anymore, that I had people who cared for me, who would stand between us, who would protect me now.

I drew in the scene around me. Every sound amplified. My eyes moved across the jury, fixing each face in memory in case I ever passed them on the street. I wanted to thank them, one by one, for the service they were giving. Gratitude swelled in my chest, for the bailiff's steady protection, and for the judge, cloaked in his black robe, carrying himself with quiet authority. In that moment, I believed he cared, not just about the case, but about me, about us, about justice.

As this victim described the abuse she endured, my mind drifted to Jody. How did she escape being charged for what she did to this victim? Years earlier, back in Apple Valley, I had told the police that Jody was a full participant, that she should have been held accountable as a registered sex offender, but she wasn't. When I searched Megan's Law, I was certain she would have at least two strikes, yet nothing appeared. Hearing this victim mention Jody in her testimony only deepened the ache. Jody had harmed so many, and still, she was never prosecuted for her.

I felt profoundly grateful that this witness had been willing to stand beside me in keeping Don behind bars. Though she and I never spoke, her mother found me afterward in the parking lot. With earnest eyes, she said, "Thank you for being here, for helping us keep him from hurting anyone else."

Her words lingered. For so long, I had carried the weight of this fight as if it belonged to me alone. But in that moment, I realized we were bound together, two survivors of different versions of the same nightmare. I felt less alone. This wasn't just my battle; it was something bigger. Together, we were making sure Don would never harm another child again.

I thanked her, my voice catching. "I'm so grateful we were able to stand as a team. Now we wait for the jury to decide his fate. No matter what, we've done everything we could." I hugged her tightly, then climbed into Davis's SUV with Robert, carrying with me a small but steady measure of peace.

We pulled out of the courthouse parking lot, heading straight for the airport to catch our flight. As I gazed out the window, my eyes softened. Gratitude welled up for all who were involved. I wished everyone could feel my gratitude.

It had all come together. After so much fear and strain, I finally felt relief. My team, our team, had turned something unbearable into a moment of strength. "We did it!" I blurted out to Davis.

"No, you did it," he replied. For the first time, I saw his face ease into peace. He actually looked happy.

"No, Davis, we did it. Thank you. I feel so much better now."

As we drove on, I turned to the window. Orange County, once the place I dreaded most, no longer looked quite so heavy.

After a stretch of quiet, Davis spoke. "Lisa, you should write a book."

I turned toward him, startled. "What? Really? Why do you say that?"

He hesitated, eyes on the road. "I don't know... I just think you should."

I let my curiosity rest, not wanting to press Davis for more. The truth was, I had thought about writing a book before, but the idea scared me. Out of the corner of my eye, I saw Robert smile wide and nod. He'd heard this suggestion from others, too. Still, it felt strange to hear it now, dropped into the silence as if out of nowhere.

Deep down, writing a book had always felt like something I was meant to do, yet I kept putting it off. The impressions to write came often, gentle but persistent nudges I couldn't ignore. I knew I could only do it if God wanted me to, and if He carried me through it.

I said, "If I write a book, Davis, will you read it?"

He responded with a smile, "I will read it if you sign it!"

"Okay. Deal. I will let you know when it's ready. Then I'll give you a signed copy, and pay you back for lunch by taking you out to dinner."

Davis nodded firmly. "Deal! I look forward to it."

We pulled up to the departing flights, and Davis quickly jumped out of the SUV to open my door.

"Davis, what happens next?" I asked.

As he lifted our luggage from the back, he explained that the trial would probably continue for a couple more weeks, after which the jury would be tasked with reaching a verdict. Though I felt lighter than I had in days, I knew the verdict could trigger me. I wanted to be in a safe place, at home, when the decision came down. The thought haunted me; Don could still walk free, even after all this.

I told Davis my concern and asked if he would let me know when the jury went into deliberations so I could be ready. He met my eyes and reassured me, "Absolutely. I totally understand. No problem, I can do that for you."

"Thank you, Davis. I know I've been raw emotionally. It's confusing even to me. I've just had such a hard time lately. I'm sorry if I caused you any stress."

He nodded with quiet understanding.

"I'll probably be back at work by the time the verdict comes in," I admitted. "I'm not sure how I'll react. I hope I'll be stronger by then, but I want to be prepared."

"I'll let you know when the jury goes into deliberation, Lisa," he promised. "And when the verdict comes, I'll tell you the results myself."

He shook our hands and wished us well. To me, Davis wasn't just an investigator, he had become a true ally, even a friend. "Same to you, Davis. Thanks again," I said.

As Robert and I walked away, Davis called out just loud enough for us to hear; "You did it, Lisa. You did it."

Lisa,

I see you leaving that courthouse, relief softening the edges of the last few weeks. You had faced him, spoken the truth, and stood alongside another survivor who braved the cost of testifying. Her mother's words in the parking lot "Thank you for being here and helping us keep him from hurting anyone else" were more than polite gratitude. They were a deep acknowledgment from someone who knew exactly what it took. And what cost you paid.

Support in a trial doesn't just come from one person, it's a network. The compassion of the judge, the steady watch of the bailiff, the attentiveness of the jury, the persistence of your attorney, and the consistency of an investigator like Davis all worked together to keep you safe, heard, and believed. That kind of care doesn't erase the difficulty, but it makes the process bearable. It gives you room to tell your story without being crushed by it.

When care is present, it builds trust, fosters healing, and strengthens resilience long after the trial ends.

You walked away that day with more than a completed testimony, you carried the proof that Little Lisa was no longer standing alone. You had a team, and together, you turned the most dreaded place into one of your strongest victories. I'm so proud of you!

CHAPTER 53

The sun was sinking low behind us as we landed in Phoenix. Warm evening air wrapped around me, and to my surprise, a smile spread across my face. For the first time in over a month, I felt hope. *I will be okay.*

The emotional high carried me for a couple of days before I eased back into the question of what came next. Not long ago, right before the trial, I had been certain everything, including myself, was ruined. The words *I am ruined* had played on repeat in my mind as I waited for court. But now, that refrain had shifted. I no longer felt doomed beyond repair. In its place was the quiet possibility of healing. Slowly, my energy returned. My appetite stirred again. Determination began to take root. I was ready to make a fresh start.

Still, the waiting for the trial to conclude was an ordeal. I tried to distract myself as I eased back into work, but the first day back was thick with shame and dread. The walk to my boss's office felt impossibly long. I imagined every colleague already knew what had happened, what I had said, what I had endured.

I coached myself quietly; *It doesn't matter, Lisa. Their reactions are about them, not you.*

To my surprise, my boss welcomed me with warmth and respect. Her compassion was a balm I hadn't expected, and it steadied me. She gently brought up the incident where I had lashed out at her, but before she could even finish, the words spilled out:

"I'm so sorry. You did not deserve that treatment."

She responded gently, "Lisa, thank you for that, it's like it never happened." She even offered a listening ear if I ever needed one. To help me ease back in, she lightened my workload at first, giving me time to adjust to full-time again. She also acknowledged how stressful it must be to wait for the verdict, which made me feel seen.

In those waiting days, I often replayed the recent positive experiences I'd had with Orange County. Work was hard to focus on, but the memories of me and my team carried me through. They became a shield against the shame of what I had said to my boss, and against the quiet fear that others at work might be judging me. Holding on to those moments of support and strength was healing. With them, I felt hope pushing me forward.

The unexpected camaraderie I felt from Orange County wrapped around me like warmth. *We're a team after all. I'm not alone. I will be okay.*

Returning to my office each day grew easier, but time still dragged while I waited for the trial to end, just as it had dragged before it began. The weeks leading up to court had felt like years, and now the wait for news that the jury was going into deliberations was just as heavy. Weekends were the hardest; I knew there could be no decision on those days. A part of me hoped they were painful for Don too, and I didn't feel guilty for it.

When dark thoughts whispered, *he'll probably go free,* I did my best to steady myself. I reminded myself of the truth I could cling to; there is eternal justice. No. Matter. What.

I was in the middle of an assessment about forty-five minutes from home when a call came through from an Orange County area code. *Finally,* I thought, *the jury must be in deliberations.*

I waited until my appointment was finished and I was back in my car before pressing play on the voicemail. The voice of the victim advocate came through, steady and urgent: "Lisa, the verdict is in!"

The verdict is in? Wait, what? Davis had promised he'd let me know when the jury went into deliberations. I trusted him. And now, instead of Davis, it was the victim advocate calling me with the verdict. Why her? Why not him?

I called her back immediately, my heart pounding. Her tone in the message had already given it away, I was going to like the outcome. I barely had time to breathe, let alone speak, before she blurted out, "The jury found him guilty!"

The joy I had longed for rose up but stayed trapped inside my chest, sealed off. I couldn't reach it. Instead, all I felt was the sting of being let down. I had trusted Davis to make sure I was safe at home when I heard the verdict, and I shouldn't have. *Dumb, dumb me.* Just like that, I was back in the mud, sinking deep.

"I didn't even know they were deliberating," I said to the victim advocate, stunned.

"Oh, they started late last night," she snapped back.

"That's really great news, I'm glad to hear it. But I had expected Davis to let me know when the jury went into deliberations so I could be home and prepare myself emotionally. I'm upset about that because I am still at work and not near home."

I could almost feel her eyes roll through the phone. "Oh, well... I guess he must've forgotten. He's really busy, you know. This is good news, Lisa."

He could have texted me anytime, I thought. *How could he not know that?*

"I know it's good news, thank you," I managed, and hung up.

I stared out the window, caught between wanting to scream and wanting to cry. I should have been celebrating, but all I felt was betrayal, again. It was as if every good feeling had been sucked out of me. I wanted them back, but I was helpless. I didn't want to care that he hadn't kept his word... but I did.

Then the tears came, hard. I couldn't stop them. I had appointments scheduled; I wouldn't have scheduled them if the plan had been respected. But the plan was changed without my consent. No apology. Again.

My boss had known the plan and had agreed to let me stay home on verdict watch, understanding how important it was for me to be in a safe place. Yet OC disrupted it anyway. Disrespected again.

Now what? I couldn't work. What would I even say to my boss? I couldn't stop crying. *I'm a loser,* my mind whispered.

I felt cut, deep, all the way to my core.

This could have been such a different moment, my special moment, and it was taken from me. I started the drive home, praying I'd make it before I completely broke down. *Why did I trust these people?*

God, I need You now. Where are You?

Tears poured as I gripped the wheel. It was a guilty verdict. I was truly grateful the jury did the right thing, yet I felt like I was unraveling. *Is this what losing my mind feels like?*

I finally made it home, pushing through the blur of burning tears. I went straight to my closet and collapsed.

After a little bit, I gathered just enough strength to email my boss:

> *I'm so sorry. I won't be able to complete today's assessments, and I'm asking for tomorrow off. I know this is a huge ask and an inconvenience for you, but I just found out the verdict. As you know, I was supposed to be told when deliberations began so I could prepare, but I wasn't. The verdict is good, but I'm really triggered anyway, and I need a few days. Do what you need to do; I understand if I lose my job. Apologies again.*

Then I crawled back into the closet and surrendered to the tears again.

When Robert came home and into our room, I whispered, "Robert, I'm so sorry. I feel like such a loser. The jury found him guilty, he won't be getting out. But I'm a mess. I'm back in the mud."

He came into the closet and lay next to me, holding me quietly. "Tell me more," he said. I explained everything to him. He knew the plan. He was prepared for the plan, not for this deviation. "Lisa, I'm so mad at them! You didn't ask for too much at all! I was there when Davis said that he would tell you when deliberations were, and how you explained that no matter the verdict, you would need to be home to process it safely. He promised Lisa, I heard him. I'm so sorry he let you down like that."

That was enough to settle me. All I needed was validation, and he gave it freely. I drew in a deep breath and rested gently with him, letting the calm seep in. After a while, he guided me to the bed, kissed me goodnight, and then quietly went out to handle dinner with the boys.

That night, my sleep was filled with dreams. I was back in a crowded courtroom, surrounded by other victims telling their stories. I kept glancing behind me, Jody was there, but always just out of sight. In the box sat Don, smiling at me, then slipping in and out of view. I tried to avoid his gaze, but at times I couldn't. I felt exposed.

My stress climbed. I wasn't sure if anyone was there to support me. I was part of the masses, listening to the sorrow of others, waiting for my turn. I shifted in my seat, slouching low, hoping to disappear. Sometimes I saw her, sometimes I saw him. Neither fully visible, both haunting me.

Then suddenly, all eyes turned to me. It was my turn. I froze, not knowing what to say, not even sure what they wanted from me. The judge leaned forward, looking down with authority yet gentleness. His words startled me: "We are so sorry for everything, for all that you have been through."

My mouth fell open. I hadn't expected this. In my mind I whispered, *thank you*. Then I broke, sobbing, until the dream dissolved and I woke in tears.

The judge, kind, noble, compassionate. *Thank you.*

And then the question rose heavy in me: *Now, how do I go on?*

Lisa,

Stepping off that plane you felt hope for the first time in weeks. You were ready to reclaim your life, to go back to work, to slowly rebuild. And then, in one phone call, your carefully laid plan for safety around the verdict shattered. You were promised a chance to prepare, to be in a safe place, yet the news came abruptly, in the middle of your workday. That betrayal stung as deeply as any verdict could heal.

This is the hidden side of post-trial life; PTSD doesn't vanish when the case ends. A guilty verdict doesn't erase the need for safety or the careful planning that protects you from being re-triggered. Returning to work while still navigating the trial's emotional aftershocks takes immense energy. Shame, fear of judgment, and lingering hypervigilance makes every step feel heavier.

Compassion, from someone, can be the difference between collapsing under the weight and moving forward. Just as your boss met you with grace and your husband with validation, survivors need workplaces and relationships that allow space for vulnerability.

Recovery is rarely linear. Complex trauma, especially when entwined with betrayal, can resurface even in moments of victory. But with steady support, treatment, and patience, those waves of pain become easier to ride out.

The verdict didn't erase the hurt of how you found out, but it didn't erase your strength, either. You stood through the storm, and you're still here. That matters more than the moment you lost.

CHAPTER 54

My boss gave me a few days to recover, and I prayed it would be enough. She was so understanding, reassuring me not to worry. Still, I couldn't shake the heaviness. *Why am I feeling so awful again?*

By Monday morning, I dragged myself up to her office. "I'm so sorry," I said, my voice low.

She looked at me with kindness. "Lisa, why don't you reach out to Davis? Let him know how you're feeling."

I had considered reaching out, but doubt held me back. What if he's annoyed with me? Still, both my boss and a friend encouraged me, reminding me that I deserved to voice my feelings. With their support, I gathered the courage to try.

I planned my message carefully. I wanted him to know I wasn't blaming, only sharing: I know you're on to the next case, and I truly wish you the best. I don't want to be a bother. I'm sure you didn't mean to hurt me by not following through with the plan, it must have been an oversight. But my boss and friend urged me to share my feelings because I deserve that chance, and because it may help future victims. We can all learn from this experience.

Finally, I took a breath and sent him a text:

> *Hi Davis, I appreciate all you have done for me. I am sad you didn't let me know when the jury went into deliberations. I had wanted to prepare by taking time off until the verdict. You promised you would tell me when they started deliberations and then that you would tell me the verdict. I have been very upset about not being notified; my boss and friend suggested I tell you my feelings. Thanks, Lisa.*

Davis's reply came short and sharp: "Do not contact me again."

Do. Not. Contact. Me. Again. The words echoed in my mind, over and over. I dropped my phone as my head spun, I literally saw red.

I cursed myself. *I should have waited until I was home to text him.* Every part of me wanted to fire back; *Please, Davis, let's not end on this tone. I wanted it to be a happy ending.*

But I didn't. I couldn't. *Don't do it, Lisa. You're pitiful,* I told myself.

I began obsessing over how I might word another text, something clearer, softer, more persuasive. *Maybe he just doesn't understand how deeply this affected me? I tried to tell him.*

I even considered texting him again and again until he responded. *No, Lisa. That would be a loser move. Pitiful.*

I paced back and forth, my mind spiraling. There was no end to it, this compulsion to be understood, this hunger for a response that would never come. *He's not going to respond with compassion, Lisa. Accept that this is what you get from some people.*

My emotions raged, screaming to be seen, cared about, but never satisfied. *I can't live like this. I don't want this.*

My throat tightened, my chest squeezed. *Don't do it, Lisa. Don't ever try to talk to him again.*

I deleted his number immediately, afraid I might reach out in a weak moment, desperate to make it right.

But I wanted to text him.

I wanted to call him.

I wanted to scream at him.

More than anything, I wanted him to apologize, to recognize where he had gone wrong, to just say *sorry.*

Oh my gosh, I can't believe this. My stomach churned with nausea. How could he say that to me? I couldn't wrap my mind around it.

We were friends... weren't we? Or was I fooling myself? Was I crazy?

The weight of it pressed hard against my soul, and I suffered under its heaviness.

I forwarded my boss the message from Davis. She couldn't believe it either, her anger rose on my behalf.

"Lisa, I'm so sorry. I thought it would go better than this, or I never would have encouraged you to reach out. I just don't understand why he couldn't simply say sorry."

I texted back, "Thank you. I really appreciate that you care, it makes me feel less crazy."

After talking with my boss, I sat down, a chill running through me. I dropped my head into my hands. *Lisa, don't spiral deeper.*

I reminded myself: he was an undertrained vicarious trauma survivor. Maybe, with time, he would regret his words and reach out to make it right. But no message ever came. I never heard from Davis again. I honored his command, *Do not contact me again*, and kept my silence.

Darkness crept back into my life. I snapped at the people I loved most, knowing the anger wasn't theirs to carry. *Lisa, put the anger where it belongs.* It didn't belong to my family, and it didn't belong on me. So, I resolved to act. I would call the Orange County District Attorney's office. As many times as it took to get a resolution. I would speak directly to the district attorney himself. He needed to hear me. I wanted him to understand my experience, to care, and to do better for the victims who would come after me. I called his office directly and was told my message would be given to him. I never heard back. So, I began again with Peter.

Day One: Peter's assistant told me he couldn't talk to me because of the possibility of an appeal.

"But Peter said there wouldn't be an appeal!" I protested.

"There's always a chance of appeal with any case. Not sure why you thought that," she replied.

"From Peter." I replied back.

Day Two: I called Peter's boss. Insufficient response.

Day Three: Davis's boss. Insufficient response.

Day Four: Peter's boss's boss. Insufficient response.

Day Five: Davis's boss's boss. Insufficient response.

Day Six: The captain of the unit. Insufficient response.

Day Seven: And on and on to anyone who would take my call. Insufficient response.

"Let me talk to your boss… Please put me through to Tony Rackauckas, the District Attorney," I insisted each time. I was determined to reach him. Every day, I left messages for Tony Rackauckas, never a response.

Each one heard me say, "I just want to make a change. Don't you understand? I deserve to be heard! I was hurt," I told them. "I have important feedback as a victim and for how I was mistreated. And I know how to train people to support those going through trauma, all based on science!"

Maybe I sounded crazy to them. I didn't care.

Days eight, nine, ten… I kept calling. Some of the men I reached showed compassion; others sounded irritated. But no one helped me. I was passed from one person to another, never reaching the district attorney.

I kept calling the DA's office directly, again and again, convinced that eventually I would get through. But with each unanswered attempt, my resentment grew. It seemed obvious he was on a power trip, indifferent to me and everything I had endured. The very idea that he was meant to stand for victims felt laughable when he wouldn't even speak to one. The woman who managed his office kept assuring me she was leaving messages, but nothing ever came back. One morning, my voice cracked, betraying my rage, and I began to cry on the phone, pleading with her to make sure he received the message. Then, like every other day, I went to work after my morning Orange County call.

Later that morning, my husband called to tell me the police had shown up at our house for a wellness check. Someone had reported I was suicidal. I was stunned. Yes, I cried, but I never said I wanted to die. This wasn't concern, it was retaliation. Instead of taking two minutes to speak to me or show an ounce of compassion, the DA chose to sic the police on me.

I never get what I ask for, especially validation. The wellness check barely registered; I felt nothing. I caught myself wondering what would happen if I actually told them I was suicidal. I already knew; they'd have to "assess" me. And police are terrible at assessing. Maybe they'd call a crisis team. Maybe not. Either way, it would be a waste of time. I know exactly how to answer their questions to get whatever outcome I want. The thought made me laugh darkly as I drove off to my next appointment, to assess a child for crisis.

Was I in crisis? I wasn't even sure I could tell anymore. Switch on; work. Switch off; call. Switch on; smile, be kind. Switch off; collapse into despair. *You can do it, Lisa.* But can I? I hoped I was infuriating the entire Orange County District Attorney's office. My pain, my rage, my grief, they needed to land where they belonged, not on my family, and not on me.

I couldn't make sense of how they were treating me. It broke something inside me. The pain felt inescapable, and I longed for someone, anyone, to help me find a way out. I tried to swap revenge thoughts for the belief that change was possible, that there could be a positive outcome. There *had* to be. I wasn't going to take this treatment anymore. I told myself; focus on change, not revenge. But the revenge thoughts crept back in, circling me. I was teetering on the edge, afraid of becoming a headline for all the wrong reasons. *Don't let the bad consume you, Lisa. Focus on the good.*

Sometimes, I gave in to the revenge thoughts. Like a pressure cooker letting off steam, those dark fantasies gave me a fleeting sense of relief. I pictured myself at the breaking point, yet I swore I wouldn't stop calling. If no one would help me, maybe one day I'd just drive down to the Orange County courthouse myself. I knew they'd treat me no differently in person than over the phone. I thought about handing out flyers. Camping in front of the courthouse until Tony Rackauckas spoke to me. All ideas, but they felt small, pitiful. *I* felt pitiful. Their power meant more to them than my well-being. But I could choose another way. They didn't care, and they needed to. Someone had to make them care.

My darkest fantasy was; I'd bypass the front desk, avoid the eye-rolling and the snickers. I'd wait for Davis in the parking lot. No speeches. No pleas. Just a confrontation that would leave him shaking. I would be packing a gun. No words, just actions. I wouldn't be the one to shoot. I would walk up to him and just pull out my gun and point it right at him. He would be left with no option. He wouldn't be able to laugh it off. He would know, in that instant, what it felt like to be powerless. And he'd have to react, then discover my gun was never loaded after I was crumpled on the ground. The idea felt like relief; no more being a nuisance, no more being ignored. My message would be impossible to miss.

I caught myself calculating the drive, the timing, the logistics, and then questioning how I'd even feel if I went through with it. I hated the desperation that had brought me there. I hated everything; how my message would be twisted, how responsibility would be deflected, how no one would care. After an act like that, they'd say I deserved it, and maybe I'd even believe them. I didn't want to be that person. I didn't want my kids to inherit that story. Yet there I was, standing at the edge of a cliff in my mind, staring into the drop and wondering if I had it in me to jump.

No, Lisa. No.

I forced my mind back to the belief that someday Tony Rackauckas would listen, that he'd want to make it right. I focused hard on nonviolence, on every positive attempt at change I could think of. I could never actually harm Davis or anyone, but the fact that such thoughts even crept in unsettled me. Still, I refused to give up. Not until I'd spoken to Tony Rackauckas.

A few weeks after I started my daily calls, another assistant district attorney talked to me. Really talked to me. He was different. He spoke with compassion to me. He apologized for how I had been treated. He listened without interrupting. He agreed to keep me updated on the case because I couldn't take another random contact in case it was appealed and they thought it would be a good idea to re-contact me. Peter said he wouldn't, through his assistant, but how could I trust that? This assistant DA said he completely understood and would make notes in the file to keep me updated. After talking on the phone a few times, we settled on monthly updates. I would email on the first of each month and he would let me know what he could find out. He made sure I knew I could email him anytime. I could call, and if he was able to, he would talk. If not, I was to leave a message. That's all I needed. I wanted to talk to Tony Rackauckas but I settled on the knowledge that someday he would apologize for ignoring me, a victim in the county he presided over. Someday, he would be sorry he never brought himself to speak to me, thought of himself as higher than me, and apparently thought less of me. *There is eternal justice.*

During this time, I also turned to the Victim Advocates, and the experience was even worse. I begged, I pushed, I clawed my way up their chain of command, and still, they shrugged me off. These were the very people paid to be *mental health professionals*, the ones who were supposed to support deputy district attorneys and investigators in handling victims. Instead, they treated me like a nuisance. It was disgraceful. Their indifference and annoyance wasn't just unprofessional, it was negligent. A betrayal. The Victim Advocates, of all people, showed me they couldn't be bothered to advocate for victims at all.

I wrote a letter and sent it everywhere I could think of; the district attorney, the *Orange County Register*, the *LA Times*, talk shows, Governor Jerry Brown, Attorney General Kamala Harris, and even Gloria Allred, the famed civil rights attorney. Nothing. No response. Crickets.

Except one. Tod Spitzer's office called, he was a former assistant district attorney, now an Orange County councilman. A reporter from the *Register* had forwarded my letter to him. For a moment, I felt relief. Finally, a break. Someone's listening! Someone sees me!

But it ended almost as quickly as it began. After his staff's polite acknowledgment, Spitzer himself, like Tony Rackauckas, refused to speak to me directly. His office did nothing to help, nothing to push for change. A few assistants tried to sound encouraging, but it was empty talk. That was it. He got away with silence. Another man in power who didn't have to face me.

Eventually I laid it down, for my own sake. Carrying their silence was eating me alive. I couldn't keep chasing people in power who had already decided I wasn't worth their time. Releasing it didn't mean their treatment, their silence, or their cruelty was acceptable. It meant I was choosing not to let their indifference destroy me. At least one councilman bothered to pretend to be concerned. A hollow gesture, but still something. And the kind assistant DA was my new advocate. I told myself, even with all the doors slammed shut and the arrogance, I will keep fighting to make change in my own way. I didn't give up, I refocused.

Lisa,

You reached out to Davis with vulnerability, hoping for resolution, for understanding. Instead, you were slammed into a wall of rejection. For someone already carrying the weight of betrayal trauma, that kind of dismissal rips open old wounds in an instant.

Your reaction, the looping thoughts, the desperation to be heard, wasn't weakness. It was your nervous system scrambling to rewrite the ending, to stop the story from closing in pain. When you directed your rage toward the system instead of yourself or your loved ones, you were placing the feelings where they belonged. That was self-preservation, that was part of your healing.

Complex trauma blurs time. One rejection today can feel like every rejection all at once. The pull toward extreme thoughts isn't who you are; it's a sign of overwhelm. Pausing, grounding, seeking safe support, those practices help keep old pain from hijacking the present.

What you wanted was simple; validation, respect, a listening ear. When the nice assistant DA finally gave you that, your shoulders dropped, your breath softened. Compassion doesn't erase the wrong, but it can loosen its grip, allowing space for healing to begin.

You didn't get what you deserved. But you held the line of nonviolence. You fought for yourself. And you kept moving toward change. That matters. You matter.

CHAPTER 55

I opened my heart a little wider, aching for help. I prayed. In the past, prayer had been my lifeline, but since the latest contact from Orange County, my words to God had been few. This time, I asked for clarity, for comfort, for His will, because mine was tangled and broken. *Help me keep Your commandments. Show me the next right step.*

As I loosened my grip on the daily calls to Tony Rackauckas, I reminded myself, he will not escape accountability forever. One day, he will have perfect knowledge of the pain he caused. *It's okay, Lisa. Good will still win. This battle isn't worth the toll anymore.* With that surrender, a wave of comfort washed over me, as if God Himself had leaned close and whispered reassurance.

I practiced "letting go." I chose to trust that things would work out for the best. Step by step, I kept moving forward on the path of healing, and even lifting up prayers for those I once called enemies.

"Robert, is everything going to be okay?" I asked as we drove toward a weekend getaway, a retreat I desperately hoped would reset me. I pictured the creek we planned to visit, its water washing away the heaviness that clung to me, awakening the real Lisa beneath the mud.

It had been a few weeks since I stopped the daily calls, yet I caught myself asking Robert for reassurance more often since the trial. The good moments came more regularly now, but I struggled to trust they would stay. I cherished every bit of peace of mind I managed to hold onto, fragile as it was. I was still wobbly. Better, but not yet back to who I had been before Orange County intruded once again.

After the trial ended I started working on getting reimbursed for my lost wages for the work I missed before and during the trial, but was met with so much resistance! But I wasn't going to give up. I wasn't going to accept the denials from the California Victims of Crime Department. I would do what it took, no matter how many denials, to get my lost wages. Their no, their rejection, cut to my core. I could get lost in the pain if I thought about it too long. I would keep appealing. The California Attorney General's office told me that the crime happened thirty-five years ago, so they didn't think they should help with lost wages, or any other support. I imagined the California Attorney General, Kamala Harris telling me to my face, "You should be over it." The outrage at the thought only fueled me to continue pursuing my rights. I only wished she or someone high up would take the time to say anything to me.

I asked Robert, "Am I so dumb to let this still affect me, thirty-five years after the crime?" My voice cracked under the weight of the contradiction. *They need me every decade to help keep this sexually violent predator behind bars because of the damage he causes to his victims, but somehow, as his victim, I'm not supposed to be damaged anymore? Not supposed to be affected by this process? Is that what they're saying to me? Are they right?*

Robert shook his head gently. "No, Lisa. Their ignorance doesn't make sense. They trigger you by the process of re-contact and testifying. And you can't say no to helping protect others. I understand."

Did they really believe I was trying to milk the system for a vacation or free therapy? The thought left me questioning myself, even my sanity. Shame pressed in, and rage boiled beneath it. I felt so flawed. And since they made it so complicated to pay for therapy, I fought through it alone. Maybe the right therapist could help, but where were they?

What I did know was this; I had to advocate for myself. This was part of my healing, self-advocacy. I wasn't going to disappear quietly.

Outside the car window, the scenery shifted from Saguaro cactus to tall pines. *Lisa, focus on this weekend, on this moment,* I reminded myself. I was getting better at compartmentalizing when I needed to, though I knew I'd lost ground. I rolled the window down and let the cool air rush over me. In my mind, I imagined the residue of pain clinging to me lifting off of me with the wind, dissolving like water evaporating under the sun.

I was startled when Robert declared, "We will be okay. You are okay. You did the right thing, and you are figuring out what you need to do. I believe in you. I believe in us."

I wanted to believe him but I was so tired of my story and the pain it caused. *I bet everyone is annoyed by me too.* Doing the right thing and trying to make positive change was my only hope. *I have to focus on what good can come, or the bitterness will consume me.*

I reminded myself that I was blessed to be a woman in the United States, with opportunities so many others are denied. At least I had the chance to try to push for change within the system. Maybe, just maybe, they would rethink some of their actions because of my persistence. The whole thing felt drenched in the bad, but I forced myself to dig through it, determined to carve out even the smallest bit of good.

I did my best to quiet my mind. *You are okay, Lisa.* I closed my eyes and pictured the wounded little girl inside me. I held her close, rocking her gently, whispering that she was safe now. Slowly, my body softened, and I drifted into sleep, the sound of the wind following us as we climbed higher toward our destination.

After a peace-filled weekend, I continued to fight the attorney general's office to get wage reimbursement. They calculated what they might pay, if they decided too, by subtracting my hard-earned vacation time I used to cover some lost wages. I scoffed at the insult.

Nine months later, I opened one of the dreaded California victim envelopes, and to my shock, there was a reimbursement check inside. *Is this for real?* Relief and disbelief hit me at once, but the feeling faded as I looked closer. After months of appeals, of being forced to beg again and again for help with the financial hit we took, the check barely scratched the surface. My hard-earned vacation time was gone, and this meager offering was supposed to make it right? The injustice of it seared through me.

Still, it was something, a hard-won, imperfect victory. I chose not to fight this battle anymore. At least not like this. But the greater fight was far from finished. I would turn this injustice into a cause, use it as fuel. For my own survival, I needed to reframe the story. I was no longer just a victim failed by the system, I was a survivor, a therapist, and I would use my voice to help others in any way I could and to educate the professionals who needed to understand.

Good would come from this. I would see to it.

Lisa,

You carried yourself through battles that drained your spirit and tested your strength. Again and again, the system dismissed you, demanded more of you, and minimized the toll it took on your life. Yet you kept showing up. You refused to vanish into silence.

Letting go of battles when you needed to didn't mean giving up. It meant protecting your energy and choosing where to fight. That choice takes wisdom and courage, especially when the system fails. But you rest in knowing that eternal justice will one day make all things right, compensating for every loss, every dismissal, every wound that went unseen. What the world withholds, God will restore.

The injustice you faced is real, and you would not stand for it. When systems deny or delay support, they inflict new wounds and deepen old ones. Your outrage is valid. Your exhaustion is valid. And your decision to rise above it, to turn injustice into a cause and transform pain into purpose, is what makes you powerful.

You are learning to hold both truths; that healing is fragile and uneven, and that you still carry the strength to keep moving forward. Even when you doubt yourself, even when you're tired of your story, you are shaping something lasting.

Lisa, you are not just surviving, you are creating change. Every time you speak, advocate, or reframe your story, you are making good come from the hurt. That is your power, and it cannot be taken.

CHAPTER 56

"When I first started seeing you, I thought I would never feel okay again. Thank you so much." My client's voice rang with clarity and confidence, a striking difference from the day she began therapy. Now, there was light and hope in her eyes, and she was steadily moving forward with her goals.

I leaned back in my comfy office chair, savoring the softness of the moment. Breathing deeply, I told her with full sincerity, "It's been an honor to work with you and I'm so grateful to have helped you in any way I could. You are so very welcome." I gestured toward the *welcome* painting by the door and added, "This is forever, okay?"

She hugged a pillow tightly to her chest, and I shifted gently in my seat as we allowed the pause to settle between us.

"Absolutely, I'll keep in touch," she said as she stood, then asked quietly for a hug.

"Take care ok? You got this!" She sniffled and nodded before giving me one last smile as she headed out the door.

I quietly closed the door behind her, feeling like the luckiest woman in the world! What an awesome job I had! This client had come to me with a history of repeated sexual abuse that had caused debilitating symptoms. I knew her pain when I saw it. And I knew that she could find healing. I was so grateful not to be scared off, like other therapists had before, because of the deep pain she expressed as part of her healing.

Session after session, I sat with her in her pain. I witnessed her grief and felt the gut-wrenching sorrow that at last began to rise and release. She learned to place her feelings where they belonged, no longer forced to bury them just to survive. I could still hear the sobs accompanying her process and the happy a-ha moments as she found compassion for her wounded self. Her powerful rage never frightened me, I knew it was necessary for her to feel it. We shared the joy she found as she finally figured out how to soothe herself and offer kindness inward. With each session, I watched hope grow stronger, her belief in herself deepen, her determination to heal take root. As her confidence blossomed, she began reclaiming the life abuse had once stolen from her. She was no longer just surviving, she was stepping fully into the life she had always wanted, and the one she had always deserved.

Those words, *Thank you so much*, repeated in my mind as I stared out of my office window into the sharp blue sky between the billowing clouds. *See Lisa, it's been worth it.*

My own therapist had looked at me with terror in her eyes when I sought her help while waiting to testify at Don's last trial. The intensity of my pain seemed to overwhelm her, as if it was foreign territory. When I expressed rage and my distress and how I was incapacitated, she just sat there, staring at me like a deer in headlights.

Despite her training in Somatic therapy and EMDR, she didn't use any of the tools she had. Instead, she sat paralyzed beside me in session. She was able to validate me somewhat, pointing out the betrayal trauma caused by Orange County's re-contact and mistreatment. She even noticed how being used and discarded by the system mirrored the very pattern of my abuse. It felt good to be seen in that way.

But I was still left without real support and no tools, drowning in unending distress. She offered no clear path forward; no sense of when or how my PTSD symptoms might ease. I began to feel hopeless in her care, like a burden she didn't know how to carry. The sessions seemed to continue out of obligation rather than confidence. So, I stopped seeing her. I know she wanted me to heal, but the truth became undeniable; I was far beyond her scope of practice.

Sitting in my office that day with my client, I knew without a doubt that healing from intense pain was possible. I had lived it. I knew healing could still unfold even after re-triggers and much time had passed, and I understood the weight of ongoing suffering. My own counselor hadn't known how to reach me in the depths of my trauma, but I did. I had walked that road myself, and in my own imperfect way, I could now be a steady guide for others on their journey toward healing.

I understood.

Lisa,

Look at what you've done, you took the very pain that once made you feel hopeless and turned it into a way to light the path for someone else. You sat with her in her darkest moments without flinching, because you knew exactly how heavy those moments could be. And how necessary they were to the healing process. You didn't rush her grief, shrink from her rage, or try to fix her too soon. You let her feel what she needed to feel and find a way to self-compassion.

Your own healing taught you what no textbook could. You learned that deep pain can be met with deep presence, and that healing is really possible. Even when others didn't have the tools or scope to help you, you found ways to help yourself, and now, you give those tools to others.

You keep showing up for yourself, whether through journaling, prayer, counseling, and the steady rhythm of compassion for yourself. You trust what works, you hold onto hope, and you walk beside those still finding theirs.

You know that healing isn't about never hurting again, it's about knowing there is a way through. You've learned steps and tools to steady yourself when the pain resurfaces, and with time and proper treatment, the symptoms lose their edge and they ease. You've turned pain into purpose, one session, one survivor, one honest moment at a time.

CHAPTER 57

It was a beautiful day in my brand-new house. Sunlight streamed through the window, its warmth brushing my face like a gentle caress. I was struck by how bright and clear the world looked, every detail sharp and alive. I drew in a deep breath as I gazed at the flawless blue sky, marveling at its brilliance. The birds singing outside seemed more melodic than ever, their wings casting giant shadows inside the house as they soared overhead. Magnificent creatures, I thought, what a gift to witness them.

As I looked around my house, excitement bubbled up inside me. I could redecorate everything, my space, my way. The possibilities stretched out before me, and fun turned quickly into pure elation. My house, my choices, anything I wanted. I felt so lucky. My creativity soared, images flashing through my mind like pages of a glossy magazine, each one brimming with ideas. I could change the colors, reinvent the rooms, even tear down walls if I chose. The freedom thrilled me.

Lighthearted, I skipped into the kitchen and poured a cup of fancy new herbal tea. Its comforting aroma wrapped around me, a mix of cinnamon and floral. With a splash of cream, the taste came alive on my tongue, warm, rich, and soothing. My whole body exhaled in bliss.

As I spun around, movement outside the window caught my eye. New neighbors! A spark of excitement rushed through me at the thought of meeting them. I even giggled at myself, imagining they might show up with the perfect piece of art for my fresh design. I felt so hopeful. I would be friendly and introduce myself, even if they didn't have anything to contribute to my decor.

I glanced out the window again and realized how much of their backyard I could see. Strange, almost too clear. My eyes landed on a deck, had that always been there? It must be new.

Wait, what am I seeing? My heart dropped, heat rushing through me until my skin turned clammy. I stumbled back a few steps, squeezed my eyes shut, then forced myself to the window again, straining to see. At first everything blurred, as if my vision refused to cooperate. Then, slowly, the shapes came into focus, two silhouettes. My sight tunneled in on them. They carried coffee cups, smoke curling around their hands. The posture, the outline, so achingly familiar. Something felt wrong.

Driven by a need to know, I climbed onto the counter to get a better view.

No. No. No.

It couldn't be. No, I refused to believe it. Was this some kind of cruel setup? *Lisa, you know happiness never lasts.* My face pressed closer to the glass, desperate to prove myself wrong. But there was no denying what I saw. A tremor ran through me, my head shaking in disbelief as my body began to tremble.

It was Don.

Hello darkness, my old friend.

Don. And Jody.

Why hadn't I been warned? Could they really be my new neighbors? No, no, it couldn't be. I scrubbed my eyes hard with a towel, but the image stayed. My eyes burned at the sight of them. There he was. There she was.

A low moan rose from deep inside me just as their hollow, haunted eyes lifted and met mine, as if they could feel my stare. Their smiles curled, smug and knowing, as though saying, *You will never escape us.* Their gaze pierced through me, and a shiver ran across my skin.

I gasped and bolted upright in bed, my heart hammering. Just a dream. Another nightmare.

Sweat and tears streaked down my face as the pounding in my chest refused to calm. The fear clung to my gut like a stone. Oh God, no. Please don't let this ever happen. A voice inside whispered back, You will survive no matter what, Lisa.

But why this dream again? Why now? Please don't let it be a sign. I curled into myself, clutching my pillow, waiting for the chills to leave my body. Still, the thought pressed in: Anything can happen, and you can't stop it.

I acted on my only power and looked at Megan's Law. Just in case. These dreams always ended with that action and I hoped each time the result would be the same; Don Gordon incarcerated.

I had lost contact with the kind assistant DA. Five years after he'd promised to keep me updated, he was gone. A year earlier, I had reached out to thank him on Human Trafficking Awareness Day, grateful for the lifeline he had been. My email bounced back with a notice; the day before, he had retired from the Orange County sex crimes unit. The day before.

He had assured me he would let me know of any major changes, even his leaving, and insisted he never would. But he hadn't. Maybe he forgot. I tried to shake it off, telling myself it wasn't intentional, that it wasn't a deliberate snub. *Let it go.*

That day, I took my disappointment and carried it to the march for trafficking victims. I poured my energy into the rally, shouting the chants the leader called out and stomping my feet with each step through downtown Gilbert, grounding myself in the rhythm of the march.

Reaching out to the kind assistant DA was no longer an option, so I went straight to Megan's Law. I was grateful to have this tool, yet frustrated that it was still part of my life at all. On October 10, 2022, I typed in his name.

Nothing.

Okay, I typed it again. Still nothing.

What? Even if he was out, he had to be registered. There was no way he could vanish from Megan's Law, not like Jody and Glenn had. But deep down, I knew I shouldn't be surprised by anything.

I tried again. No Donald Lee Gordon. Not in California. Not in Utah. Not in Illinois. Nowhere.

My breath caught. *Okay, Lisa, think.*

I emailed the contact link on Megan's Law, asking why he wasn't listed. But almost instantly I realized I couldn't wait that long, if I even got a response. The emotions surged fast and hard, threatening to drown me. I shook out my hands, forced deep breaths, trying to keep control as the flood pressed in.

Wait! Maybe he's dead, that must be why he isn't showing up. But then again, wouldn't they have told me? *No Lisa, you know they wouldn't.* Either way? I couldn't sit with the uncertainty. I grabbed the phone and called the Orange County sex crimes unit immediately. I had no idea who would answer, but I needed to know right now what was going on. I couldn't imagine him being free and not registered. My heart raced as I prayed, *Please, let me find out quickly so I don't have to keep worrying.*

A woman picked up the phone.

"Hi… I'm a previous victim of crimes handled by your office. I'm trying to find out if a sexually violent predator is out, or dead, or what's going on, because he's no longer showing up on Megan's Law."

There was a pause on the other end, then she asked for my name, her voice tinged with surprise.

"Well, my name is Lisa Plumb, though back then, as the victim, I was Lisa Baer. People probably just remember me as the 'crazy victim,' but whatever. I just need to know, did Don die or what? Please."

"Oh… okay, let me check." Her voice grew hesitant, almost mumbling, as if unsure she should be telling me. "I'm not seeing him. Oh, wait, he isn't on Megan's Law because… he's deceased."

"He's dead?" My mouth dropped open. Then, before I could stop it, a smile spread across my face. "Oh, heck yeah! When did he die? Where?"

"I really can't tell you any of that, I'm sorry,"

"Ok, but he is dead, for sure?"

She whispered, "Um yes."

"OK, that's all then, I guess, thank you so much." Click.

He's deceased!

Those words rang through my ears like a detonated bomb and suddenly it was as if stress I didn't realize I had been carrying began melting right off my body. I hadn't realized how heavy the weight had been until it lifted. I felt so light! I half believed I might float right up into the air. *Oh wow... I don't ever have to worry about Orange County contacting me again. I don't have to fear running into him, or worse, seeing him move in next door.*

Tears welled as I whispered, "Oh, dear God, thank you."

Lisa,

That nightmare held the weight of decades, the fear that safety could vanish, the dread of the next intrusion, the haunting sense that peace could be shattered at any moment. Your body remembers, as it always has, preparing for danger and survival.

When you learned he was truly gone, the relief that rose in you was not cruel, it was holy. At last, your body could release a burden it had carried for far too long. Relief after the loss of someone harmful is not shameful; it is your nervous system recognizing safety.

Your intuition, through dreams, gut feelings, and sudden flashes of knowing, has always been your early warning system. Even nightmares, though painful, have meaning. They can help the brain work through what was overwhelming, bring hidden fears to light, and even practice survival through their vivid scenes. They are exhausting, yes, but also one of the mind's ways of processing what was left undone. They can be reshaped, by rescripting endings, grounding before sleep, or uncovering the truths they carry. They are both signal and symptom, and with support, they can become part of healing instead of only suffering.

Lisa, you are free now, to feel the joy of safety. You are free to exhale, to trust peace, and to build a life where your dreams are filled with light instead of fear.

CHAPTER 58

I didn't judge myself for my relief at his death. He was in his eighties. He chose his life. Eternity would sort it out. I was free of him on this earth, and I rejoiced! I didn't have him or my parents, or contact from Orange County to worry about anymore. I felt the sweet relief. I messaged my editor, called my husband, posted on Facebook, and breathed calmer. I didn't hope it was a painful death. I actually felt sorry for him. To be so disturbed and addicted to evil, to give up your life for a pursuit that destroys children, that is very sad. I am much more fortunate to be a survivor than a perpetrator. *I'd hate to be him.*

I celebrated by going to the beach. The ocean breeze was splendid, perfectly ruffling my hair. I stood on the dune gazing out to sea, lost in the horizon of where the ocean met the sky. I felt at home here, in my special, sacred space. I felt happy. It seemed the ocean was joyous to have me near. Love flowed from its waves and splashed over my feet.

The ocean had always been there for me. I closed my eyes and breathed in the salty air, remembering Little Lisa in her polka dot bikini toddling around, squishing the sand between her toes. She enjoyed grasping for sand crabs and getting buried in the sand up to her neck. Then teen Lisa came to mind. She made herself one with the sand for hours, soaking up the sun as she napped, and let the heavy air caress her. Now, as an adult, the ocean embraced all of me, and I did too. Compassion and joy flowed through me as I looked back on my past selves. *It's been so hard, but there is so much good too.* And I always have the beach.

A shock of salty wind burst past. I opened my eyes, and something sparkled out of the corner of my vision. I turned to my right and saw what looked like a crown. How beautiful! I was surprised that a child's toy would wash up on the beach like that. I squinted my eyes. *Wait, is that a shell?* I felt a playful urgency to run towards it. As I ran, I raced a wave and beat it. I scooped it up and looked closer. The most beautiful shell I had ever seen!

For me, ocean? I felt a yes, and knelt to caress it, then brought it to the center of my chest, holding it like a baby. I stood up, closed my eyes, and whispered, *Thank you.* A wave washed over my feet and then up to my knees. It was meant for me. The ocean's special gift.

I joyfully ran towards my husband and showed him, playfully piping up, "Look at this shell the ocean gave me!" It looked like it was lined with pearls, cascading along the side of the shell. And it was huge! Almost as big as my hand. It glistened and shimmered brightly and colorfully like a rainbow was dancing across it.

"Oh wow, that's so beautiful Lisa!" He put his arm around me and stood quietly, admiring the ocean's artwork.

I sat down as he went to take pictures of our beautiful beach. I was in love with this day, this beach, and my life. And I loved myself. At another time in my life, I might have doubted that I deserved such a gift from the sea. But now, I just felt grateful, playful, and full of self-acceptance.

I thought back to how deeply I had once loathed myself, how little I trusted myself. Looking back at little Lisa through adult eyes, I often described her as a "puppy dog", trailing after others, desperate for scraps of approval, ashamed of her own needs and silenced voice. Like a puppy that's been abused she still came back to the abusers, seeking affection, approval, and love but only more frantically. I had been taught that abuse was love, and with nothing to compare it to, and no one to protect me, I believed it. Carrying that level of self-contempt and confusion was suffocating, yet loosening its grip required something I hadn't understood. I heard more than once that self-forgiveness was vital to healing, but for years I could not grasp why or what that meant.

I now knew that self-forgiveness is the act of facing reality, the truth that the little girl I once was had no power, no voice, and no ability or responsibility to stop the abuse. She reacted just as any child would. She did her best to survive. Her brain was still forming; she could not see with perspective or act with the strength of a fully developed adult. Recognizing this truth allowed me to loosen the grip of the harsh judgments I had carried for so long. At last, I could trade self-blame for compassion, and condemnation for understanding. I was never a dumb, worthless, or a bad girl.

I closed my eyes and took a deep breath. I recalled when I was younger than five, in a favorite frilly dress, spinning around and dancing, my hair going wild. I now felt unconditional love and compassion for her. She was a child in a world that should have protected her, but didn't. There was no way she could have done any better, and she deserved my love and understanding. She needed it. She blamed herself because no one told her the truth. I now saw her as the innocent and perfect little girl she was! *I love her, I really do!* I dug my toes into the warm sand and embraced Little Lisa. "I understand you," I told her. "I'm proud of you and I love you so very, very much."

We found the treasure, the treasure of self-compassion. All of our efforts have been worth it. Little Lisa now trusted adult Lisa because adult Lisa saw her, valued her, and now has her best interest in mind. We will always have the knowledge we have gained about healing truths that no one can ever take away. And I know where to turn for comfort; myself. At last, I understood that I could never truly hold the compassion of others until I first filled the hole inside me. Self-compassion has to come first; without it, every kind word and every gesture of care slips through the cracks of unhealed shame.

I know now that I will always be there for me, like the ocean. I cannot carry the ocean with me, but I can carry love for myself, offering comfort, protection and care from within. And when I need it, I can return to the shore, feel the breeze against my skin, breathe in the salt air, and gaze at the sparkling water. My own safe place. My own constant. The ocean will always meet me with love, and so will I.

ACKNOWLEDGMENTS

I would not have been able to complete this book without the very loving support of my family, especially my husband who has always been kind and gentle with me.

And Kim Clement, my editor coach, who held my hand more than I thought I would need and lent out her prefrontal cortex without complaint.

And for all survivors, especially the photographers' victims, you are not forgotten.

I thank all of you so much.

Lisa is a victim and survivor of child abuse who decided to become a trauma therapist. Nudged by God through the process of becoming, she helps others the best she can. She leans on wisdom from so many scientists and teachers who have done the work that we all benefit from. Like Issac Newton said, "If I have seen further, it is by standing on the shoulders of giants."

www.ingramcontent.com/pod-product-compliance
Lightning Source LLC
Chambersburg PA
CBHW071707120626
46550CB00001B/132